Empowering Knowledge Workers

New Ways to Leverage Case Management

BPM and Workflow Handbook Series

Empowering Knowledge Workers

New Ways to Leverage
Case Management

Foreword by
Derek Miers

BPM and Workflow Handbook Series

Published in association with

Workflow Management Coalition

20 Years of Thought-Process Leadership

Edited by
Layna Fischer

Future Strategies Inc., Book Division

Lighthouse Point, Florida

Empowering Knowledge Workers
New Ways to Leverage Case Management

Copyright © 2014 by Future Strategies Inc.

ISBN-13: 978-0-984976478

Published by Future Strategies Inc., Book Division

3640-B3 North Federal Highway #421
Lighthouse Point FL 33064 USA
954.782.3376 fax 954.719.3746
www.FutStrat.com; books@FutStrat.com

Publisher's Cataloging-in-Publication Data

Library of Congress Catalog Card LCCN No. 2013955072

Empowering Knowledge Workers

New Ways to Leverage Case Management

/Layna Fischer (editor)

p. cm.

Includes bibliographical references, glossary, appendices and index.

ISBN 9780984976478

1. Adaptive Case Management. 2. Intelligent Systems. 3. Knowledge Work 4. Business Intelligence. 5. Business Process Technology. 6. Production Case Management. 7. Productivity Improvement 8. Predictive Analytics 9. Business Process Technology. 10. Process Mining

   Palmer, Nathaniel; Swenson, Keith; Harrison-Broninski, Keith *et al* (authors)

   Fischer, Layna (editor)

Table of Contents

Section 2: Appendices

Foreword

"What's the business problem you are trying to solve?"

I first read that as a quote by Intel CIO Kim Stevenson, I believe, and it stuck in my mind. I particularly like that it gets to the heart of the discussion, quickly. Far too often I find myself fielding queries where the people on the other end of the phone have decided on a technological solution (a hammer), and are now looking for a problem (the right nail).

The business doesn't want a hammer or a nail, they want something of tangible value—they want the *house*. Without clearly demonstrating tangible value, it matters little to them where the solution contains this product or that techno buzzword. They don't care for how cute your big data credentials are, or whether your mobile mojo has trumped your social ace in the hole. Big data, mobile, social—these are not the house (nor the solution) more aptly likened to the context within which the house sits.

Of course, we need that application delivered to our customers on a digital device nearby to them. Of course, we want that engagement to leverage the history of what we've done with that customer in the past – their wants and preferences taken into account. Of course, we want to leverage what we know others in the same context considered the right choice. But we also expect the customer to channel-hop to the Web, and then perhaps wander into a branch or store, and ring up about it to see where things are at (WISMO—what is the status of my order).

The customer expects that you are going to maintain that context across all those channels. The customer doesn't care for how you are organized by departments and product lines. The customer doesn't give a damn about the fact that your system of record always does things like that. Customers tend to find the decisions taken long ago by programmers quite irrelevant. In the end, they vote with their feet and go elsewhere.

And that brings us to case management—case management technology delivers a compelling and accessible range of features that help manage a dynamically unfolding context.

This enables organizations to manage those unpredictable and unexpected service nuances that help differentiate a service proposition from that offered by competitors. Their systems usually leave people in control, exercising their judgment when needed but also automating the repetitive elements of the work.

For historical reasons, Forrester calls it Dynamic Case Management (DCM) and despite the protestations of some protagonists there is no difference to Adaptive Case Management (ACM). Although I didn't know it at the time, I started developing a generic Case Management system in 1990. I wrote a paper called the *Business Case for Case Handling* in 1996.

What's different now is that these platforms have steadily evolved to the point that they now deliver a compelling proposition. But we are only seeing the tip of this iceberg in the dynamic/adaptive case management area. Let's face it—technology is the easy part. The real challenge is how you bring the people with you... how you get them to imagine a different way of engaging customers. How do you get all the processes and people aligned to deliver consistently compelling experiences? While the transformation is usually driven top-down, the engagement part needs to happen bottom up.

My point is that it's much easier to reimagine the future than it is to reengineer the past. In the end, just like all projects are business projects, all problems are people problems. People want to be engaged in co-creating the solution rather than having it imposed upon them. If you do that right—the engagement part—then the technology component becomes easy. Instead of it being your change project, it's their business development agenda. Instead of resistance to change, the challenge becomes one of channeling their enthusiasm.

It's those soft skills—empathy, facilitation, and coaching—that are the keys to success. Helping managers see the world differently is critical; creating the alignment and engagement usually starts at the top.

The good news is that case management technology enables that to happen. It enables empowered employees to adapt and evolve the way they do work. It truly is a democratizing force in the world of increasing automation. It provides a mechanism to balance control and empowerment at the same time as enabling the people involved to better serve their customers.

Derek Miers, Forrester Research

Empowering Knowledge Workers

Introduction and Overview

Adaptive Case Management is ultimately about allowing knowledge workers to work the way that they want to work and to provide them with the tools and information they need to do so effectively.

Empowering Knowledge Workers describes the work of managers, decision makers, executives, doctors, lawyers, campaign managers, emergency responders, strategist, and many others who have to think for a living. These are people who figure out what needs to be done, at the same time that they do it, and there is a new approach to support this presents the logical starting point for understanding how to take advantage of ACM.

Keith Swenson points out, "We are seeing a fundamental shift in our workforce, and in the ways they need to be managed. Not only are companies engaging their customers in new ways, but managers are engaging workers in similarly transformed ways."

In award-winning case studies covering industries as a diverse as law enforcement, transportation, insurance, banking, state services, and healthcare, you will find instructive examples for how to transform your own organization.

This important book follows the ground-breaking publications, *Taming the Unpredictable*[1], *How Knowledge Workers Get Things Done*[2] and *Mastering the Unpredictable*[3] and provides important papers by thought-leaders in this field, together with practical examples, detailed ACM case studies and product reviews.

WHERE IS ACM TODAY? REALITIES AND OPPORTUNITIES
Nathaniel Palmer, Business Process Management, Inc.

Today, more than a half-century after Drucker first coined the phrase "knowledge worker" (in 1959) the share of the workforce represented by this group has grown considerably, to as much as half of all workers by some measures. So, too, have grown investments targeting knowledge worker productivity. Yet despite this, we remain far from realizing the level of improvement seen in manual labor over the course of the last century.

Nathaniel Palmer shares his intensive research on how knowledge work is performed and how to bridge the gap between controlled and ad hoc ACM. He explores work patterns applicable to case management and how the emergence of Adaptive Case Management represents the paradigm shift from adapting business practices to the design of IT systems, to building systems that reflect how work is actually performed.

---

[1] *Taming the Unpredictable, Real World Adaptive Case Management: Case Studies and Practical Guidance,* published by Future Strategies Inc., 2011 www.FutStrat.com

[2] *How Knowledge Workers Get Things Done: Real-World Adaptive Case Management* published by Future Strategies Inc., 2012 www.FutStrat.com

3 *Mastering the Unpredictable:* How Adaptive Case Management Will Revolutionize the Way That Knowledge Workers Get Things Done, published by Meghan-Kiffer Press, April 2010

INNOVATIVE ORGANIZATIONS ACT LIKE SYSTEMS, NOT MACHINES
Keith D Swenson, Fujitsu America

The author asks - do you conceptualize your organization as a machine? If so, you may be led down the wrong path for optimizing business processes. Machines are complicated, but truly complex systems, like an organization, a marketplace, an ecosystem, are not like machines. Evidence for this is both familiar and surprising. It is the "Enlightenment Bias" which blinds us to the true nature of organizations. For an organization to be innovative, you need to design it to be self-controlling, but not constrained to fixed predefined patterns. A new generation of tools is come to support organizations in this manner. Antifragility is a quality that emerges from an adaptive system. While it sounds crazy, there are adaptive systems all around us, and a human organization is one of those. We need to think of an organization as a system which includes both the people and the information technology.

BOTTOM-UP PROCESS DISCOVERY USING KNOWLEDGE ENGINEERING TECHNIQUES
Thomas Bech Pettersen, Steinar Carlsen, Gunnar John Coll, Helle Frisak Sem, Norway

We have found acquisition techniques from knowledge engineering (KE) useful for process discovery in our work with operational Adaptive Case Management (ACM) solutions. These techniques can easily be combined with more traditional top-down approaches from the architect's toolbox. Our overall approach uses dynamically combinable snippets of task support functionality rather than trying to create linear and static "end-to-end" processes. Events and user goals chain these snippets together. The described knowledge engineering techniques have proved useful for bottom-up discovery focusing on tasks and their actual work performance that may go hand in hand with the prototyping and development of a task support system.

JUSTIFYING ACM: WHY WE NEED A PARADIGM SHIFT IN BPM
Ilia Bider, Paul Johannesson and Erik Perjons, Stockholm University, Sweden

This paper is devoted to understanding the needs of the enterprise of the future in the area of BPM, and analyzing whether the mainstream workflow-based systems will satisfy these needs. The analysis is done based on assumption that an essential property of the enterprise of the future is agility. The agility is understood as ability to discover changes, trends and opportunities in the dynamic world and react to them by adjusting current products, services and processes, or creating completely new ones.

The paper is structured in the following way: we start with giving a pragmatic definition of the concept of business process that will be used in the paper. Then, we analyze the properties of a business process that can be supported by a workflow-based system and discuss whether business processes of the enterprise of the future will possess these properties. After that, we give some suggestions on what type of techniques could be employed in the new generation of software to support business processes. In the last section, we summarized our findings.

AUTOMATED GUIDANCE FOR CASE MANAGEMENT: SCIENCE OR FICTION?
Irina Rychkova, Manuele Kirsch-Pinheiro and Bénédicte Le Grand, University Paris 1 Pantheon-Sorbonne, France

Humans dream about an intelligent computer assistant who would support them in critical situations thanks to its capacity to reason objectively, to take into account millions of factors and criteria and to value carefully thousands of alternatives prior to make a decision. HAL 9000, in Kubrick's 2001: A Space Odyssey (IMDB 1968), is probably the most famous incarnation of such assistant. Being a fictional character, it reflects a number of great ideas of scientists from the 20th century who believed that machines one day would be capable of doing any work a man can do. Though it was shown that such a vision of computer technology is too optimistic, scientists keep working on theories and prototypes that can support practitioners in agile decision-making and smart process management.

In this paper, we propose our vision of what academic research can do for such a pragmatic and experience-driven discipline as Adaptive Case Management and to discuss to what extent fiction may become reality in what we call *automated guidance for case management*?

IDENTITY MANAGEMENT VIA ACM
Keith Harrison-Broninski, Role Modellers

Despite the current fast pace of innovation in Identity Management, new technologies still provide little support for securing the primary occupation of most knowledge workers - collaboration with colleagues, especially those in other organizations. If an organization is going to grant access to business-critical resources, it needs to know why access is needed and what will be done with those resources. This means understanding the work item that has caused the person to request access – i.e., the business process context in which access is being granted:

- The Activities the person is carrying out using the resource;
- The Roles they have been assigned, to which the Activities belong;
- The Plans (projects, programmes, processes, initiatives, ventures...) of which the Roles form a part.

This paper discusses an ACM technique that not only enhances traditional Role-Based Access Control for use with collaborative work spanning multiple organizations, but also solves a related challenge into the bargain. Increasingly, business systems are used to send messages, by email and other means, often containing sensitive content. The sender may be known, but what about the recipients? The ACM technique presented streamlines and improves collaborative work across multiple organizations in such a way that not only the sender but also the recipients of any message are automatically authenticated, authorized and audited.

MASTERING KNOWLEDGE FLOW: ALIGNING SOCIAL NETWORK, KNOWLEDGE USE AND PROCESS DESIGN
Alberto Manuel, Process Sphere

Our society is constructed around flows: flows of capital, flows of information, flows of technology, organizational interaction, flows of data. This construction is also applied inside of organizations and among its stakeholders. Flows are the sequence of interaction between physically disjointed positions held by social actors that belong or interact with organizations. These flows are what organizations are made off.

Classic analysis methods can only work in predefined or controlled environments, because organizations live in a world where interdependence, self-organization and emergence are agility, adaptability and flexibility. It is a networked composed world in the design of collaborative-networked organizations. This networked configurations comes to the composition of complex systems, from cells, to society and enterprises (associations of individuals, technology and products). In those complex systems, characteristics of emergence, order and self-organization, develop a set of network interdependent actions not visible in the individual parts. This is the reason why defining methods to analyze a domain fail if the domain and the parts change, which is what most of the times occurs once we are living in a world of variety.

In this paper you will learn how to tackle the challenge that organizations must be able to align network structure to the process type being executed and evolve the network type according to circumstances. Organizations that manage to better align these three perspectives: social network, knowledge nature and process design, are those that will be ahead in terms of execution capabilities, flexibility and adaptation to change.

Real-World Award-Winning Case Studies

AXLE GROUP HOLDINGS LTD., UK
Nominated by EmergeAdapt, United Kingdom

In January 2012, Axle Group Holding, one of the UK's largest multi-channel tyre retailers, replaced four eCommerce systems along with a back-office platform to provide case workers with a tool to deliver customer service and post-order treatment. EmergeAdapt built the eCommerce systems and a new back-office case management platform, integrated to all four sites, and to a branch and warehouse system written in DataFlex. All systems were launched in December 2012.

Separately, and while engaged on the Axle project, EmergeAdapt was asked by a UK Claims Management Company to provide the same case management platform for the end-to-end management of circa 1 million PPI claims. This solution allows 120 operators to manage case creation, through to customer contact and negotiation with the UK financial institutions defending the claims. The solution was launched in January 2013.

Both organisations are supported in production on a single multi-tenanted cloud platform, configuring their own case templates in order to deliver their unique service proposition.

CARGONET AS, NORWAY
Nominated by Computas AS, Norway

CargoNet AS is the primary Norwegian freight train operator, and GTS (Goods Transport System) is their system for logistics handling. GTS adaptively unifies contributions from knowledge workers across the organization, from marketing and sales to train configuration and composition, scheduling, real-time monitoring, handling of dangerous goods, truck operations and container quality assurance. It is an ACM system, multiplying as an ERP solution.

GTS is a mission-critical system used by most employees involved in the primary value chain, fully integrated with CargoNet's Internet customer portal. Since going online in 2002, GTS has been gradually enhanced in terms of end-user functionality.

Showcasing a non-traditional application of case management technologies, the GTS architecture is information centric. A range of tasks and tools operate on shared work folder contents. The integrated customer portal for placing orders contributes to the contents of work folders. A ruggedized mobile client is deployed in cargo handling trucks, used for container reception, placement and depot management. Another mobile client handles container damage assessment.

DEPARTMENT OF TRANSPORT, SOUTH AFRICA
Nominated by EMC Corporation, United States

The Department of Transport, based in Pretoria with offices in Cape Town, oversees all modes of transportation in South Africa. The Department is organized into branches responsible for civil aviation, maritime, motor vehicles, passenger and freight rail, and other means of public transport.

While many of the Department's processes followed a case management pattern of work, both internal and external, these processes were manual and time-consuming. Externally, constituents submit queries or apply to the Department for licensing. Internally, employees respond to requests from Parliament and the Cabinet, and submit requests and issue memos that must be reviewed and approved at higher levels of the organization.

The answer was to implement a case management solution for Department-wide document capture, case management, analytics and reporting, and continuous improvement. As a result, the Department is now able to avoid costs of manual and broken processes, better manage case workflows, ensure accountability in all case-related activities, comply with relevant regulations and guidelines, and deliver significantly higher levels of service to all stakeholders.

DIRECTORATE FOR THE CONSTRUCTION OF FACILITIES FOR EURO 2012, UKRAINE
Nominated by PayDox Business Software, Russia

Preparations for the 2012 UEFA European Football Championship «EURO-2012» required implementation of large-scale projects for construction and renovation of stadiums. These projects relied on information technology for flexibility in the management of a large number of business processes containing a lot of tasks, assignments, documents, and discussions. A key system requirement was to the ability to quickly respond to changing circumstances in the project. To meet this requirement all project management was carried out using the Adaptive Case Management (ACM) system.

FLEET ONE, USA
Nominated by 4Spires, USA

Fleet One is a midsized company that provides fuel cards and other financial services to private and governmental organizations with fleets of vehicles. The 9-person marketing department was struggling with managing their workload. They receive numerous requests from company management and colleagues in other departments for preparing marketing collateral, advertisements, exhibits at trade shows, marketing programs, etc. On an ongoing basis the department is typically working on 40 or 50 requests at a time.

Each knowledge worker in the department is working on multiple requests at a time on various schedules; and so oversight of the whole workload, both by person and across the department, is critical to managing personal and departmental resources. Flexibility is key; individual obligations are initially mapped out in the context of the final delivery, but it rarely turns out exactly according to plan. A high degree of communication and collaboration among the team is needed to juggle changing schedules across multiple projects. In October 2012, Fleet One installed an innovative knowledge worker system that enabled the department to improve their coordination, efficiency, visibility, and governance over the activities in the department. The system is producing a new class of granular performance data that is providing new insights into individual and group performance.

INFO EDGE PVT. LTD., INDIA
Nominated by Newgen Software Technologies Limited

Info Edge Pvt. Limited is India's leading online classifieds company with a strong portfolio of brands, experienced management team and a business model that is driven to further capitalize on its first phase of growth.

The company wanted a robust, scalable, enterprise class solution for Naukri.com, India's biggest jobsite and its flagship brand. They were looking for a solution to standardize five core processes namely resume writing, cover letter, application writing, and info-graphic resume and video resume script writing. The company faced challenges in handling the huge transactions related to their job applications.

Keen to plug this gap, the company implemented a solution for its strength in process definition, quick deployment cycle and flexibility. Coined "Resumepedia" this solution consisted of its Business Process Management tool and Enterprise Content Management tool. It replaced the existing workflow solution and currently has more than 100 active users.

NORWEGIAN COURTS ADMINISTRATION, NORWAY
Nominated by Computas AS, Norway

LOVISA is the ACM solution for the Norwegian Courts Administration (NCA). LOVISA supports Norwegian first and second instance courts in their case handling and court management. All court employees are LOVISA users, including judges, clerks and other staff. It facilitates communication with external stakeholders such as lawyers and lay judges through web portals, whereas police, prosecutors, the correctional services and other public bodies rely on "business to business" integration.

Supporting the complete value chain of the courts, it focuses on the active participants' decision-related parts of the juridical case handling. For each case, a work folder provides a shared work environment for the case manager (normally the judge) and other participants. These work folders provide access to worklists, case data and documents, giving users active and adaptive task support, ensuring high-quality uniform case handling in accordance with Norwegian procedural law, while leaving the specific legal contents of the case for professional judgment.

LOVISA uses a rich variety of case type templates with specific case handling functionality, ranging from simple types with short lifespans to complex types spanning over several years. The system has integrated multilingual document handling, including generating/merging documents from case data, using hundreds of document templates maintained by the NCA. It assists with delegation, deadlines, reminders and escalations—also based on task support. To assist in planning and follow-up, case folders have a generated timeline view contrasting the current state with the desired state, independently of all concurrent partial workflows operating on the case.

TEXAS OFFICE OF THE ATTORNEY GENERAL CRIME VICTIM SERVICES DIVISION, USA
Nominated by IBM

The Office of the Attorney General's (OAG) Crime Victim Services Division (CVSD) legacy workflow system was implemented in 1999 to replace a paper file processing system. Victims of violent crimes in Texas can apply for eligibility for the Crime Victims' Compensation Program, which pays medical and other bills related to the crime.

All aspects of the existing system were now unsupportable by current vendors and were becoming increasingly unstable. Due to the aging infrastructure, poor architecture, and unsupported software versions, the current system was dangerously close to failure. A software change and new approach were critical to continue meeting the CVSD statutory functions. Failure to implement or improperly implementing the project could result in a delay in processing claims for victims of crime in Texas. This could also negatively impact legislatively-mandated measures, which could put future state and federal funding in jeopardy.

The OAG is using adaptive case management (ACM) to manage the victim application process, eligibility determination, case management, medical bill tracking, and the appeals procedure. The case view of the victim within the ACM solution provides knowledge workers a 360-degree view of a victim's case, with access to all received documentation and case history. Knowledge workers and other program staff can initiate pre-defined and ad hoc tasks, with email or workflow notifications to task assignees. Managers can monitor and adjust workloads, and view program productivity through reports to the individual user level. This is a cloud infrastructure deployment of ACM. Phase II of the project will include replacement of a legacy mainframe application and a potential expansion of social networking capabilities.

U.S. DEPARTMENT OF HOUSING AND URBAN DEVELOPMENT (HUD), USA
Nominated by AINS, Inc., USA

The U.S. Department of Housing and Urban Development (HUD) is responsible for overseeing national policy and programs to address the nation's housing and community development needs, and for enforcing fair housing laws. Since 2011, approximately 10,000 staff members at HUD have relied on a highly flexible Correspondence Tracking System (CTS) to facilitate the processing of Executive Correspondence related to department-wide programs. The CTS application is built on a dynamic, configurable case management platform that was subsequently leveraged vertically within the organization to configure applications for a wide range of non-core Human Resources (HR) business process pain points. In this way, HUD was able to quickly and cost-effectively build several mission-support case management applications under a unified platform - with minimal custom software coding.

The HR Case Management System (HR CMS) applications bring transparency to HR operations, provide better communication, reduce opportunities for delay, allow supervisors to monitors workload, ensure accountability, and consolidate 20 disparate systems. The HR CMS is under the purview of the Office of the Chief Human Capital Officer (OCHCO) and has been configured for a variety of HR management functions such as Employee Relations/Labor Relations, Reasonable Accommodations, and Workers' Compensation.

The configurable platform approach to solving organizational case management problems has allowed HUD to consolidate legacy systems and save money on O&M; deliver new workflow-driven HR applications within 6 months from contract inception (exceeding expectations); and demonstrate the ability to make application changes in a timely manner without impacting other systems. To address their business process needs, HUD had previously required three separate contracts costing more than $1M per year, whereas it now relies on one contractor with less than $150K per year for maintenance.

UBS Bank, Worldwide
Nominated by Whitestein Technologies

This case study describes the successful adoption of Adaptive Case Management by UBS Wealth, a division of UBS Bank. UBS is enhancing their global operations with client-centric collaboration, operational visibility, adaptive process improvement, through the 'PM1' portfolio management suite built with the Living System's Process Suite (LSPS).

LSPS is designed for cases in which adaptive changes to data state are made by a goal-oriented software controller. This ensures that cases evolve in coordination with events and situational change in order to adapt in real-time to a goal-focused execution path.

In partnership with Whitestein, PM1 was built by Expersoft Systems, a global vendor of Portfolio and Wealth Management applications for retail and private banks, independent wealth managers, and asset management providers. LSPS provided Expersoft with the ability to model a comprehensive set of goal-oriented processes that form the core of their portfolio management system.

PM1 with LSPS integrates and extends UBS' complex ecosystem of banking applications, supporting the achievement of transversal goals within a flexible, integrated, and intuitive environment for both the bank and their customers. Each case follows a goal-driven pathway defined by the customer's specific objectives, while meeting both the unique local requirements that vary between regions, yet ensuring that each region complies with the bank's global goals and policies.

Knowledge Work and Case Management

Where is ACM Today?
Realities and Opportunities

Nathaniel Palmer,
Business Process Management, Inc.

1. INTRODUCTION

In his groundbreaking book, *Management Challenges for the 21st Century*, Peter Drucker illustrated that in the 20th century it was the extraordinary increase in productivity by manual laborers that enabled the previously unprecedented increase in the standard of living enjoyed throughout the 1900s. For the 21st century, he argued, it is the productivity of the *knowledge worker* that would define both the core mission for managers and the source of economic growth.

Today, more than a half-century after Drucker first coined the phrase "knowledge worker" (in 1959) the share of the workforce represented by this group has grown considerably, to as much as half of all workers by some measures. So, too, have grown investments targeting knowledge worker productivity. Yet despite this, we remain far from realizing the level of improvement seen in manual labor over the course of the last century.

These knowledge worker targeted investments have largely revolved around Information Technology (IT) systems and have traditionally targeted one of two areas. The first involves control and automation systems, involving software such as Enterprise Resource Planning (ERP) or the more contemporary technology of Business Process Management (BPM). These systems are designed to enforce a command and control management model to ensuring consistent work, adherence to policy and regulation, and generally repeatable, predictable modes of work. Where efficiency gains are realized, it is through standardizing how work is performed.

Yet without the flexibility to adapt to changes in the business environment, the potential impact of work automation offered for knowledge worker productivity is limited. Much (if not most) of the knowledge worker's daily activities cannot be accurately defined in advance, within pre-defined automation units. At least not with the level of structure and precision necessary to code activities into transactional environments designed for control rather than flexibility. Knowledge work is by its nature more complex, dynamic and unpredictable in nature.

As a result many of the most pivotal activities which fill the knowledge worker's day take place outside the realm of particular applications, other than the basic ad hoc tools of email, SharePoint, and other components of ironically named "productivity suites" which offer very little with regards to specifically facilitating productivity improvement.

In fact, the transactional environments that make up much of previously cited investments (such as ERP and BPM) may actually curtail the knowledge worker's effectiveness, by placing procedural limits and restrictions where none need to exist and contributing to frustration levels and knowledge worker attrition. It is in part due to these limitations that Drucker was a long-time skeptic of the potential for IT to sufficiently address knowledge worker productivity. Yet Drucker was not opposed to collaboration, per se, but rather to the command-and-control orientation of transactional environments. As he often posited (and to quote specifically one of his *Harvard Business Review* op-eds), *The modern organization cannot be an organization of boss and subordinate. It must be organized as a team.*

Those words go directly to the notion of top-down management via predefined, structured process automation. Effective and efficient knowledge work relies on the smooth navigation of unstructured processes and the elaboration of custom and one-off procedures. As we move to the 21st century business model, the focus must be on equipping knowledge workers with tools and infrastructure that enable communication and information sharing, such as networking, e-mail, content management and increasingly, social media. Yet supporting the inherently dynamic nature of knowledge work does not mean abandoning all aspects of governance and information management.

2. BRIDGING THE GAP BETWEEN CONTROLLED AND AD HOC

As these 'traditional' IT investments have advanced their footprint in the workplace, a gap has emerged. It can be found between e-mail and ad hoc communication tools (which, while used in one form or another by all knowledge workers, offer little with regard to task management) and the ERP/BPM realm, premised on predictable work patterns defined in advance. What has emerged to fill this void is Adaptive Case Management – solutions with capabilities that recognize the perpetual evolution that will characterize particular business processes and provide powerful support to those who must work within these environments.

For the last several years, I have studied knowledge worker productivity and work patterns. Part of this research has involved the analysis of how an average knowledge worker spends their day. We asked knowledge workers to identify the percentage of their day spent in various work modes ranging from fully automated to entirely ad hoc. With results shown on the next page, two studies conducted first in 2011 then followed up again in 2013 found that little had changed in that time.

Notably, only a third of knowledge workers' time is spent in structured work that can be or already has been automated through traditional IT investments. Of course there is in part an easy explanation for why so little is reported spent on fully automated—if it's automated, then little time is invested in performing it. Yet the larger issue here is that not just that a small percent of the day spent on automated activities, but that only an insignificant portion of a knowledge worker's activities are even automatable. That which can be automated by and large already has been. While there remain opportunities for alleviating the burden of repetitive "drudgework" by incorporating automatable work into the course of knowledge work, the bulk of the low hanging fruit of automation has largely been addressed.

Where knowledge workers do spend most of their time (two-thirds of their day as shown below) is at the nexus of both purely unpredictable work, where nothing ever happens the same way twice, the realm of *barely repeatable* processes, where work follows a pattern, but not a scripted pathway. This is in contrast with traditional structured workflow, which may be complex in its definition, yet is comparatively much more narrowly focused, by virtue of the fact that it is entirely predefined. Whereas Adaptive Case Management (as a means of facilitating knowledge work) involves specifically defined goals and milestones, inevitably the sequence to realize these changes varies from day-to-day. This spotlights the critical difference between Business Process Management (BPM) and workflow automation from Adaptive Case Management, where both structured work and structured processes combine across the lifecycle of a business process.

Work Patterns of Knowledge Workers; Percent of the Day Spent in Different Modes

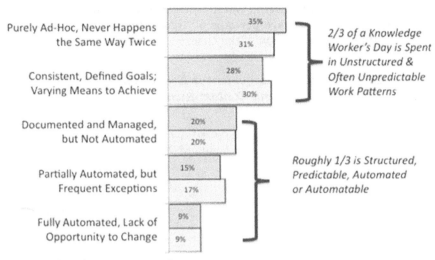

Source: 2011 - 2013 Case Management Survey

Barely repeatable processes are representative of the inherent complexity that defines knowledge work, where goals are consistent and well-established, yet the pathways to achieve them are numerous with different variations and different decision points. Often with these types of processes it is possible to define and apply policies and specific business logic around how that work is performed. This will often require the ability to define and manage specific sets of business rules, as well as high level patterns of how the process is going to flow (e.g., "milestones") yet have it still be impossible to determine in advance the exact sequence of tasks and activities. In each case, the exact combination and sequence of activities is determined by the unique circumstances of a given case.

3. WHY MANAGING KNOWLEDGE WORK IS HARDER

The difference between the manual work that was the subject of the pre-Drucker theorists such as W. Edwards Deming and Frederick Taylor and knowledge work we face today, is the abundance highly-predictable production processes. Manual work readily lends itself to standardization and the application of statistical optimization. Quality control and efficiency in this context comes from performing the same task the same way, not finding creative ways to reach the same outcome.

Investments in packaged software such as ERP, or more domain-specific applications such as those for loan origination, are predicated on adopting the specific vendor's view of how the process should be and would be performed. In fact that was their selling point – the vendor having spent a lot of time and their own R&D investment to pre-define the process.

The expectation was and is that the purchaser or adopter will change their operations according to the new process(es) contained within the application. Although BPM has offered a great leap forward in enabling the shift from vendor-defined to client-defined processes, allowing business analysts to define processes unique to the business, these advantages remain limited to the roughly one-third of work that the knowledge workers reported as being predictable, yet still fails to address the majority of their workday.

Yet contrast this with ACM, which allows retaining consistency where it is useful to do so, but brings a broader focus on events and outcomes and thereby offers support to knowledge workers in the less predictable and predefined areas of their roles. The lifecycle of a case begins when an event occurs, and as a result a case file is opened, then at that stage perhaps all that is known is the end point—the criteria that defines the resolution of the case.

Adaptive Case Management is Event-Driven, Content- and Context-Aware

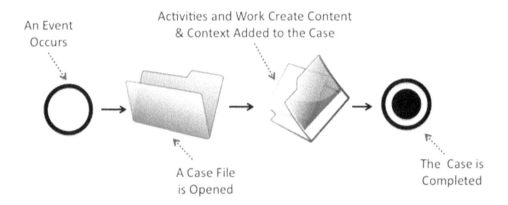

An Event
Occurs

Activities and Work Create Content
& Context Added to the Case

A Case File
is Opened

The Case is
Completed

As the case progresses, a series of activities will occur and information is generated and/or otherwise added to the case. It is that information and the context around it that determines the path(s) to be taken, and ultimately define the achieved outcome. It is only when that end goal is reached that the case is completed.

For example, when a customer reports a problem, a case is opened and what happens next is the movement toward realizing and resolving the case, but each step is only determined as the previous one is completed, not as part of a predefined sequence. In this instance an issue is investigated. It may be something that takes months to resolve or it could take hours. Along the way, potential solutions are attempted or suggested, there is communication by voice, email, or postal mail, and inevitably research is conducted. There may be any number of sub-processes or steps kicked off as the case evolves, but the sequence for those activities, how the work is performed and how it flows, is deliberately not determined in advance.

As is the case for knowledge work itself, the pattern of work supported by Adaptive Case Management that which is goal-driven yet inherently nonlinear. The route to resolution of the case evolves over time, depends on circumstances and feedback in response to previous case activity and may (and often will) go off in unpredictable directions and without a regularized time sequence. Thus the lifecycle of the case is inherently non-deterministic, where the pathway for reaching the outcome is determined by each stage, each milestone in the management of that case. The state of the case is determined by the content and the context within it, not by where it fits on a particular flow chart or process map.

With Adaptive Case Management Goals Are Predetermined, Sequence and Pathways Are Not

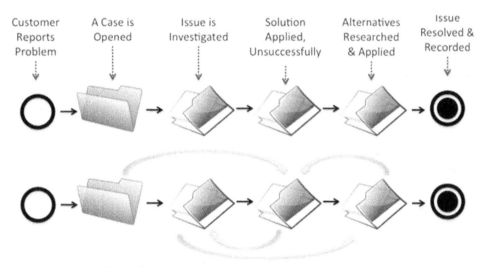

4. GETTING TO THE ROOT CAUSE OF PRODUCTIVITY LOSS

As part of the research repeated in 2011 and 2013, we asked about the hurdles and pain points that knowledge workers face relative to their productivity – i.e., what did they face in the course of their workday which caused them to be less productive than they could otherwise be. Here again we found notable consistency between studies, and most curious is that it is not the knowledge-dependent activities that would otherwise be impossible to automate.

Daily Challenges Knowledge Workers Face

Source: 2011 - 2013 Case Management Survey

Rather, the greatest productivity traps are found in the more mundane activities, simply tracking who is doing what, where they have dependencies on co-workers, where are they in the course of their work, what's the state of their work, and how are they managing the documentation that they need to support a given task. These are the things that knowledge workers find the most challenging.

These findings reinforces the fact that knowledge workers do not need to be told what to, but rather require tools that give them visibility into operations, access to information, and assistance with enabling collaboration. Here we see great alignment between the benefits offered with Adaptive Case Management and the capabilities needed for knowledge worker productivity. A prime example of the need for a more flexible investment is the rising trend for remote/field workers. Enabled by the latest mobile hardware (smartphones, tablets, iPads, etc.) remote knowledge workers are more connected than ever – the only limiting factor has been the software to allow them to fully utilize the connective and collaborative possibilities of modern technology. Adaptive Case Management is the latest evolution and is filling that gap.

5. IDENTIFYING ADAPTIVE CASE MANAGEMENT WORK PATTERNS

Not every organization has specific staff, roles, or departments explicitly identified by name or title as performing "Case Management." This has traditionally been limited to certain industries and company types, such as insurance carriers, healthcare providers, other services delivery providers, government agencies, and so forth. Five years ago, or even more recently, if you asked an executive at an organization outside of that traditional group whether or not they needed case management, chances are their response would be "We're not managing cases. So, no, we don't."

Yet it is interesting to see that nearly every organization that was surveyed now identifies work patterns directly applicable to case management and across all of these case management type patterns there is growth in either applicability or recognition over the last two years. Indeed it maybe more of the latter, greater recognition rather than actual changes in work patterns from 2011 to 2013.

Work Patterns Applicable to Case Management

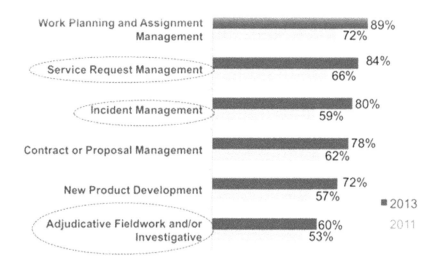

The reality is these patterns are applicable. The work patterns, the use cases, the aspect of knowledge work for which adaptive case management is needed, these are applicable to virtually every organization. We expect case management to be a market that's going to grow quite a bit and be central to this notion of how we actually start to realize knowledge worker productivity. Through their various reports *Forrester Research* has identified three central types of work that fit the Adaptive Case Management model: **Investigative**, **Service Request**, and **Incident Management**, circled in red in the chart above. Forrester's categorizations are generally validated by our own research, with their three main categories representing a superset of the top six case management work patterns identified in both the 2011 and 2013 surveys.

This three-part segmentation presents a useful framework to see the interplay between the functionality and sub-processes and use cases that you would see in each of those three categories, as well as the drivers there. For example, customer experience is probably one that you could say overlaps with incident management and service request, probably less relevant to investigations; risk management being a critical aspect of investigations as well as service request and so forth.

We have asked organizations to describe work patterns, priorities, and challenges, and in doing so gained more context, getting to the definitions behind these terms and validating which work patterns are applicable to their organizations. One aspect that is a bit outside of the Forrester segmentation, however, but is nonetheless something we've seen quite a bit in our own work is the pattern for *Work Planning and Assignment Management*. In fairness, it could fit in all or one of the three, depending on the context, the type of capabilities and functionality involved. Although it may be closest to *Service Request Management*, particularly as it relates to service delivery.

Where the profiles of staff involved (knowledge workers) revolve around service roles or customer support type roles, then service request assignment management tends to be part of Service Request Management, particularly where it augments (or increasingly is replacing) the common Workforce Optimization (WFO) applications used in service industries. If the functions of planning and assigning staff revolve around fieldwork that is *not* part of service delivery, then in our experience it is most likely around an investigative process.

Incident Management

Incident Management deals with supporting processes where things need to be handled in a particular way, but not in a way that can be fully automated. It is about applying policy, rules, tracking, being able to have an audit trail in place, being able to have consistency and traceability and visibility into how work is performed, but not overly prescriptive in every aspect of it. This may involve standard processes such as the creation, formatting, and development of documents or other areas, but it's not something for which you can apply a fully-automated process. In that case, you have a work pattern that follows a case management type lifecycle, but it's less about the subjectivity or the knowledge worker. In other words, it's less about enabling the knowledge worker to apply their own judgment and know-how to it. It's more about allowing dynamic processes to be performed according to prescribed policies and procedures.

Not every aspect of incident management falls into that category. What is common is requiring multi-channel interaction across multiple devices, being able to support cloud and mobile access, having fine-grained tracking and reporting around how information is captured and used, what rules are applied and how decisions are made. Typically, this is something that's event-driven rather than discovery-oriented, such is otherwise true with *Investigative Case Management.*

For the last two years the lack of visibility in others' work has been the top challenge faced by knowledge workers (see *Daily Challenges Knowledge Workers Face* on page 23). This is certainly true for incident management, as the ability to expedite a resolution requires visibility into the status of dependent activities being performed by others.

Lastly, we look at the notion of better records and data management practices. This is a critical issue in every organization and something that case management deals with very directly and in a very meaningful way by being able to apply context to existing content going into a system of record, and governance or structure to content that's coming out of or being produced as a result of engagement; interactions through systems of engagement.

Service Requests

Services requests and *Service Request Management* are inherently event-driven, whether it's a help desk scenario where a service request call is coming in or logged. The same would apply to customer onboarding or even employee onboarding. In each case, the exact steps and the sequence to be followed are going to be defined based on the unique aspect of the case, incident, or event. Inevitably this will involve a set of milestones, a checklist, rules and policies. In different cases, there might be regulatory requirements. There's certainly tracking of it. And in every case, you want to do it as quickly as possible, but without compromising the quality of the outcome and experience. This is one of the distinctions between case management to a service request scenario versus CRM or other tools that have traditionally been applied to the same basic business problems.

We've all been on the phone with a customer support rep and known that they're trying to get through the call as quickly as possible. Part of that is good. You want them to be expeditious. But they're moving very quickly. Largely that's because the metric applied there is not necessarily your satisfaction, but the time to resolution and being able to close that ticket as fast as possible. Very often, that works against the benefit to the customer, employee, or stakeholder involved.

With case management, it is following a goal-driven path where the goal is known when that ticket is open, the goal is to close that ticket. But the metrics applied aren't necessarily applicable and don't need to be limited to just the time to resolution. It can be applied to other aspects such as enhancing the quality of experience and the ability to bring in the combination of access to information from external systems, the ease of facilitating collaboration, bringing in other subject matter experts or others that are going to collaborate on that resolution, being able to have an accurate log of what steps are taken to have that adaptive capability where the next step is just based on the context using analytics, using past service resolutions; being able to bring all that to bear to not only resolve the incident quickly, but to do so in a way that optimizes the experience. That's a benefit of case management versus CRM.

Investigative Case Management

Investigative case management is the one that showed up consistently in both surveys as being the least applicable, yet in reality, as you deconstruct both what's involved with investigative case management and how that might be applied in organizations, it's something that is very broadly applicable.

There are some obvious aspects of it, such as where it's being used in a criminal investigation, in a fraud investigation, in an audit scenario. In all these cases, it's goal-driven and it has a definitive lifecycle. It's event-driven, but it may be something that is initiated. In other words, it may be used as a discovery process looking for events as opposed to simply starting once identified fraud or something else that has occurred.

It's most definitely not production case management. You can talk to anybody that's involved in any aspect of investigation or any kind of judicative process. They are experts and their expertise is what guides that process. Yet, it still needs to follow prescribed procedures and policies the way that information is handled, whether it's specifically the chain of custody or more mundane aspects that one piece of information might trigger five other pieces of information that need to be collected.

A frequently-cited and thus critical requirement for *Investigative Case Management* is the ability to delegate for different investigators to follow up on different pieces of information, and then that needs to be consolidated and synchronized. There may be handoffs of the case – in fact, there almost always are – and being able to maintain consistency and continuity with those handoffs. All of that is critical, as is the cloud aspect, the mobile aspect. None of this stuff is happening today with one individual sitting in front of a PC completely tethered. This is stuff that's highly collaborative, very field-oriented, and something where case management is absolutely key.

Those are the clear cases, but there are many other cases around. Even things such as new product development, new drug development – discovery-oriented processes where you want to be capturing that information. New drug development is frankly a fascinating application of case management. It's a field that we've been involved with for more than ten years and have seen the obvious parallels with adaptive case management.

It's frankly not an area where case management has largely been applied so far. They don't think of themselves as having case management type problems. They have discovery-oriented problems and innovation-oriented problems. But this is why adaptive case management is so applicable to these areas. It's not just what was traditionally deemed case work in the old model of things.

The other aspect, particularly with investigative and discovery-oriented case management and applications and use cases, is that it's very data-driven. However, we tend to take exception to this notion of being data-driven. It's the term that is in today's vernacular that we use to describe things for which information is informing how work is to be done, and the pursuit of that information really defines that work. Thus it is knowledge-driven. Ultimately, it's the context of that information that drives the process and the ability to enable that by applying analytics in a closed-loop scenario is a critical aspect and a critical benefit of adaptive case management, as we distinguish dynamic and adaptive case management from the other kinds of case management – things that might be described as case management but are falling into the other realm of CRM or content management.

That dividing line is around how you can create those closed-loop environments and scenarios in which you are able to extract analytics around information and context as it's being captured, feed that back in a way that's actionable, and allow for knowledge workers to be able to make better decisions based on the analytics. Not to prescribe exactly what they need to do, as in the case of production case management, but enable them to make better-informed decisions based on analytics. That's a critical benefit of adaptive case management.

6. BUILDING RESPONSIVE SYSTEMS

In many ways, the emergence of Adaptive Case Management represents the paradigm shift from adapting business practices to the design of IT systems, to building systems that reflect how work is actually performed. Our work today is untethered. The tools supporting it may not be. Having access on smartphones and tablets is critical. Being able to have access to that information while traveling is critical. Having flexibility of those environments is critical. When we look at the patterns of how knowledge workers spend their day, we need to think in terms of whether or not it is structured activity, such as completing within a transactional application (and we already know that is a very small part of their day) Or if an unstructured activity, is it purely ad hoc? Chance there is there some definition to it, and that it is dynamic in nature.

Look at the priorities that are in place today that are addressable by case management. In other words, don't start by asking what benefits of case management apply to you. Rather, identify the things that are priorities in you organization, then identify the link to those which happen to be applicable to case management. For example, reducing training requirements and change management otherwise associated with the introduction of new processes, policy/procedure, systems; these are matters that can be greatly improved (or otherwise prevented) by leveraging Adaptive case management. In our survey research, we have seen consistent interest in the pursuit of these productivity-oriented improvements (e.g., distinct from specific financial gains) and "soft dollar" benefits around reducing rework, increasing customer satisfaction, increasing employee satisfaction, gaining visibility into operations. What we're starting to talk about is IT in terms of *Systems of Record* and *Systems of Engagement*. Systems of record are transactional systems, ERP, HR, database, structured systems. Systems of engagement, as the name applies, are how individuals, stakeholders, employees, and customers are engaging (e-mail, customer-facing aspect of a CRM, increasingly web apps and mobile apps).

Unsurprisingly for knowledge work, this dividing line is not a definitive demarcation. It's more a fuzzy line between systems and engagement and systems record as it applies here. Generally, we can say that this highly-structured automated work is indicative of the systems of record whereas work that is more dynamic, more ad hoc, that has definition and rules but is not structured, is in the province of systems of engagement. The reason today there is so much discussion about case management in the context of knowledge work is case management provides a framework that is both a system of record and a system of engagement. The case folder provides connections to rules, policies, process, as well as the systems of record. The case management system provides for multiple channels of interaction, collecting multiple types of information whether it's a traditional document, a scanned image document, report, e-mail, voicemail. All that becomes a critical part of the case record.

Traditionally, that's out of reach for one or the other; i.e., either the system of record has no visibility or the only connection point to the system of engagement is the user. Ultimately it is still hard to use systems of record in the mobile, dynamic way we now frequently work, and it's hard to apply governance to systems of engagement. Bridging that is one of the core values of Adaptive case management, through a shared object model that enables incorporating both structured and unstructured information into the case, and with that the ability apply governance.

As described earlier, our research has consistently shown that knowledge workers spend at least two-thirds of any given day in activities which do not follow a predetermined path and which are unpredictable in nature, but still geared toward specific goals. Adaptive case management's adaptive nature assists the knowledge worker to apply know-how and make decisions that lead to the achievement of these identified goals. Better records and data management by connecting context and outcomes with actual information is at the heart of Adaptive case management's effectiveness.

The ability to identify cases, to be able to access information based on the case, based on the context of what occurred, as well as to manage information so the different files can be cross referenced and linked between cases, ultimately allows for capturing and managing the context and the know-how from the activities associated with that case. With Adaptive Case Management a given case may live on in perpetuity, retaining its last state until another event occurs to re-launch it; or it can also be used to launch another case.

For example, with a customer resolution scenario, it may be that a particular customer issue now has become a best practice for other issues, related issues, or other occurrences of that issue and that case can then be the template for how similar situations will be solved going forward. In that sense, the original case's record becomes part of the wider system of record, continuing to influence and guide (but not decide) the knowledge workers' decisions.

Adaptive Case Management Enables a System of Engagement and a System of Record (SOR) For All Forms of Content

Documents • Images • Email • Reports • Voice Mail

Business Rules, Policies & Processes   **Case Folder**   **Record of Context** (complete audit trail)

Multiple Channels of Interaction

Adaptive Case Management fundamentally differs from tools such as BPM and ECM because it is not simply a system of parallel silos, but rather a superset or master system of record, capturing both the "what" (data, files, records or, most often, links to the physical sources of those) and the "how" (metadata, audit trail, as well as the context of decisions and actions). As a result, Adaptive Case Management facilitates more productive knowledge work through the ability to identify and organize content distinctly from other cases—whether shared or unique, it is connected to the specific business context in which it was used.

In this way, Adaptive Case Management even when it is connected with other information management systems and functions still provides a transactional thread across multiple systems of record. The direction for ACM allows the work to follow the worker, providing the cohesiveness of a single point of access. Adaptive Case Management does not impose whether this work is virtual or physical but pulls together all the end points, information, environments and provides the long-term record of how work is done, as well as the guidance, rules, visibility and input that allow knowledge workers to be more productive.

7. CONCLUSION

Adaptive Case Management allows productivity improvements to be measured in both financial and non-financial terms, including reduced re-work, improved customer, and employee satisfaction. In part, by bringing areas of work previously "under the radar" when performed in purely ad hoc environments into greater visibility, Adaptive Case Management offers the ability to prioritize activities across multiple cases, balancing workloads, as well as monitoring quality, timeliness and speed.

There is a broad and collaborative synthesis of case data that is at the heart of what makes Adaptive Case Management "adaptive" and is also the basic driver for why it needs to be so. Adaptive Case Management is ultimately about allowing knowledge workers to work the way that they want to work and to provide them with the tools and information they need to do so effectively. Increasingly, this means having access to social media and outside information sources. There is a significant amount of work currently conducted through *LinkedIn, Twitter* and other social sources as well as resources selected by individual workers that create input and contextual information. It's a critical part of the case record, but is not part of any centrally-managed IT infrastructure.

Critical benefits, and fundamental unique include factors should as delivering a *shared object model* for both structured and unstructured data, so that content from any number of sources can be incorporated not only within the case folder, but the case context as well. By having a comprehensive context around the case folder, rather than simply a "blind" container of files and data, allows for *goal-based outcomes, defining targets and milestones* using the combination of business rules, data, content and analytics.

Ultimately this *enables actionable analytics* seeing meaningful information and context, in a cohesive environment where action can be taken. Adaptive Case Management offers the ability to have analytics around that work, around the content and the context of the case, and to have that be in an actionable framework where you're able to see the result of interactions and actually make decisions in real-time.

Further, and this notion reinforces the fact that *cloud-based delivery is a must*, Adaptive Case Management enables field-based activities by providing access to mobile devices, participating in from any device, anywhere – delivering work to where and how the work is done today. Rather than creating yet another island of automation, Adaptive Case Management *allows the work to follow the worker, providing the cohesiveness of a single point of access* to critical files, content, and application capabilities. Ultimately, to allow knowledge workers to work in the way most conducive to delivering their best performance, rather than being weighed down by the limits of antiquated or otherwise unresponsive systems.

Innovative Organizations Act Like Systems, Not Machines

Keith D Swenson, Fujitsu America

Do you conceptualize your organization as a machine? If so, you may be led down the wrong path for optimizing business processes. Machines are complicated, but truly complex systems, like an organization, a marketplace, an ecosystem, are not like machines. Evidence for this is both familiar and surprising. It is the "Enlightenment Bias" which blinds us to the true nature of organizations. For an organization to be innovative, you need to design it to be self-controlling, but not constrained to fixed predefined patterns. A new generation of tools is come to support organizations in this manner.

ANTI-FRAGILE

An organization hires knowledge workers so that they will think outside the box. However, a BPM system that automates work in a predefined patterns is precisely the box they are hired to think outside of. This paper will deal with "BPM for intelligent workers" and particularly why an approach called adaptive case management (ACM) might be a good fit. Before concluding this, we need to understand some rather surprising things about human organizations. Let's start by exploring the concept of   . This term was coined by Nassim Nicholas Taleb in his 2012 book "Antifragile: Things That Gain From Disorder."

We all know the meaning of 'fragile': When you stress something that is fragile, it might break. What is the opposite of fragile? Most people will readily suggest that the opposite of fragile is 'robust.' When a robust object is stressed it does not break; it remains the same.

There exist things that are even less fragile than robust. These are things that when subjected to stress, they not only resist change, they actually grow and get stronger. They actually get better when subjected to stress, and remain better after the stress is removed.

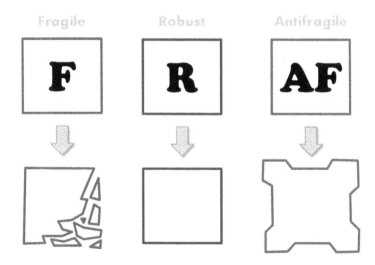

What kind of crazy notion is this? Common sense says that everything eventually wears out and breaks down. It may not happen all at once, like a china teacup, but it is inevitable. Friction on the bearing of a wheel will eventually wear down and fail. Wind on a canvas tarp will eventually work the material and rip the weak spots. Yet, on further consideration, there actually are many things around us that demonstrate antifragility.

Consider muscles. If you exercise, the result will be increased size and strength of the muscles used. To learn to play the piano, you practice. Reading a book on piano technique is not effective. Only by actually sitting at the keyboard and working through songs will you gain proficiency. To learn to play tennis, you have to get out on the court and start hitting balls.

Learning in general is antifragile. Quizzes and exams are purposeful stresses that help to prepare a student for when they will have to face real situations. Simply reading the answers of past tests will not work as well as practicing by taking those tests. Performing a fire drill is clearly an unwanted extra stress that takes people away from their main job, but the result will be an organization better prepared for such an emergency. A fire drill teaches these behaviors far faster and more effectively than any amount of textbook learning.

Things that actually get better as the result of stress are known as adaptive systems. Antifragility is a property that emerges from a complex adaptive system. Complex adaptive systems are all around us; ecosystems, biological systems, organizations, marketplaces, social networks, the economy, even our own muscles and brain. We will explore how these are dramatically different from machines.

MACHINES

To create a good machine, you break the design into a set of discrete parts. Each part is made very precisely and accurately from a hard and durable material to perform a particular function. Parts fit together as perfectly as possible, with just the right gap to minimize friction and other degrading forces.

A good analogy for an idealized machine is a fancy mechanical watch. There are many gears, each made to fit precisely together with the other gears.

The better watches have a jewel movement, which use a very hard stone at the pivot points. Built correctly, the watch will run for a very long time, and be very accurate.

It is, I hope, obvious that machines are not adaptive systems. No matter how many times you wind a clock mechanism, it will run down and need winding again. Less obviously, we should understand that organizations are not machines, even though we like to think of them as machines. Unlike machines, organizations can learn and flexibly adapt to situations. The introduction of a new CEO, with a different management philosophy, can have the effect of redefining many jobs in the company, without any explicit orders being given. The roles that people play are not like the parts of a watch. People routinely fill in for others while they are away on vacation. Organizations do not wear down; they may come to an end in many different ways, but they never simply wear out. Organizations routinely do many things that a machine could never do.

STABILITY

Organizations do not achieve stability the same way that machines do. Remember mechanical stability comes from designing parts very precisely and forming them from very hard materials. Even so, this stability is a temporary thing: the machine will eventually wear out.

An adaptive system achieves stability through what is called *homeostasis*; this stability comes from a balance between different adapting forces. Homeostasis is how your body maintains the same temperature, even when you move from a hot room to a cold outdoors, without any need for a central thermometer mechanism to control it. Homeostasis is how an ecosystem remains viable even though varying climate conditions. Good weather may cause an increase in vegetation. In response the population of grazers might increase. Later, the population of predators might increase as well. The next year weather might be less productive, and grazing populations would be down, and so would the predators. These population proportions are not maintained by any central plan, but instead by a balance of different adaptive forces working off each other.

Improperly thinking that adaptive systems should be treated like machines is a large part of what I call "Enlightenment Bias." This is a way of viewing the world using ideas from Descartes, Newton, and other Enlightenment philosophers who promoted the idea that behind every complicated phenomenon is a set of simple rules that define the behavior. These ideas were revolutionary at the time and led to a tremendous expansion in understanding of natural laws.

With Scientific Management, these ideas expanded into where large complicated operations are seen to be decomposable into smaller, simpler steps that can be precisely and rigorously defined. Scientific management is a part of our culture. We all learned that you should first plan, and then act. If you fail to act, then the fault can be attributed to poor planning. Plan better and you will act better in the future.

The ultimate expression of the Enlightenment Bias is in BPM systems where management attempts to define every possible detailed action that workers might make, and to find the optimal sequence of these actions. These designers imagine the organization as a kind of machine. They try to define very precise and very durable parts for that machine. This works for automating routine processes, but more and more organizations are turning to support for knowledge workers who do work that is anything but routine. At the level of knowledge workers, the organization is not a machine. It behaves more like an adaptive system, and applying machine principles can actually harm the organization.

> "The only sustainable competitive advantage is an organization's ability to learn faster than the competition."
> Peter M. Senge, The Fifth Discipline

ADAPTIVE SYSTEMS CRAVE STRESS

Adaptive systems not only respond well to stress, they actually need stress. This seems surprising when stated that way, but we already know of many examples around us.

If you don't use muscles, they atrophy; they shrink and become weaker. A large muscle uses resources, and that is a waste when that muscle is not necessary. Growing and *shrinking* muscles are the balancing adaptive forces that allow the body to optimize resource usage. Yet if muscle strength declines too far, it is possible to be injured by something that a normally healthy person would not be hurt by. So exercise is an important part of remaining healthy.

If a forest is protected from fires, the undergrowth grows up, and makes the forest more susceptible to fires, and if a fire breaks out it is likely to do far more damage. The policy of preventing all fires in a forest has had the disastrous consequence of indirectly causing far larger and more damaging fires that are harder to recover from. In a very real sense, protecting a forest from fire makes it grow weaker. To maintain the strength of a forest, you need to have regular, modest sized forest fires.

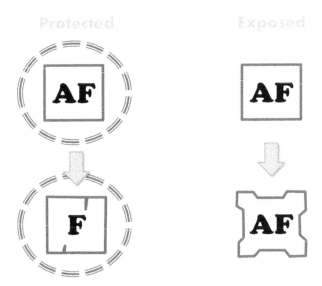

Here is the surprising conclusion: adaptive systems need a certain amount of stress. *If they are protected from all stress they become fragile.*

The same is true with organizations. I mentioned earlier that fire drills are required to ensure that the employees are prepared for the case that an actual fire occurs. Suspending all fire drills will cause the organization to be less prepared for fire. Emergency response teams that do not drill themselves on different simulations and scenarios in advance, would find themselves ill-prepared to meet the next unexpected situation.

If a football team wants to win the tournament, it does so by practicing and playing many scrimmage games on the field. If it spent the time instead sitting still, resting, and conserving muscle movement, team members would be less likely to win the game. Unlike a machine, a team is an adaptive system, which gains from being exercised, and is actually harmed if it does not exercise.

Such exercise must include variations. Olympic swimmer Michael Phelps was forced by his coach to swim in unexpected circumstances: sometimes with the lights turned off, sometimes woken up in the middle of the night without warning. This intentional variation in training has been credited with his ability to win a gold medal in the Beijing Olympics even though his goggles cracked and filled with water.

Business teams crave this as well. Running simulations and scenarios as a business team is a well-known way to improve team performance. Doing things differently allows the team to understand how to coordinate on the fly. Then, if a situation comes along where the team has to do things differently, they are more prepared to meet this challenge.

THE ORGANIZATION AS A SYSTEM

In order to continue this discussion, some clarification of the terms is necessary. Some readers will automatically associate the idea of a system with the information technology (IT) system. However in the rest of this chapter, when I use the term system, I mean the combination of the organization, the people within the organization, and all of the IT systems as well. It is the entire organization that might be fragile or antifragile, not just the computer systems.

> Ask not what the information system does for the organization; instead ask only how the organization performs better with the information system.

Remember that the overarching goal of BPM is to make the overall organization (the system) more effective. We strive to make the business better at providing the products or services that are the purpose of the organization. When we model a process, we are modeling the activity of the business, and not just the computers. When we measure the efficiency, we measure the output of the business, and relate that to the cost of the business. If making the business more efficient meant making the IT systems less efficient, we would do this without hesitation, because our goal is effectiveness of the organization.

This is particularly important when we discuss fragility, antifragility, and adaptiveness. It is the entire organization, the people together with the technology, which is adaptive. An adaptive system automatically senses and responds to new situations, but it is important to remember the people are an essential part of that adaptiveness. While some might dream of IT systems that automatically adapt to new situations, it is not necessary that they do this without human intervention. A large part of making the organization successful with adaptive case management is going to rely on the fairly mundane capability of letting knowledge workers simply do what they want to do, without constraints.

It is the entire organization, the people and the technology, which should not be viewed as a machine, but instead as a system, like a forest, or an ecosystem. Organizations are complex, and they have many interrelated parts that depend upon each other. In doing this we are leveraging Systems Thinking (ST) a philosophical approach to understanding the behavior of organizations (see Fritjof Kapra, "The Web Of Life", Stafford Beer, "Brain of the Firm").

THE BEST PRACTICE CONUNDRUM

It is ironic that the very purpose of most business process management initiatives is find the single best practice, and institute that best practice by forcing employees to follow it. Here we get to the central theme of this chapter and if you remember nothing else, remember this:

*Enforcing a single best practice on an organization can make it **fragile**.*

This can be hard to understand if you think of an organization as a machine. After all, a diesel truck will perform best (no matter how to define best) at a particular speed in a particular gear. A truck driver's goal is to find that optimal mode and use it as much as possible. But organizations are more like muscles than trucks.

I mentioned Michael Phelps above. A coach searching for the single best practice might run a lot of tests, and find out that Phelps swims best at 2:00 in the afternoon, after sleeping to 10am and when the pool temperature is 72 degrees. He might then institute this best practice, asking Phelps to rise at 10am every day, swim and 2:00, and keep the pool at 72 degrees. But doing this would not prepare Phelps for many important aspects of actually competing in the Olympics. If the final swimming environment was not at 2:00pm, or he would not be able to sleep until 10am, then he would find himself less prepared.

The same thing happens in business teams. If a process is put into place that enforces that 'A' is done first, then 'B', and then 'C', the people working in the office come to expect it to always be this way. By acclimatizing to *always* having this pattern, the organization loses the ability to handle cases in any other order.

If you continually take antibiotics, your immune system gets weak possibly allowing you to die from a minor but novel infection. In a complex adaptive system constant stress is not to be mistaken as overreacting to noise but must be understood as environmental tuning information. We need to re-learn that in a complex world the notion of a single logical cause or a predictable outcome of an action is suspect. Constant, random stress is information that aligns the small anti-fragile system with the changes in its environment

The central point of Taleb's book was that antifragile systems crave stress, and if you withhold stress, they wither or become dangerously unstable. He went further to say: "Stability is a Time Bomb." While an adaptive system is able to readily accommodate modest perturbations, if you protect the system from those changes, attempting to provide a static environment, then the system becomes fragile and dangerous.

If you scour management literature, you find this is not an uncommon idea. Management guru Tom Peters' 1988 book "Thriving on Chaos" discusses organizations that thrive on the churn and turmoil around them. It is common to suggest that an organization need occasional "shaking up" to keep it healthy. Roger Martin, Dean of the Rotman School of Management says that "Mastery without originality becomes a cul-de-sac." Jim Collins says that if we will "engage [workers] in a vigorous debate, we will find a way to make this company great." Agile software methodology works on understanding that software development is complex and unpredictable, and does not try to define everything perfectly in advance.

PLANNING AS PART OF WORK

Part of the reason for attempting to identify and isolate the single best practice is to eliminate the need to spend time planning what to do. If there is a fully elaborated best practice, then there is no need to waste time planning. Planning is viewed as a waste, and if planning can be eliminated, then workers can spend all the time doing productive work.

That, at least, is the theory, but many leaders have expressed opposition to this point of view. For example, the following two quotes:

> "No plan survives contact with the enemy."
> Helmuth von Moltke the Elder

> "Planning is essential, plans are worthless."
> Dwight D. Eisenhower

The military is the place where you might expect to see the most rigorously defined and standardized modes of operation, but these respected leaders go out of their way to stress the importance of the planning activity itself. The importance is not just the end result–the plan–but the actual activity of planning itself is important.

Translated to modern terms, it is almost as if Eisenhower was saying that it is important to model your business processes, but when you are done you can throw the resulting models away. It is not the models that have value, but the activity of doing the modeling that provides the value.

From this we can conclude that planning itself should not be eliminated, but in fact should be done as part of work. A best practice should be enforced without question, but instead as a guideline that might, or might not, be followed. There should be a point where the team sits down and evaluates whether the best practice is going to work in this case, and if not, to come up with an alternative. Planning needs to remain part of what the knowledge worker does.

INFORMATION TECHNOLOGY TO SUPPORT THIS

We hire knowledge workers to think outside the box. A IT system dedicated to anticipating every move of a knowledge worker in advance will simply an elaborate box constraining on what the knowledge worker can do. If we want organizations that are strong in the face of varying market conditions, if we want them to be responsive to new situations, then instead of enforcing a single best practice, the IT system should allow for myriad different practices.

This is very surprising and quite disturbing. It flies in the face of everything we learned about finding and instituting the best practice. There are two approaches one might take to allow may varying paths, one I call the "radical" approach, and another I call the "innovator" approach.

The radical approach is to suggest that the information itself system should mix things up a bit. That is, it should randomly alter some parts of the business process in order to see what happens. This would exercise the workers in the same way that a vaccine exercises the immune system. Workers would certainly learn how to accommodate variations in the process, and they would certainly be able to accommodate future changes. In the long run the system might identify a novel, improved business process, however this approach is wasteful.

The less radical approach is the "innovator" approach in which knowledge workers are allowed to do the process differently if it seems necessary to them. This relies on the knowledge worker coming up with an idea about what might be a better way to do things. In my own personal experience many knowledge workers have plenty of ideas on how things might be done better. The innovator approach would allow them to try out their idea and see if it works.

This is not really a new idea either. Before the advent of BPM systems, managers would redesign their processes as needed when they thought they could do it better. Generally, if successful, they would be rewarded for "taking initiative." An IT system that enforces a particular best practice can actually stand in the way of these innovators, which is why we need specialized system that allow for these kinds of changes.

ADVANCES IN INFORMATION TECHNOLOGY

System architects have a wide spectrum of technology available to support business. Each technology approach is useful for a different kind of business problem. In order to organize and make this easier to understand, I have organized them according to the degree of predictability of the business problem they solve. At the left end you have entirely predictable work which needs to be done exactly the same way every time: the process has always been done that way for years, and (probably) always will be done that way. The other end of the spectrum is complete unpredictability where there is no way to know from moment to moment what will have to be done next.

Predictability and repeatability go hand-in-hand. Any work which is repeated the same way thousands of times, is predictable by definition. Work that is not done the same way every time, that is frequently repeated, is consequently less predictable. Something that is done only once in history is the most unpredictable of all.

The approach to developing any system will depend on how much change the system will have to respond to over time. Extremely predictable, stable environments can benefit from powerful but inflexible approaches. As the anticipated amount of change rises, it becomes more important to use a technique which offers greater flexibility. More flexible approaches have less precision to exactly match the needs of the situation. The approach depends entirely on the amount of change.

Most job situations lie between the extremes of completely predictable/repeatable and not predictable/not repeatable. We can break the field into seven domains according to the technology that might be used to support workers:

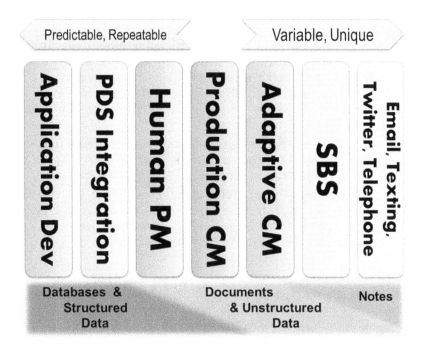

1. Traditional Application Development is not a special process approach, but rather the absence of process technology. If work is very predictable and stable over time, one can use traditional development techniques (e.g. using any third generation language like Java, VB, PHP, etc.) to create a supporting application. The cost of development might be high, but the benefit of having very precise control of the capabilities will yield efficiency that over a large number of cases will pay back the up-front costs.

2. Process-Driven Server Integration (PDSI) is a form of programming that uses process models to provide flexibility to cope with changes in the distributed server environment. These process models deal with low level data; pick up a record from one place, transform it, and send the result to another place. The modeling is done by a programmer who understands data structures and transforms, although a business person might be able to review the model for conceptual correctness. Straight-thru-processing (STP) and Enterprise Application Integration (EAI) are other names for this category.

An example of a business problem in this domain is fulfilling the purchase of a cell phone: coordination is needed between one system to allocate a phone number, another system to set up an account, another system to order the phone, and yet another system to arrange for delivery. Ideally the process model automates this completely and quickly.

3. Human Process Management (HPM) uses a process map showing actions assigned to people. Humans are in many ways less predictable than servers. In PDSI, the process will decide which server to handle a task, send the request and 99.95% of the time it will be done. However, for humans, it is not uncommon for a task to be assigned to one person, then reassign to another, then forgotten about until a reminder is sent, and then finally complete by someone else who works with the assignee. Human process management is designed for the idea that one can't state in advance exactly who will do the task.

Usually this technology has strong support for roles which is a way of directing the assignment to a structure that can be easily changed from day to day, without having to edit the process. Humans need a task list in order to decide which task to do next, deadlines to indicate that something has been sitting too long, and reminders to actively prompt for something that is late. Escalation is a feature that allows a task to be automatically reassigned if it takes too long. It is worth noting that none of these features are needed in the PDSI domain: if a server fails to respond, then sending a reminder will have no effect.

A good example of HPM is expense report approvals: there are a number of people involved who do different tasks like approving. There are reminders if people are slow, and tasks can be reassigned if someone changes position.

4. Production Case Management (PCM) is for when the process itself cannot be completely defined in advance, but the set of possible actions one might want to do can be defined. The user has to decide, based on experience, what the right next thing to do, and to pick that from a menu of possible actions available at that time.

It is called production case management, because it is designed for high volume situations. Like Human PM there is a separation between the people who determine the possible actions (the developers) and the people who use the actions (the users).

A good example of a business problem needing PCM is a help desk or customer support center. There are set of possible actions, such as refund the customer, order a replacement, escalate to development, etc. The customer support agent is there primarily to answer questions, but if warranted, can call one of these steps into play. The agent is a knowledge worker who learns the specific trouble modes that people are likely to encounter, and learns to determine the right course of future action for each case.

5. Adaptive Case Management (ACM) - not only are the processes unpredictable, but even the actions that need to be done are not known in advance. Knowledge workers can actually create new goals that have never been needed before.[5] An ACM system allows knowledge workers to experiment with new ways of working. It does not constrain the workers to any given business pre-defined process. The process can be changed by any participant, and changing the process is a natural part of everyday activity.

When we say that the process can be changed by any knowledge worker, it is necessarily understood that no special skills or knowledge must be necessary for making these changes. Users must be not only be allowed, but also able to make those changes. This requirement rules out most of the more formal ways of modeling processes which require specialized training.[13] The process must be expressed in a way that a completely untrained knowledge worker can modify at will. One might think of this not as process modeling, but instead planning. Knowledge workers don't work on pre-planned units of work, but instead planning itself is part of doing the job.

An example needing ACM is that of a doctor defining a treatment plan for a patient with a particular set of symptoms and history. The treatment plan is a kind of process, but the doctor cannot wait for a programmer to implement it. In an ACM system, the doctor is able to create the treatment plan directly and without IT help.

6. Social Business Software (SBS) is the last category between ACM and email: it is a domain that has very little or no explicit process support, however there is a greater amount of collaboration and time sequencing than manual email. This domain has people collaborating on permanent artifacts, and often using network connections to control access. This is collaborative software, and it includes basic document management systems without a fixed plan. There may be representations of goals, but they are created on the fly and discarded after use.

7. Email, Telephone, Texting is on the right end of the spectrum, and has no process support at all, no permanent structures, simply communication. This is the default that many current processes are forced to use, but this approach puts the greatest burden on the user, and yields the least amount of analytic data to monitor and improve processes.

ADAPTIVE CASE MANAGEMENT

From all of these, it is exactly adaptive case management (ACM) that provides the best support for intelligent workers. It does not constrain the workers to any given business pre-defined process. The process can be changed by any participant, and changing the process is a natural part of everyday activity.

A lot of systems talk about their ability to change, but in most cases they assume that a specially trained person will do the changes. Here, when we say that the process can be changed by any knowledge worker, it is necessarily understood that no special skills or knowledge must be necessary for making these changes. The users must be not only allowed, but also able to make those changes. This activity rules out most of the more formal ways of modeling processes which require specialized training. The process must be expressed in a way that a completely untrained knowledge worker can modify at will.

We don't think of this as process modeling, but instead planning. Knowledge workers don't work on pre-planned units of work, but instead planning itself is part of doing the job.

This approach is very hard to accept by those who view an organization as a machine that operates on a set of simple principles. It is contrary to the idea that there is a single best way to do something, and our goal is to find the one best way and make sure that everyone does it. Failure to accomplish goals in the organization is seen by these people as an inability to follow the best course.

> "The future is uncertain—but this uncertainty is at the very heart of human creativity"
> Ilya Prigogine

SUMMARY

We started by defining a few concepts:
- **fragile**—the quality that when disturbed has a propensity to break. Kicking around a fragile object reduces or destroys its value.
- **robust**—the quality that when disturbed it remains the same. Kicking a robust object has no effect on it at all.
- **antifragile**—the quality that when disturbed it improves. Kicking an antifragile object actually makes it more valuable.

Antifragility is a quality that emerges from an adaptive system. While it sounds crazy, there are adaptive systems all around us, and a human organization is one of those. We need to think of an organization as a system which includes both the people and the information technology.

Not only do adaptive systems respond well to stress, they actually degrade when all stress is removed. Like muscles that need exercise, an organization needs a certain amount of variation in order to remain healthy.

Adaptive case management is an approach to supporting knowledge workers that does not constrain the working patterns to a predefined best practice. Instead, it allows knowledge workers to evaluate what the options are in this case, and to plan a course of action that might be unique for this case. It then focuses on communications about the plan, and in support of the plan.

This approach is likely to be very uncomfortable to traditional scientific managers who view their organization as a machine that has a single best mode of operation. Instead of a machine, we should think of the organization as a system with complex interactions. Experienced managers already know that knowledge workers are not simple gears in a clock, but instead are capable of far more than would be expected, if they can only be given the ability to experiment and try to do things better.

> "A military force has no constant formation, water has no constant shape: the ability to gain victory by changing and adapting according to the opponent is called genius."
>
> - Sun Tzu, The Art of War

Bottom-up Process Discovery using Knowledge Engineering Techniques

Thomas Bech Pettersen, Steinar Carlsen, Gunnar John Coll, Helle Frisak Sem

ABSTRACT

We have found acquisition techniques from knowledge engineering (KE) useful for process discovery in our work with operational Adaptive Case Management (ACM) solutions. These techniques can easily be combined with more traditional top-down approaches from the architect's toolbox. Our overall approach uses dynamically combinable snippets of task support functionality rather than trying to create linear and static "end-to-end" processes. Events and user goals chain these snippets together. The described knowledge engineering techniques have proved useful for bottom-up discovery focusing on tasks and their actual work performance that may go hand in hand with the prototyping and development of a task support system.

BACKGROUND

Traditional approaches to process discovery are typically top-down, such as use case descriptions (Cockburn 2000), business process mapping / modeling using BPMN or other notations, user stories, user story grouping, etc. In the knowledge engineering community, analysis methods are often bottom-up by nature (Schreiber 1993), (Schreiber 1999). We have found these bottom-up techniques from KE useful for process discovery in realizing enterprise ACM solutions.

In several of our practical ACM applications (Sem 2012a), (Sem 2012b), (Sem 2013a), (Sem 2013b), (Pettersen 2013), (Sem 2013c), the customer's subject matter experts (SMEs) have been engaged in describing a shared data model as well as growing their own vocabulary related to their professional tasks, business rules and organization roles. These solutions are all based on our own ACM framework – FrameSolutions (FS). Using the FS architecture, knowledge is stored as relatively independent fragments, known as "snippets", turning these into assets both for discourse and for implementing future system functionality. This helps maintain focus on the customer's knowledge assets in terms of value creation, not only on best practice use of technology for "requirements engineering".

Working in this way rapidly provides handles for the SMEs and business analysts to identify the key ingredients of a knowledge organization, paving the way for value-driven system development: What are the different user groups? What tasks do they solve on a daily basis? What are their frustrations? How are the tasks related? Who is allowed to initiate which tasks? Who collaborate on the problem solving needed to perform these tasks? Which task components are reusable? What added task support to my application will produce the greatest business benefits?

THE BOTTOM-UP APPROACH IN A NUTSHELL

The bottom-up approach to process discovery starts with the recurring difficult tasks and how these are carried out, in dialog with SMEs as representatives of knowledge workers. The analysis brings out reasons why the selected tasks are performed and the resulting events generating further tasks. In this way, we can harvest smaller fragments, or snippets, of the larger work processes of the customer organization.

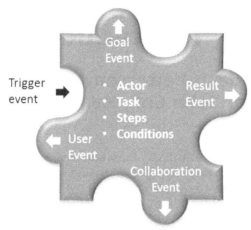

Figure 1: Process snippet concept, to capture a limited segment of work, including its conditions and products.

We have found it practical to limit each process snippet to cover a task that can typically be performed by one person within the scope of one day or less. Usually, larger tasks can either be split into smaller parts or be initiated and finished several times.

Below is an illustrative example of how such process snippets can be put to use in a simple ACM scenario, with no previous analysis of the complete top-down process structure.

EXECUTION OF EMERGENT PROCESSES

As the work progresses through the various tasks to be performed, a full-fledged process emerges as a daisy chain, shaped by the current context. Each resulting event generated by the task of performing one process snippet may in turn be the start event triggering a new task of performing another work item.

An example of such an emerging process is the following. The front desk-person receives a call: a trigger event. He performs the initial conversation task, supported by a process snippet ensuring that the necessary initial information is exchanged and identifying where to put the call through: a result event. This event serves as the trigger event for the department to which the call is put through, initiating someone there to perform the task of continuing the conversation and performing a suitable process snippet for this purpose.

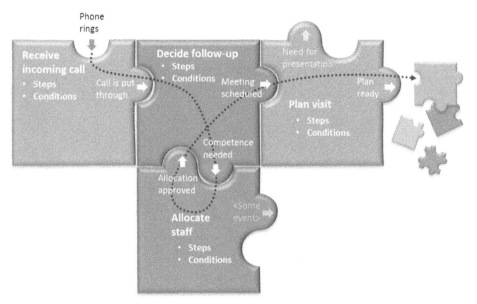

Figure 2: Process snippets combine emergently, to suit the work process as it unfolds.

A SUITABLE APPROACH FOR CASE DRIVEN ARCHITECTURES

Knowledge based systems differ from purely algorithmic systems in that they allow open ended search for a solution rather than deterministically executing a prearranged business logic sequence (Dehli 2000). A rule engine cycles through a partitioned collection of relatively autonomous pieces of knowledge, to find possible ways to achieve a goal. The more comprehensive the knowledge base, the more probable it is that the system can come up with satisfactory support. But a complete solution cannot be guaranteed. In complex ACM domains no two problems are quite alike, so the contribution of the knowledge worker remains significant, and each manifestation of system support is partly unpredictable.

Thus, the paradoxical starting point of our approach is, that *some* knowledge is better than *all*. This is because an up-front complete solution in a typical ACM context will be forbiddingly expensive and an almost meaningless exercise to specify. System development must involve SMEs and knowledge workers as soon and as closely as possible, starting with smaller islands of knowledge and staging the development for gradual enhancement of the knowledge base during system lifecycle.

Working bottom-up is an ideal approach for involving SMEs in our hunt for useful pieces of process knowledge. A limited set of snippets is initially captured, using patterns described below. The system is launched to a user community as soon as its knowledge base is deemed to have reached critical mass – when the proportion of supported to unsupported work will make the system worthwhile for the knowledge worker.

Inside any ACM supported work scenario, the mix of supported and unsupported activities will vary. The knowledge worker will always play a significant role from initial problem to achieved goal, and may undertake quite significant parts of work "outside" the system, particularly early in ACM system lifecycle. Figure 3 is a trivial example that illustrates this:

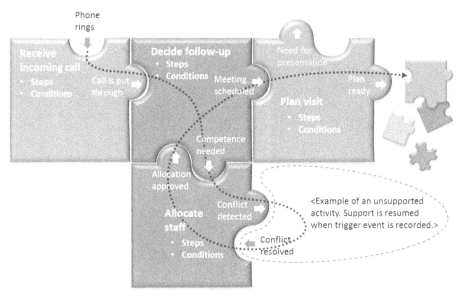

Figure 3: Process snippets combine emergently, and the knowledge worker takes action outside the system to bridge a gap.

ANATOMY OF KNOWLEDGE ENGINEERING PATTERNS FOR TASK DISCOVERY

We now go on to discuss some patterns we have found useful for capturing process snippets together with SMEs, cultivating operational work support systems in a bottom-up way.

A pattern is a description of a general relation between a problem and a possible solution. These practical patterns relate to the different phases and elements in the KE process. The patterns presented are by no means complete, but give an impression of how we think that such patterns could be useful in task discovery.

Each pattern is described by the following elements:
- **Pattern name:** describes the pattern in terms of what problem it solves.
- **Context:** a description of where or when the pattern is useful.
- **Problem:** a more detailed description of what problem the pattern applies to.
- **Discussion:** could be an explanation or discussion of the problem, the solution or alternative solutions.
- **Solution:** describes what actions should be taken when facing the problem, in the given context.

We maintain and document our library of knowledge engineering patterns using a wiki solution, which is also useful for knowledge sharing between development projects. The wiki has a set of more general knowledge acquisition patterns (originating from "expert system" work in the 1980s) as well as more high-level patters for task discovery. The patterns below are all imported from our wiki.

KNOWLEDGE ACQUISITION PATTERNS

Pattern name: Making implicit information explicit

Context: Used in the problem of classification of metal fractures in an expert system for Det Norske Veritas (Fjellheim 1988).

Problem: How to make all evaluated variables explicit in an expert's problem solving situation.

Discussion: Trying to elicit how the expert worked was difficult because he did not make all evaluation explicit through an interview phase. Obvious things for the expert did not get communicated to the knowledge engineer.

Solution: Make the expert analyse the cause of the metal fracture per telephone. In this way the expert must ask explicitly for all information that he needs.

Pattern name: Picking out the right SMEs

Context: Generally applicable.

Problem: If several experts are available, with varying levels of expertise, which expert(s) should be chosen.

Discussion: An expert with many years of experience usually has the expertise to solve problems in his domain very quickly. But the problem may be that he has "compiled" his knowledge in such a way that a long chain of inference is likely to be reduced to one single association. This "feature" can make it difficult for an expert to access and verbalise his own problem solving strategy. Faced with a difficult problem, the novice fails to solve it, the journeyman solves it after a long time and the master solves it immediately (Kuipers1984).

Solution: Try to pick an intermediate expert.

Pattern name: Pin-point critical parts of compound problem solving

Context: A problem type consists of several interdependent components, and solving it is a matter of days or weeks rather than hours.

Example from DNV: Assessing longitudinal strength of a projected oil tanker.

Problem: For recurring protracted problem solving processes, how to select which parts to address initially, to construct really useful process snippets.

Discussion: For protracted operations, the knowledge engineer cannot be present during the whole process. The expert's post-hoc self-reporting may be idealised and less useful, particularly in terms of helping less knowledgeable personnel do the job. The novice does not yet know enough to ask the right questions.

Solution: Assign a representative, real-life problem to a novice, with telephone, chat or email access to a seasoned expert. Let the novice log his work, particularly the situations where he gets stuck, his worries, questions and the replies he gets. Use simple log sheets, to ensure consistent recording of salient information. This leaves a useful trace for subsequent probing and explication.

Pattern name: How to start-up knowledge acquisition

Context: Useful in domains where some amount of written documentation exists.

Problem: What should be the first activities to start with in knowledge acquisition?

Discussion: When first consulting an expert it can be boring for the expert to explain every professional/domain term he uses. If the knowledge engineer is already familiar with the most common terms in the domain it will be easier to communicate with the expert.

Solution: Start with a document study so that the knowledge engineer has a basic understanding of professional/domain terms used in the domain. Ensure that the knowledge engineer does not fall into the trap of trying to impress the expert with his new proficiency.

Pattern name: Length of interviews

Context: General.

Problem: How long should an interview be?

Discussion: It is often hard to keep meetings within the bounds of the predefined time-slot. But we have all experienced how performance deteriorates if the schedule is not respected. One should not try to cram too many issues into an interview. Having shorter and more frequent interviews generally stimulates both productiveness and continuity.

Solution: Keep interviews short (less than one hour).

Pattern name: Doing teachback

Context: The knowledge engineer is trying to understand how a complex procedure is carried out in a VLSI Design.

Problem: How should the teachback of a procedure be performed in a teachback interview?

Discussion: Ideally, teachback repeats back the procedure, but there is a danger of degenerating into two mutually irritating monologues. Therefore three auxiliary methods are used (Johnson 1987):

- The knowledge engineer summarizes on the spot, distinguishing between physical detail and conceptual detail.
- The knowledge engineer uses a different form of expression than the expert. Everyday terms may serve the purpose.
- The knowledge engineer "chimes in" on the end of a sentence.

Solution: Try to use other forms than just repeating what the expert has said.

TASK AND PROCESS DISCOVERY PATTERNS

Pattern name: Organizational Context

Context: You are responsible for capturing structured work process descriptions for your customer's organization, to be implemented in an ACM solution.

Problem: To provide a starting point for where to identify relevant work tasks that are candidates for further elaboration into a structured form and ultimately into a machine-readable declarative form.

Solution:
1. Establish the outer borders of the (part of the) organization to support.
2. Identify the categories (or groups) of actors within the organization to support.
3. As separation criteria, consider (items not ordered)
   - Actor qualifications (seniority, hierarchical position, education level, ...).
   - Actor overall task set (clerk, data entry, case officer, expert, resource, manager, ...).
   - Events that cause this actor to perform work (external, internal, autonomous).
   - When each actor interacts with the various domain entities and tasks, during their lifecycles.

Example: In a police case proceedings support application, the following actor categories were identified:
   - Constables - typical tasks: case entry, initial interrogations, road accidents...
   - Inspectors - interrogations, case reorganization, search reports, searches, confiscations, arrests

- Group Leaders - distribution of tasks among inspectors, investigation directions...
- Prosecution Lawyers (Chief Super Intendants) - charges, indictments, prosecutions, search warrants, confiscation warrants, arrest warrants, legal considerations...
- Office Personnel - data entry, coding, mainframe system users, consistency checking, ...

The next step is to further identify and study the tasks for each of the actor categories.

Another way to initially structure the problem would be to study the life cycle of the relevant primary domain object, in this case the criminal case proceedings entity:

- Initiate - alternative ways to initiate a criminal case: offence report, missing person, road accident...
- Investigate - interrogations, case reorganization, search reports, searches, confiscations, arrests, laboratory orders, ...
- Prepare for trial - charges, indictment, and prosecution, informing the Counsel for the Defense...
- Post-trial - appeals, ...
- Enforcement - pronouncement, recording in judgment book, certificate of judgment...

Pattern name: Identify Process Snippet Candidates

Context: You are responsible for capturing structured work process descriptions for your client organization, to be implemented in an ACM solution. You have established a basic structure from which you can link or organize the work tasks, e.g. after having applied pattern *Organizational Context*.

Problem: Now, you are out to find the set of process snippets pertaining to a given category of actors in the organization, or pertaining to a given part of the main life cycle of the primary domain entity.

Solution: An informal solution: "Sit down with an insightful representative of the given category of actors, ask her/him to close her/his eyes, and list the events that cause her/him to perform some task. Thereafter, ask her/him to describe (in keywords) the possible tasks resulting from each event."

A more formal solution:

1. Select an actor category.
2. Establish a list of events that may cause actors of this category to perform some task.
3. Define whether these events are:
   - external (i.e. initiated by some entity external to the organization in question)
   - internal (i.e. initiated by some actor inside the organization in question, or by some domain model entity state change)
   - user-initiated (i.e. caused by a decision made by this actor, and not included in the above categories)
4. For each of these events, identify the task or tasks performed by this actor in order to handle the event.
5. As far as possible, specify an initial (sequential) list of steps that are performed as part of the task. By step we mean a single "unit of work" that can be performed uninterrupted, that can be performed by one actor alone, and in a context where the task does not change during the execution.

6. Start over with the next actor category.

Example:

The front desk staff at a debt collection company typically react to the following events:

1. Incoming phone calls - external event
   - Questions on the current state of the case proceedings
   - Complaints (informal)
   - Information from 3rd parties
2. Incoming letters - external event
   - Complaints
   - Applications
   - Address change notices
3. Threats
   - Incoming legal notices - external event
   - Bankruptcy notices
   - Death notices

The above events are handled by the following process snippets:

1. Manage communication (Event: Incoming phone calls)
   - Questions: Ask for the caller's name and birth date; look him/her up in the register to find the officer in charge, and put the call through.
   - Complaints (informal): Inform that complaints are only handled when received in writing. Information from 3rd parties: Make a note of the information in the case file in question (you need the name and birth date of the debtor to look it up). If the type of information is diffuse, or if there is a lot of information, put the call through to the officer in charge of this case.
2. Register incoming letters (Event: Incoming letters)
   - Letters pertaining to the organization as such, and no specific case, are handled by general routines (outside the scope of the ongoing analysis project).
   - All letters pertaining to cases: Register the incoming letter in the journal. You will need the name, birth date or more information about the debtor in question to link the letter to the case in question. Scan the letter contents to see whether you can annotate the letter registration according to the predefined categories. This will help the case officers, and it will improve the organization's overview of the total mass of documents.
   - If it is not evident which case the letter would belong to, keep it in the "unresolvable" bin which some dedicated officer will regularly scan through.
3. Register legal notices (Event: Incoming legal notices)
   - Bankruptcy notices: Use the social security number or organization number in the bankruptcy notice to check whether the person or organization in question is a debtor. If so, open the case and record the bankruptcy notice as a top priority task to follow up.
   - Death notices: Use the social security number in the death notice to check whether the person in question is a debtor. If so, open the case and record the death notice as a top priority task to follow up.

From the above lists of events and tasks, it can be inferred that this actor category has a highly reactive work pattern, i.e. they do not have any significant responsibility for pro-activeness in a professional context. The opposite would be the case for police investigators, except for the fact that they rarely initiate cases themselves, but a very high portion of the tasks they perform on a case are user-initiated.

Pattern name: Elaborate On a Process Snippet

Context: You are responsible for capturing structured work process descriptions for your client organization, to be implemented in an ACM solution. You have established the (initial) set of work tasks to be supported, and a preliminary list of steps contained in these tasks, e.g. after having applied pattern *Identify Process Snippet Candidates*. For each of these tasks you are now out to refine it, together with client representatives. The aim is to create task descriptions that will be reasonable and relevant for the end users in the client organization.

Problem: Agree upon the steps and the sequence of steps in a task.

Solution: Reevaluate the initial list of steps established for the task, and check for relevance. Does it result in a natural flow of steps to produce a successful result?

Does the execution of this task include steps that cannot be performed by a single individual, e.g. because of roles and abilities? In that case, carefully evaluate if you should split the task.

Do the names (descriptions) of the steps convey the right information and mind-set for the end user who will perform the step, and for users that may at a later time open the task to check the progress status?

For each step, discuss
- which, if any, domain services can provide functionality for the user to complete the required action indicated by the step?
- whether there is a lead-time (i.e. time before this step needs to be exposed, e.g. waiting time to cater for interaction through mail with external parties)
- whether the step is mandatory
- whether the step is repeatable
- whether any side-effects are produced (e.g. documents).

Store the task description with its step declarations/definitions in an appropriate form. In our work this is done using FrameSolutions' knowledge editor.

Pattern name: Augment a Process Snippet with Rules

Context: You are responsible for establishing structured work descriptions for your client organization, to be implemented in an ACM solution. You have established a detailed structure for the tasks to support, e.g. after having applied pattern *Elaborate on a Process Snippet*. Thus, it is now clear what tasks to support, and the basic structure of these tasks has been captured.

Problem: You want to control the execution of the tasks in the support application by adding conditions that link the task execution to the state in the underlying domain representation.

Typical condition forms are:
- Preconditions: statements that must be true before the action of an activity can be performed
- Postconditions: statements that must become true before the execution of an activity can be considered successful

Solution: For each step in the task description, find out whether there is a specific state that should be established in the domain model (and possibly also in the task execution model),

1. as precondition
2. as postcondition

For each condition,

- establish a response to give to the user when the condition fails.
- establish an action set to perform when the condition fails, e.g. to restore some state in the model.

LESSONS LEARNT

Many traditional methods for process discovery are top-down and directed towards and discovering comprehensive end-to-end business processes. Such methods are often hard to combine with parallel prototyping and realization of a supporting operational solution, whether ACM or more traditional BPM. The described knowledge engineering patterns for task discovery are bottom-up and easily mixable with the stepwise delivery of an operational work support solution. Realizing work support solutions working top-down may be accused of taking a "boil-the-ocean" approach. We have found that working bottom-up has several practical benefits:

- **Start small, start from anywhere** – after having established part of the organizational context, a detailed analysis of the various users' goals and tasks can start from anywhere and several smaller areas can be investigated in parallel by different joint teams involving the customer's subject matter experts.
- **Work performance focus** – emphasis on user tasks, goals and the various reasons to start work.
- **Value-driven delivery** of an operational work support solution. Analysis and prototyping may expand in directions prioritized in accordance with their value potential for the customer organization.
- **Emergent processes** – focusing on supporting tasks and how tasks and events may spin off other related collaborative tasks results in emergent overall end-to-end processes that are more likely to reflect real work practice than their top-down designed and deployed counterparts.
- **Workflow as a side-effect** – with emergent processes forking new processes or tasks, the workflow becomes a side-effect of executing the tasks.
- **Smart relay batons** – whereas traditional workflow solutions route work packages as passive relay batons, our process snippets also provide a proposed way of performing the work, supported by active task definitions.

CONCLUSION

For a given work case instance, rigid end-to-end process support will either succeed as predicted, or fail completely. It is brittle. Even with alternative paths and bypasses, the success rate will depend on how many possibilities have been explored and pre-captured. This in itself is a tall order, given the open-ended nature of knowledge based work. Even worse: too rigid support can deprive the knowledge worker of initiative and control, with impoverished learning and degrading knowledge as ensuing long term effects for the organization. A rigidly defined system does not get better through use.

Working bottom-up, on the other hand, produces system support that may never become complete, but is adaptive, resilient and evolutionary. Adaptive, because the snippet sequence is not predetermined but composed on the fly, continually taking new events into account. Resilient, because any unexpected turn of events can be handled and put right by the knowledgeable user. Evolutionary, because snippets can be added and refined incrementally, as the independent knowledge modules they are.

In conclusion, where a top-down end-to-end model sets up a more or less rigid course of events or paths, the bottom-up approach produces a flexible repertory that offers considerable space for improvisation, learning and improvement. In our experience, this freedom of action is productive in achieving the enthusiasm of the knowledgeable user, stimulating good practices in the knowledge organization.

REFERENCES

(Cockburn 2000) Alistair Cockburn. Writing effective use cases. Addison-Wesley Professional, 2000

(Dehli 2000) Dehli, E., Coll, G.J. Just-in-Time Knowledge Support, in Rajkumar, Roy (ed.) Industrial knowledge Management: A Micro-level Approach, Springer-Verlag 2000

(Fjellheim 1988) Fjellheim, R.A., Coll, G.J., Johansson, B.G. Modularity and User Initiative in an Expert System for Fracture Analysis, in Pham, D.T.: Expert Systems in Engineering, Springer-Verlag, Berlin 1988

(Johnson 1987) Leslie Johnson and Nancy E. Johnson. Knowledge Elicitation Involving Teachback Interviewing, in Alison L. Kidd: Knowledge Acquisition for Expert Systems.

(Kuipers 1984) B. Kuipers and J. Kassier, Causal Reasoning in Medicine: Analysis of a Protocol, Cognitive Science, 8:363-385

(Schreiber 1993) G. Schreiber, B. Wielinga, J. Breuker. KADS: A Principled Approach to Knowledge-Based System Development (Knowledge-Based Systems). Academic Press, 1993

(Schreiber 1999) Guus Schreiber, Hans Akkermans, Anjo Anjewierden, Robert Dehoog, Nigel Shadbolt, Walter Vandevelde, Bob Wielinga. Knowledge Engineering and Management: The CommonKADS Methodology, MIT Press, 1999

(Sem 2012a) Helle Frisak Sem, Steinar Carlsen and Gunnar Coll. Norwegian Food Safety Authority, Nominated by Computas AS, Norway. In Fischer, L. (ed): How Knowledge Workers Get Things Done - Real-world Adaptive Case Management, Future Strategies Inc, Florida, 2012

(Sem 2012b) Helle Frisak Sem, Steinar Carlsen and Gunnar Coll. On Two Approaches to ACM. ACM 2012 1st International Workshop on Adaptive Case Management and other non-workflow approaches to BPM, Tallinn, Estonia, 2012

(Sem 2013a) Helle Frisak Sem, Steinar Carlsen, Gunnar Coll and Thomas Bech Pettersen. ACM for railway freight operations, in Intelligent BPMS, BPM and Workflow Handbook series, Future Strategies Inc, Florida (2013)

(Sem 2013b) Helle Frisak Sem, Steinar Carlsen, Gunnar Coll, Håvard Holje, Eli Landro, Heidi Mork and Thomas Bech Pettersen. GTS - Cargonet AS Norway, http://adaptivecasemanagement.org/awards_2013_winners.html.
Ibid Empowering Knowledge Workers, page 115, Future Strategies Inc, Florida, 2013

(Pettersen 2013) Thomas Bech Pettersen, Helle Frisak Sem, Steinar Carlsen, Gunnar Coll, Margit Matras and Tove Moen. LOVISA - Norwegian Courts Administration (NCA), http://adaptivecasemanagement.org/awards_2013_winners.html.
Ibid. Empowering Knowledge Workers, page 163, Future Strategies Inc, Florida, 2013

(Sem 2013c) Helle Frisak Sem, Thomas Bech Pettersen, Steinar Carlsen and Gunnar Coll. Patterns boosting Adaptivity in ACM. 2nd International Workshop on Adaptive Case Management and other non-workflow approaches to BPM, OTM 2013, Graz, Austria.

Justifying ACM: Why We Need a Paradigm Shift in BPM

Ilia Bider, Paul Johannesson and Erik Perjons, Stockholm University, Sweden

INTRODUCTION

The workflow-based system is the major paradigm in use in today's Business Process Management (BPM) practice. There are several reasons for this phenomenon:

1. This paradigm is connected to the wide-spread operational view on business processes, where a process is considered to be a sequence of operations (activities) for reaching a goal, alternatively for transforming inputs into outputs.
2. Secondly this view is imbedded in the industry standards, like UML, BPMN.
3. This view, because of 1 and 2, is being built in modeling tools, workflow engines, and BPM suites which are enthusiastically marketed by both small and large vendors, including IBM and Oracle.

As a result, very little space is left to the BPM approaches based on views other than workflow (operational view). The latter encompasses Adaptive Case Management (ACM) (Swenson 2010).

There is a deeper reason for the operational view to be widely accepted in business. It is connected to the idea that BPM is a tool for optimizing the usage of enterprise resources by using standardization, specialization, and automation, which is including in such BPM directions as Six Sigma and Lean. These directions continue the tradition that F. Taylor and H. Ford introduced in production.

There are a number of problems with fixation on optimization, for example:

*   Standardization minimizes deviation from the standard. It works very well in the condition of the expanded market as in case of the Ford's model T, for which the customer could "choose" a color from one option available (black), but might not work well in a mature market with tough competition.
*   It takes resources (in time and effort) to devise and introduce in practice a fully optimized process. This investment could be justified if the process could be run for a long time, as, again, in case of Ford model T. However, when the process is radically changed after running a short period of time, this investment may be lost.

The above drawbacks of the focus on optimization might not be essential in the case of relatively stable (static) environment of the past, or even present. The question is whether it suits the enterprise of the future, which is supposed to work in a highly dynamic global environment with tough competition and continuing technological progress.

This paper is devoted to understanding the needs of the enterprise of the future in the area of BPM, and analyzing whether the mainstream workflow-based systems will satisfy these needs. The analysis is done based on assumption that an essential property of the enterprise of the future is agility. The agility is understood as ability to discover changes, trends and opportunities in the dynamic world and react to them by adjusting current products, services and processes, or creating completely new ones.

The paper is structured in the following way: We start with giving a pragmatic definition of the concept of business process that will be used in the paper. Then, we analyze the properties of a business process that can be supported by a workflow-based system and discuss whether business processes of the enterprise of the future will possess these properties. After that, we give some suggestions on what type of techniques could be employed in the new generation of software to support business processes. In the last section, we summarize our findings.

PRAGMATIC DEFINITION OF BUSINESS PROCESS

There are many definitions of what a business process is, each of them highlighting different aspects of this phenomenon (Bider & Perjons 2009). The most common view on business processes is the operational one, where the process is considered as a partially ordered sequence of operations/activities aimed at reaching some goal. The latter view serves as a basis for workflow-based Business Process Support (BPS) systems. However, the operational view does not suit other types of BPS systems, for example, ACM systems (Swenson 2010). In this section, we introduce the concept of business process and BPS systems in a pragmatic manner so that it does not contradict specific definitions and can suit many practical purposes.

Actually, the term business process encompasses two concepts (which often confuses outsiders), business process type and business process instance (or case). We give both concepts the following pragmatic definitions sufficient for the issues discussed in the paper:

- Business Process Type (BPT) is a plan/template for handling business situations of a certain type
- Business Process Instance/case (BPI) is a situation (being) handled according to the plan/template

The plan/template can include information on any or a combination or all of the following:

- A situation that warrants application of the plan, i.e. triggers a new instance creation
- A goal to reach
- Sub-goals and an order in which they could/should be achieved (goal decomposition)
- Operations/actions/activities that should be completed for achieving goals/sub-goals and the order in which they should be completed (operational decomposition)
- Rules of responsibility/participation (both for sub-goals and operations)
- Rules of collaboration/communication between participants pursuing common goals/sub-goals (communication/collaboration channels)

For example, consider a situation of developing a customized software system for a particular customer. A general plan for handling this situation can be presented as a simplified flowchart in Fig. 1. To this flowchart, any number of details can be added, e.g. the first step in Fig. 1 should be carried out by requirements engineers, the second step should produce use-case diagrams, or the third step requires using Java as a programming language. The more details are added, the more rigid the process will be. For example, setting the requirement that all programming should be done in Java will force the developers using this language even in cases where it does not fit, e.g. for development of operating systems.

Figure 1: a plan/template for handling a situation when there is a need to develop a customized software system

The plan/template can reside in any or in a combination of all of the following:

- In the heads of members of staff who participate in the process instances of the given type (tacit knowledge). This knowledge guides the process participants in what can/should be done or/and what is prohibited, without them thinking about any explicit rules.
- As written documents, including process maps and other kind of process description (explicit knowledge) on the paper or inside a computer, e.g., in the form of web-based hypertext. These documents contain explicit instructions of what can/should be done or/and what is prohibited to do.
- In software systems/services used to support running process instances (built-in knowledge). The usage of such systems/services forces to do some actions in a certain way and/or in a certain order, or/and prohibit to do it in other ways.

In other words, the knowledge on processes can range from being completely tacit (e.g., resides in the heads of the process participants), to being totally explicit (e.g., depicted in detailed process maps).

We define Business Process Support (BPS) system as a software system that helps the participants of a business process instance to follow the plan/template defined by the business process type. It can, for example, automate certain operations or support coordination/collaboration between the workers who participate in the same process instance. Note that using a BPS system does not imply that the whole process definition needs to be incorporated in the system, and the system needs to supports all operations included in the process.

DO WORKFLOW-BASED SYSTEMS FIT AN AGILE ENTERPRISE?

Properties of a workflowable process

The workflow-based systems are built upon the operational view on business processes, the most widespread definition of a workflow being "a sequence of operations, declared as work of a person, a group of persons" (from Wikipedia (Wikipedia 2012)). Term workflowability was introduced (Baresi et al. 1999) as a characteristic of a business process that suits best to be supported by a workflow-based software system. Below, we list properties of an ideal business process that can be represented as a workflow chart, e.g. an UML activity diagram, Petri Net, or in BPMN notation. The list is based on analysis from (Baresi et al. 1999, Bider & Perjons 2012), and includes the following properties:

1. The process can be split in well-defined steps or operations common for all instances of the process type.
2. For each step, inputs and outputs are fully formalized (e.g., a document, an application form, a drawing).
3. It is fully determined what outputs and from which steps serve as inputs for other steps. Thus, casual dependencies are established between the steps.
4. Execution of each step does not require any other information than the one included in its formalized inputs.
5. Two steps are not allowed to be executed simultaneously (in parallel) if outputs from one of them serve as inputs for another. Besides this rule, parallel execution is encouraged. Loops are also allowed.
6. Each step is executed by a special group or one person. From the optimization point of view the latter alternative is more preferable. If in addition each such group or person is responsible only for one step, even greater degree of optimal usage of human resources can be achieved (via full specialization).

The set of properties above can serve as a checklist to ensure that a process is suitable for employing a workflow-based BPS system. If the above properties are confirmed, the process can run as on a conveyor belt, allowing optimization of the usage of human resources.

Designing a workflowable process requires full formalization of all inputs and outputs, and decomposing the process into relatively small steps so that each step can be entrusted to a particular role, and as many steps as possible can run in parallel, being independent of each other.

It is unrealistic to expect that such a design can be produced in one go and without several rounds of unsuccessful trials. In addition, the list of properties above sets some limitations on how a process could be conducted. For example, if a process in Fig. 1 is considered to be workflowable, it won't be allowed to start the design phase before the full set of requirements has been established. It also means that all requirements should be explicitly defined, and designers do not informally communicate with requirements engineers to clarify the meaning of the requirements, as the latter might not be available for questioning (are engaged in other projects somewhere else).

Enterprise agility from the business processes point of view

We consider enterprise/business agility as a property of an enterprise to function in the highly dynamic world (Sherehiy et al. 2007). The agility concerns both being able to adjust the enterprise to changes in the surrounding environment, and discovering new opportunities constantly appearing in the dynamic world for launching completely new products/services. Becoming agile requires setting a structure that allows discovering changes and opportunities as soon as possible and react on them appropriately.

From the process thinking perspective, agility can be achieved through the interplay of business processes that belong to three different levels: *operational*, *improvement* and *strategic* (Bider, Bellinger & Perjons 2011), as presented in Fig. 2. Each level has its own sensors that monitor the internal and external environment and, when needed, start Business Process Instances (BPIs) to deal with a discovered situation. Both sensors and BPIs work according to Business Process Templates (BPTs), see Section 2. The description of each level is as follows:

1. *Operational* processes - sales, production, product development, HR (e.g., hiring), etc. A sensor discovers the need (customer needs - sales, or internal needs - HR), and initiates a relatively structured process instance to attain the operational goal (making a deal, or hiring a new employee). These process are usually called core processes, i.e. processes that directly produce value for the enterprise stakeholders.

2. *Process improvement* (optimization) processes. A sensor here is based on the performance indicators established to measure efficiency, productivity, or other parameters of the given business process type. If the performance is not according to the expectations, a process improvement (re-engineering) process instance starts with the goal to change a process definition(s) used by operational processes. The process instances here can follow some known methods (like Six Sigma, or Lean).

3. *Strategic* processes. A sensor here is based on the macro view on the whole organizations. If the overall performance is below expectation, a strategic process instance is fired with the goal to make more radical changes in the organization. The latter can include radical changes in process definitions, removing obsolete processes, introducing new ones, rearranging departments, substituting key managers, introducing new technology, etc.

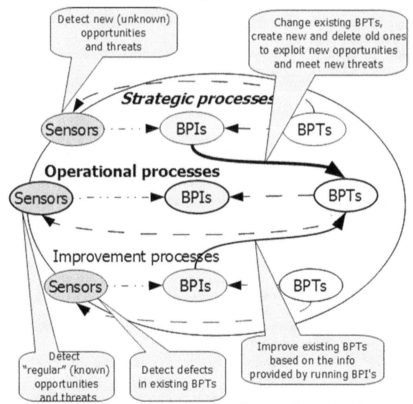

Figure 2: process structure of an agile enterprise

The interplay between the levels works as follows. A sensor of a strategic process discovers some trend, future change or a new kind of opportunities and starts an appropriate strategic BPI that can, in turn, radically change BPTs of operational processes. The operational BPIs start running according to the new BPTs and give information to the improvement sensors. The latter initiate improvement BPIs aimed at optimizing the new operational BPTs. Improvement continues until the new operational BPTs become optimized, or the next radical change occurs. Naturally, BPTs of strategic and improvement processes can be changed and improved in the same manner as operational BPTs (which is not shown in Fig. 2).

Is there always time to optimize a process in an agile enterprise?

Making a business process workflowable needs time, thus this activity falls into the category of improvement processes. Creating a workflowable process can constitute a valid approach to getting a process optimized only in situation when the needs for radical change come infrequently. In the highly dynamic business environment that is expected in the future, there might not be much time to make the process workflowable before discovering that it is time to drastically change it or remove it altogether. An agile organization of the future needs to be content with non-workflowable processes, as long as it is easy to set them into operation and introduce radical changes in them. It should also find another way of providing technological support for its business processes than employing a workflow-based BPS system.

Does achieving workflowability always produce an optimal process?

Let us return to the example in Fig. 1 of the software system development process. In Section 3.1, we have already discussed that deciding on this process being workflowable sets some limitations on how it is conducted. One of them is that the requirements phase should be totally finished before the design is started. From the point of view of optimizing usage of human resources, this limitation sounds like a good solution. Starting the design phase before the requirements have been established means taking a risk that requirements discovered later may force redoing parts or all of the already done design.

Suppose now that the workflowable system development process is used for creating a new product for the market in a highly competitive dynamic environment. Then not taking the risk of starting design before finishing the requirements engineering means taking the risk of coming with the new product too late. To minimize the risk of redoing too much of the design, the agile enterprise needs to find the solutions opposite to achieving the workflowability, namely:

- The dependent steps should be allowed to run in parallel.
- The input/outputs for them should be less formalized and partly rely on on-going personal communication between requirements engineers and product designers.
- The same people are allowed to be engaged in different step (less specialization), especially if they run in parallel. This will facilitate tacit transfer of the outputs from one step as inputs into another.

Implementing a software development process with the properties as above leads, more or less, to the agile system development process.

Is optimization of an individual process good for the whole enterprise?

Let us consider another aspect of the system development process aimed at producing a product for the market. Suppose we have created a very good set of requirements that would ensure that a new product will satisfy the needs existing in the market. Suppose also that the new system is fairly complex, and it takes a long time, say a year, to develop it. While the developers design, code and test, the needs in the highly dynamic market would continue to evolve creating a risk that the new system will be outdated when it hits the market. In this situation, there is a need to provide the development team with information on the changes in the market demands so that they can adjust the product to the evolving needs even when the process is in the design and coding phases. Below, we discuss a possible way of arranging this information flow.

We use Fig 3 to investigate where in an organization the knowledge we need to feed to the development team resides. Fig 3 presents a simplified view on an organization as consisting of assets and business processes (more exactly, business process instances) currently running in the organization (Bider, Bellinger & Perjons 2011). The most interesting assets in our case are people that are normally organized in units/departments. We differentiate two types of processes: internal (like product development) and boundary (like sales, or field services). The boundary processes run partly inside the organization and partly outside it (in the surrounding environment).

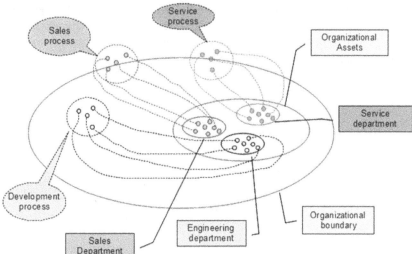

Figure 3: traditional scheme of manning business process

People engaged in the boundary processes spend most (or at least part) of their time outside the organization and have a possibility of obtaining tacit knowledge on the current needs and problems. Usually, each process is manned by people from a corresponding department, i.e. sales processes are conducted by the staff from the sales department, field services are conducted by the staff from the service department, product development is conducted by the staff from the engineering department, etc. In such a situation, people who man the boundary processes and have a chance of acquiring the tacit knowledge that might be needed for the development do not directly participate in the development process.

There are two options to solve the problem above. One is to arrange internal processes for transferring the knowledge on changes in the outer world. This will require converting the tacit knowledge into an explicit form, e.g. analysis, recommendations, etc. before sending it to the development team. In addition, there should be some unaffected schemes to encourage such transfer. Both add overheads and make the organizational structure more complicated.

The other solution is cross-manning of business processes as is represented in Fig. 4. Cross-manning means that people participating in the development process participate also in the boundary processes (e.g. sales and/or field services). It can be sales people, or service engineers that participate in the development process, or (and) the developers that also participate in the sales and (or) field services processes. The advantage of cross-manning is that there is no need for additional internal processes for knowledge transfer. Development team gets the knowledge directly through participating in the boundary processes. The disadvantages are that business processes should be adjusted to allow participation of the "foreigners". This might lead to each process becoming less optimal on its own. There can be loss of efficiency in each of the processes. However, this loss might be a small penalty for ensuring the shortest time to the market for the product that will also be right for the market.

Effective transfer of knowledge on the current needs and problems to the development team is not the only effect of cross-manning. The sales, or field service team that possesses the knowledge on the products under development may start transferring this knowledge to existing and future customers far in advance of the product reaching the market. This will create expectations and ensure smother transferring of knowledge on how to use the new product in practice.

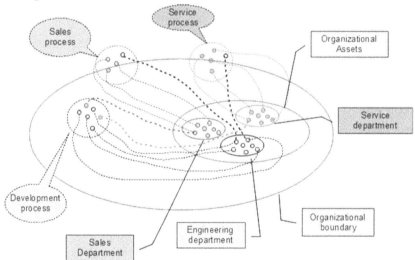

Figure 4: cross-manning of business processes

Cross-manning of business processes have serious implications on the way the processes are to be developed, maintained, and supported by IT-tools. The two most important implications are:

1. Each cross-manned process has multiple goals to achieve. For example, a sales process—besides its main goal to sell a product (or service)—has a goal of giving the development team knowledge of the current customer's needs/problems, even if they cannot be satisfied by the existing assortment of products/services. What's more, it has a goal of informing and educating potential customers about products soon to come.

2. The process team becomes heterogeneous, i.e. it includes people with different backgrounds, experiences and goals.

The above implications mean that the idea of a process as a conveyor belt that could be optimized for one particular goal can no longer apply. Coordination and collaboration among people engaged in the processes come to the forefront. This means that all participants should fully understand different goals, should see the progress of their achievement during the process run, and can help each other in achieving these goals.

SUGGESTIONS – SHARED SPACES AND AGILE PROCESS DEVELOPMENT

As is shown in the previous section, it is highly probable that business processes in the agile enterprise of the future will not be workflowable. This should be taken into consideration when deciding on IT systems to support these processes. Instead of passing task assignments in predefined sequences to various participants, a BPS system in an agile enterprise should facilitate collaborative work. Namely, it should provide the process participants with means that help to track the progress in each process instance and exchange information, knowledge, experience, and ideas.

Computer science has, for a long time, promoted the idea of using shared spaces for supporting collaboration. The idea was first introduced in the field of Computer Supported Cooperative Work (CSCW) and Groupware, see, for example, (Takemura & Kishino 1992). With advances of Social Software, like Facebook, Wiki, etc., this concept became more wide-spread. We believe that a system with a shared space properly structured for a given business process would satisfy the needs of participants of this process.

An example of how a shared space in a new generation of BPS systems could be structured is shown in Fig. 5. The top part in Fig. 5 represents the upper level structure (a map) of the shared space for the process called "New product introduction". The lower level details are organized as step forms that are attached to the process steps, boxes in the upper level map, as shown in the bottom part of Fig. 5.

As follows from Fig.2, changes in the environment may require radically change some or create completely new business processes. In a highly dynamic world, there is not much time to follow traditional approach to developing a new process and a support system for it. Some version of the process should be set in operation relatively quickly, and modified after some experience of running it has been obtained. This warrants transition to the agile development of business process and their support systems, as shown in Fig. 6, see also (Bider 2012).

The traditional approach follows the Nonaka's (Nonaka 1994) cycle of knowledge transformation from tacit to explicit and back to tacit (Fig. 6 was influenced by the Nonaka diagram in (Nonaka 1994)). The agile approach follows Polanyi's ideas (Polanyi 1969) and relies, as much as possible, on the tacit knowledge transformation which allows to obtain results quicker, even if they are not the optimal ones. In the agile approach, the process design is merged with the BPS system design and BPS system manufacturing (coding).

For the agile approach to be practical, there needs to be a tool that facilitates the "merged" activities without requiring that people who use this tool to have knowledge and experience of software system development. Ideally, the tool should be easy to use for "ordinary" process participants. This, for example, would allow a cross-manned heterogeneous process team to adjust the process and its support system to their preferences. An example of such a tool is described in (Bider, Johannesson & Perjons 2011), screen dumps in Fig. 5 being from a process implemented with the help of this tool.

Figure 5: An example of a process's shared space

CONCLUSION

We started with the question whether workflow-based BPS systems would satisfy the needs of the enterprise of the future. To answer this question, we:

- Defined properties of a business process that makes it suitable to be supported by a workflow-based BPS,
- Assumed that an essential property of the enterprise of the future is agility,
- Analysed whether business processes of an agile enterprise have the properties that makes them suitable for the workflow-based support.
- The results of this analysis show that, most probably, the enterprise of the future will need some other kind of BPS than workflow-based systems. We also suggested a type of BPS that could suit the purpose, which is currently under test in real practice.

The limitations of the research presented in this paper are that it is impossible to prove the conclusions above, as only the future itself can show whether agility is an essential property of the enterprise of the future, and whether the suggested type of BPS systems will be widely adopted by practice.

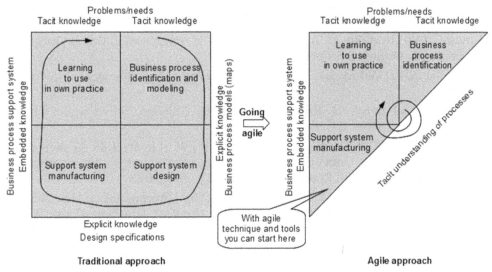

Figure 6: From traditional to agile process development

ACKNOWLEDGEMENTS

A short version of this paper (Bider et al. 2013) was presented at the first international workshop on Adaptive Case Management and Other Non-work-flow Approaches to BPM in Tallinn in September 2012. This version was published in proceedings of the workshops of BPM 2012 by Springer.

REFERENCES

(Baresi et al. 1999) Baresi, L. et al. "Workflow design methodology". In: Grefen, Pernici, and Sanchez, eds. Database Support for Workflow Management: The WIDE Project, Kluwer, 1999, 47–94.

(Bider 2012) Bider, I. "Agile Process Development: Why, How and When. Applying Nonaka's theory of knowledge transformation to business process development". In: SIGBPS Workshop on Business Processes and Services (BPS'12) December 15, 2012 Orlando, Florida, USA, pp.13-17. http://personal.cb.cityu.edu.hk/jlzhao/sigbps/bps12/bps.pdf

(Bider et al. 2013) Bider, I., Perjons E. and Johannesson P. "Do workflow-based systems satisfy the demands of the agile enterprise of the future?" In: Rosa La, M., Soffer, P., Eds. Business Process Management Workshops - BPM 2012, LNBIP 132, Springer, 2013, 59-64.

(Bider, Bellinger & Perjons 2011) Bider I., Bellinger G., Perjons E. "Modeling an Agile Enterprise: Reconciling Systems and Process Thinking", LNBIP Vol.92, Springer, 2011, 238-252.

(Bider, Johannesson & Perjons 2011) Bider I., Johannesson P. and Perjons E. "A strategy for merging social software with business process support", LNBIP, Vol 66, Part 4, Springer, 2011, 372-383.

(Bider & Perjons 2009) Bider I. and Perjons E. "Evaluating Adequacy of Business Process Modeling Approaches", Handbook of Research on Complex Dynamic Process Management, IGI, 2009, 79-102.

(Bider & Perjons 2012) Bider I. and Perjons E. "Preparing for the era of cloud computing: Towards a framework for selecting business process support services", LNBIP, Vol. 113, Springer, 2012, 16-30.

(Nonaka 1994) Nonaka, I. "A dynamic theory of organizational knowledge creation", Organ. Sci., 5(1), 1994,14–37.

(Wikipedia 2012) Wikipedia, May 2012 http://en.wikipedia.org/wiki/Workflow

(Polanyi 1969) Polanyi, M. Knowing and Being. Chicago, University of Chicago Press, 1969.

(Sherehiy et al. 2007) Sherehiy, B., Karwowski, W., Layer, J.K.: "A review of enterprise agility: Concepts, frameworks, and attributes", International Journal of Industrial Economics, 2007, 37, 445- 460.

(Swenson 2010) Swenson K.D. ed. Mastering the Unpredictable: How Adaptive Case Management Will Revolutionize the Way That Knowledge Workers Get Things Done. Meghan-Kiffer Press, Tampa, Florida, USA, 2010.

(Takemura & Kishino 1992) Takemura H., and Kishino F. "Cooperative work environment using virtual workspace", Proceedings of the 1992 ACM conference on computer-supported cooperative work, 1992, 226-232.

Automated Guidance for Case Management: Science or Fiction?

Irina Rychkova, Manuele Kirsch-Pinheiro and Bénédicte Le Grand, University Paris 1 Pantheon-Sorbonne, France

Humans dream about an intelligent computer assistant who would support them in critical situations thanks to its capacity to reason objectively, to take into account millions of factors and criteria and to value carefully thousands of alternatives prior to make a decision. HAL 9000, in Kubrick's 2001: A Space Odyssey (IMDB 1968), is probably the most famous incarnation of such assistant. Being a fictional character, it reflects a number of great ideas of scientists from the 20th century who believed that machines one day would be capable of doing any work a man can do. Though it was shown that such a vision of computer technology is too optimistic, scientists keep working on theories and prototypes that can support practitioners in agile decision-making and smart process management.

In this paper, we propose our vision of what academic research can do for such a pragmatic and experience-driven discipline as Adaptive Case Management and to discuss to what extent fiction may become reality in what we call *automated guidance for case management*?

1. WHAT MAKES THE PERFECT CASE MANAGER?

To provide a common ground for our readers, we start with a definition of Case Management: OMG defines case management as "A coordinative and goal-oriented discipline, to handle cases from opening to closure, interactively between persons involved with the subject of the case and a case manager or case team". Case management processes have multiple applications, including "licensing and permitting in government, insurance application and claim processing in insurance, patient care and medical diagnosis in healthcare, mortgage processing in banking..." (OMG 2009). Navigating a spacecraft to a distant planet can make a perfect example of case management process too.

Efficient case management in industry is hampered by attempts to deal with case management process the same way as with regular business process. The main feature that distinguishes case management processes from traditional business processes is their unpredictability. Unlike a business process that, once designed successfully, can function for years following a predefined scenario, case management processes have to constantly adapt to various "unknowns". These "unknowns" may include client situation and needs, fashion, economical and technological trends, expert skills, available equipment, environmental conditions (temperature, humidity, pollution, radiation), etc. Here the term Adaptive Case Management (ACM) comes to play.

In the literature, Adaptive Case Management discipline is often compared to Business Process Management (BPM). From the theoretical standpoint, BPM and ACM demonstrate conceptually different views on the system design. Similarly to the "chicken or egg" dilemma, they try to resolve a question about what comes first: process or data? The view adapted by BPM is process-centered; it implies that data emerges and evolves within a process according to a predefined scenario, similarly to a product evolving on a conveyor belt. ACM view, in contrast, implies that process scenario evolves at run time in response to emerging circumstances or case-related data.

Dependence on changing data and other (possibly unknown) circumstances makes automated support for case management processes extremely challenging. Therefore, the features of a case management support system often include case artifacts organizer/repository, task scheduler/allocator, report generator, document sharing, business calculator based on business rules etc. Definition and assessment of alternative scenarios and decision making remains a responsibility of a human expert – a case manager. Let's look in detail at what makes a perfect case manager:

The first characteristic we derive based on our experience and discussions with professionals is *objective and well-argued reasoning*. A case manager has to be well informed about the case: he/she must take into account multiple variables in order to evaluate a situation and to decide on the further case handling scenario (e.g. an activity to perform, information to request, expertise to call for etc). He should also possess a vast experience in similar cases in order to predict possible alternative scenarios and estimate their likelihood. This resumes in the second characteristic: *capability to value alternatives under uncertainty*. And the last characteristic we add here is *capacity to learn fast, by turning both good and bad experience into expertise* that will eventually improve quality of manager's decisions in the future.

HAL 9000 could probably make a perfect automated case manager but this is still fiction; what about science?

2. FICTION OR SCIENCE?

We wish to assert from the beginning: no, we are NOT going to replace a case management expert by a program. However, we intend to push the limits of existing case management systems so that they could guide this expert and help him/her to learn quicker and to make better decisions faster.

Imagine an IT system that drives you and your team through a case like a GPS Navigator: it collects data from the different sources, identifies your current position (i.e. case status), anticipates traffic jams (i.e. resource deficiencies or other potential risks), calculates alternatives routes (i.e. case development scenarios), values them with respect to your current situation and objectives and proposes you options (i.e. set of activities) to help you in achieving your objectives with a maximum likelihood.

Compared to a GPS Navigator, the Case Navigation System (Figure 1) has to process parameters and events, whose sources can vary from customer calls, social media posts, stock market feeds and traffic reports to messages from RFID and other mobile sensors. Due to heterogeneity and complexity of processed information, this system has to come up with much more sophisticated navigation scenarios, too. Nevertheless such a vision is far from fiction: it is grounded on the intersection of mature scientific disciplines that we are going to examine below.

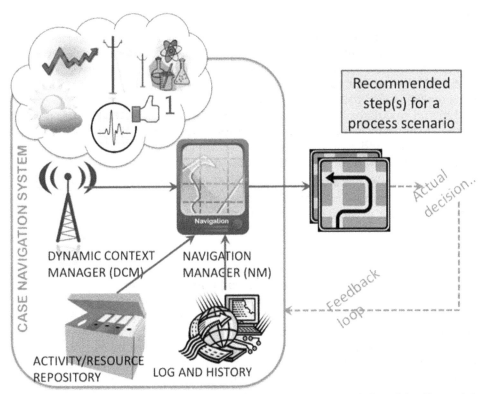

Fig 1: Case Navigation System guides an expert providing him/her with a set of activities leading to a (current) objective with a maximum likelihood.

Before discussing the scientific background, however, we take a closer look at the components of the Case Navigation System we propose. The logical architecture of our system follows the principles of Event-Driven Architecture (EDA), a successor of SOA. It is based on the capacity to sense the environment, produce, detect, process the events and react to these events.

Dynamic Context Manager (DCM)

Similar to a GPS Navigator, the Case Navigation System operates based on accurate definition of the current state (or position) of the case in its relevant coordinate system as well as its next state. Such state is defined by values of different case-related variables that can be of the two types: a) internal or controlled by the case (e.g. absolute coordinates, speed and direction of a car, generated report, calculated price, discount, offer) and b) contextual, or produced by the case environment (e.g. accidents, traffic jams, changing weather conditions, stock market fluctuation, new evidence, change of customer's situation).

The contextual variables can change spontaneously or due to external reasons; they can have mild or severe effect on the case and therefore need to be considered in order to define the case scenario. On the other hand, considering too many contextual parameters can make the case management unbearably tough. The idea is to select, measure and monitor "right" contextual variables at the "right" case states. This is the role of dynamic context manger (or DCM) component (Figure 1).

At a given time, the context variables processed by DCM plus the values of internal case variables are transmitted to the navigation manager (NM).

Navigation Manager (NM)

The Navigation Manager (Figure 1) makes navigation decisions and determines one (or several) plausible activity to execute with respect to the current objectives and navigation conditions[1]. Specifically, when such a decision is required, NM takes into account the current case state, the context of the case defined by the DCM, and the available activities (i.e. what can currently be done?). It runs a predictive algorithm and calculates different scenarios of case development and their possible outcomes. Eventually it selects those scenarios that will have a highest probability to result in the desired outcome. It suggests corresponding activities and their assignment to actors from the activity/resource repository (Figure 1).

As an expert uses his/her intuition or previous experience to make the right guess, the accuracy of scenario/outcome predictions of the NM can be improved by using previous experience in similar cases that is stored in the Log and history component (Figure 1).

Log and History

This component is the memory of the case manager: it contains descriptions of scenarios of previous cases (successful or not) and can be "mined" in order to answer the questions "was similar situation already happen?" and if yes, "what did we do?" and "what happened next?". Log/history mining techniques are a valuable toolkit for determining patterns in cases and predicting further development of the case under certain initial conditions. Therefore it is important to accurately record every event, decision made and activity that follows to this log at run time. This is depicted with a dashed line tagged "feedback loop" in Figure 1.

Activity/Resource Repository

This element represents a catalog of activities that can be performed during the case handling and resources that can be used (actors, equipment etc.). Each activity is characterized by:

- A set of conditions under which it can be performed (e.g. when a specific event happens, when a certain resource is available, when the value of x is greater than...etc); this set of conditions is typically called precondition.
- A set of conditions or outcomes that will be produced upon its termination; this is typically called postcondition.

NM uses preconditions and postconditions to determine the "right" activities to perform in the current case state.

Resources are also characterized by the conditions when they can be used. For example, actors (or human resources) are described by their skills: this enables a dynamic activity-actor assignment. Activity/resource repository can be extended any time by defining new activities and adding new resources.

Algorithm

Following the concept of Navigation System, we represent case management process as moving in a coordinate system where each coordinate takes values of some case-specific parameter (e.g. client income, inflation rate, time of the day, availability/amount of some resource etc.).

A single point or a group of points in this coordinate system corresponds to a case state (or status) at a given moment of time. We say that "the case develops" if its

---

[1] We consider that objectives of the case are not fixed and can change during the case handling.

state changes over time. There are three types of triggers that can lead to state change: case management activities, internal events and external (contextual) events. The examples of these triggers and their corresponding state transitions are shown in Table 1.

Table 1: Examples of Triggers

Trigger type	Trigger example and subsequent state transition
External events	Applicant files complementary information about his income -> clerk processes the information -> the application gains "high income" status and "Priority processing" state of the case is triggered
	Temperature rises above critical -> "Emergency" state of the case is triggered
	Interest rate of the bank changes -> "Contract re-validation" state of the case is triggered
Internal activities	Manager invalidates the application -> "Demand refused" state is triggered
	Agent (or system) recalculates discounts -> "Contract re-validation" state of the case is triggered
	Team executes an emergency operation procedure and reduces the temperature -> "Normal operating" state is triggered.
Internal events	Contract validity date has expired -> "Contract re-validation" state is triggered
	"Out of stock" reminder is generated by the system -> value of the corresponding "resource amount" variable is changed to "0".

The case management can be seen as navigating from one state to another, aiming to achieve some case objectives (a target state).

The functionality of our Case Navigation System can be summarized in the following abstract algorithm:

1. Select the relevant case-specific parameters, observe and measure them and identify the current case state (DCM + NM);
2. Identify probable scenarios (sequences of states) taking into account, if possible, previous experience (NM + Log&History);
3. Exclude the scenarios that are forbidden or not feasible for the current case according to business rules, regulations, availability of resources etc. (NM);
4. Select the scenarios that can lead the case towards its target state with the highest probability (NM);
5. Identify one or several alternative activities that trigger such successful scenarios and recommend them to the case manager (NM + Repository);
6. Record the case manager's decision (Log&History).

The algorithm above should be repeated in a cycle, and can be triggered

- by a case manager requiring an assistance;
- by DCM, after registering some potentially important contextual or internal event.

3. SCIENTIFIC BACKGROUND

The idea of automated guidance for ACM is grounded on the intersection of several scientific disciplines. In particular, we propose to explore formal methods, formal concept analysis (FCA) and dynamic context modeling.

Table 2 shows the steps of the algorithm for the Case Navigation System presented above and indicates the research challenges and theoretical background for implementing these steps.

Table 2: Theoretical Foundations required for Case Navigation System

Step	System Element	Research Challenges/Background
Select the relevant case-specific parameters, measure them and identify the current case state	DCM + NM	*Challenges:* Dynamic model of the context; Representation, capturing and processing of complex internal and contextual events; Rules for inclusion/exclusion context subjects/elements into consideration; Formal Specification of case coordinate system. *Disciplines:* Dynamic context modeling; Complex Even Processing; Formal specification languages.
Identify probable scenarios (sequences of states) taking into account, if possible, previous experience	NM + Log&History	*Challenges:* Rules for state transitions; Specification of case objectives, final states and case management scenarios; Discovery of the case abstract states and case management scenarios from the log and history. *Disciplines:* Formal specification languages; Process mining; Formal Concept Analysis
Exclude those scenarios that are not feasible/forbidden for current case (i.e. business rules, regulations, availability of resources)	NM	*Challenges:* Formal specification of business rules; simulation and validation the case scenarios against these rules; Disciplines: Formal specification languages and model checking.
Select the scenarios that can lead the case towards its target state with maximum probability	NM	*Challenges:* Identification of the best next state given the current state; *Disciplines:* Graph analysis; Formal Concept Analysis
Identify one or several alternative activities that lead to such successful scenarios and recommend them to the case manager	NM + Repository	*Challenges:* Specification of activities (preconditions + postconditions) and resources; Identification of the activities that lead to required state transition with the maximum likelihood; *Disciplines:* Formal specification languages; Formal Concept Analysis
Record the case manager's decision	NM + Log&History	-

Formal Concept Analysis (FCA)

Automated guidance for ACM proposed in this paper depends heavily on the systems capability to analyze, look for dependencies and classify vast amount of data considering the case, its context, states, log and history. Navigation system also has to efficiently predict the successful scenarios and recommend to a user some course of actions based on a certain criteria. Formal Concept Analysis discipline proposes a set of methods and tool for such data processing and **predictive analytics**.

FCA is a mathematical theory relying on the use of formal contexts and Galois lattices (Birkhoff 1940). The use of Galois lattices to describe a relation between two sets has led to various classification methods: a Galois lattice gathers elements, which have common properties in clusters, called formal concepts. A partial order exists among these concepts, which form a lattice with an upper and a lower bound. Since their creation, Galois lattices have been used in numerous contexts to extract hidden knowledge from data.

Formal concept analysis provides a universal tool for clustering the objects as well it can be used as underlying semantics for a recommenders system, providing a selected subset of elements that correspond to a certain criteria. Its joint use with formal methods and context modeling is very promising in the context of case management.

Dynamic context modeling

The main characteristic that distinguishes Adaptive Case Management from Business Process Management is its dependency from the complex events and contextual parameters. The more complete information we have about the case context the more accurate the decision we can make about what to do next (Vanrompay 2011). However, too many contextual parameters can make the case management unbearably tough. Designing a context model that will adapt to the case needs by dynamically including new relevant parameters into the consideration and excluding the irrelevant ones – is an important endeavor for efficient Case Navigation System.

The process context information should be acquired, modeled and formally analyzed at run time in order to adapt case handling scenario and to ensure its flexibility (Bettini 2010). Most context models consider a subject or a number of subjects (e.g. a person, a physical or information object, a phenomenon etc.). Each subject can be associated with multiple context elements (location, status, etc.); for each context element, we observe values that can dynamically change and that can be described by meta-data. Both subject and context elements can be semantically described using ontologies.

The subjects/elements present in a current context model depend on the activity domain related to our case. An important advantage provided by dynamic context modeling is a possibility to add/remove subjects and elements to/from the context model at run time.

Complex Event Processing (CEP)

Capturing and processing complex events in business organizations have been recently addressed by Complex Event Processing (CEP) discipline (Luckham 2011) (Bates 2012). The goal of CEP is to handle the streams of information from different sources, to identify meaningful events and to respond to them as quickly as possible. Complex events can emerge at different layers of an organization and can combine various simpler events such as customer calls, messages, social media posts, stock market feeds, traffic reports, weather reports, etc. Integration of the CEP technology into BPM has a great potential (Janiesch 2011) as it can result in development of decision-support systems and other recommendation systems for efficient business process management.

Detection-oriented CEP is a class of CEP solutions focused on identification of *pattern situations* from combinations or sequences of events. Complemented by dynamic context modeling for run-time definition of complex contextual events and by FCA for identification and evaluation of case handling scenarios that can follow a detected pattern situation, detection-oriented CEP represent a valuable technology for automated ACM.

Formal Methods

Process modeling (graphical or formal) prior to its implementation is important since it helps to understand and communicate the meaning of the process. Formal modeling (or specification) is yet more beneficial: it allows a process designer to check if a given process meets specific conditions, respects (business) rules and if it can result in desired outcome.

Formal specification of a case management process assumes definition of the coordinate system, abstract states and conditions that trigger the state transitions during a case handling. This specification can be done using a formal specification language and further validated using formal methods.

In computer science, formal methods are a particular kind of mathematically based techniques for the specification, development and verification of software and hardware systems (Clarke 1996). The examples of formal methods include Z notation, B-method, Alloy specification language etc.

Formal methods can be used for step-wise system design: they provide a formal specification of the system to be developed at different levels of details and allow for accurate refinement (transition from one level to another). The resulting formal specification can be used to verify that the requirements for the system being developed have been completely and accurately specified. Along those lines, formal methods can be used to verify that the proposed case-handling scenario meets the objectives of the organization while respecting the contracts and regulations associated with it.

4. DISCUSSION

The vision presented above results from an academic research of our group and its implementation only begins. Our objective is to extend the capability of ACM supporting systems and to transform them from useful assistants to experienced guides and reliable advisors.

While trying to answer the question "what makes a perfect case manager?" we highlighted the following characteristics:
- objective and well-argued reasoning;
- capability to value alternatives under uncertainty;
- capacity to learn fast from the experience.

The Case Navigation System pictured above focuses on these characteristics: dynamic context manager supports objective and well-argued reasoning about the case; thanks to predictive scenario calculation and mining of previous scenarios, accurate predictions about case development can be made by NM; thanks to registered log and history, scenarios can be improved in the future.

So what?

This is probably the main question that bothers a reader during the last couple of pages. Could these ideas, which look like a mixture between good imagination and scientific terminology, leave the research lab one day? We will try to answer this question.

Our group works in collaboration with other researchers in order to provide solid theoretical foundations, algorithms and working prototypes for the Case Navigation System depicted in this article. First, we are going to create models and algorithms for a *generic system*, which does not consider any concrete application domain. The next step is to create a prototype of the Navigation System for a concrete domain (e.g. banking, insurance, administration, legislative etc.).

The prospective prototype, however, cannot be considered a working system until it is *simulated, validated and tested* on multiple, first, toy and then, real life examples. Simulation and validation phase will be followed by the learning phase, where the algorithms will be tuned based on the existing cases. This will potentially improve their accuracy. These research and development activities are summarized in Figure 2.

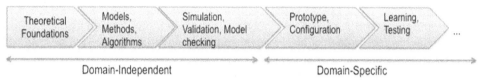

Figure 2: Research and development activities for the Case Navigation System

Challenges

The main challenges we have to face can be roughly divided in three categories:

- Theoretical challenges related to overall problem complexity and number of "unknowns" to manage.
- Technological challenges (e.g. scalability and robustness of algorithms, availability and quality of appropriate ICT technologies)
- Challenges related to adoption by the users (e.g. user perception of complexity versus utility, appreciation and willingness to adopt).

We give some examples related to our scientific objectives first:

In spite of their effectiveness, approaches based on a formal semantics, model checking and theorem proving are rarely used in practice due to their complexity and high implementation cost. Indeed, formal specification languages are typically based on first or higher order logic: reduction of a real life problem (i.e. a case and its handling) to a logical formula represents a complex task and requires specific skills from a designer. So far, formal methods have been successfully used in design and development of safety critical systems.

The main critique of the approaches based on Formal Concept Analysis is related to their scalability. Computation and update of Galois lattices are complex tasks, especially if the input data is large and evolves frequently. This can be seen as a serious drawback in development of automated guidance for ACM. To cope with this problem, several approaches based on filtering techniques have been proposed. Recent works demonstrate a possibility to generate Galois lattice from a data stream in real-time. In particular, some tools like FCA Stream Miner tool (Melo 2013), which implement this approach, have been successfully used for anomaly detection in telemetry data.

Scalability of context acquisition platforms can be pointed out as an issue for context-aware ACM. Indeed, the DCM component of the Case Navigation System described above needs to observe an important number of elements, identify and handle complex business events. This potentially involves connecting multiple distributed information sources. Recent solutions developed in the fields of pervasive systems and sensor networks demonstrate that it is possible to handle hundreds of sensors for observing context information.

Another critical challenge is related to the *heterogeneity* of contextual information: the DCM component has to deal with a multi-scale context, where information can range from simple coordinates coming from a GPS to complex client or market descriptions coming from cloud platforms, social networks, RFIDs and personal mobile devices. Such heterogeneous information has to be represented using multiple scales, demanding expressive models. This is an ongoing issue considered by numerous research teams. Some of the issues related to handling multiple heterogeneous information sources are addressed by Complex Event Processing discipline.

The problems described above mostly illustrate the theoretical challenges. Regarding the technological and adoption challenges we refer to Gartner's Hype cycle. Figure 3 illustrates the Hype cycle for emerging technologies for 2013[2] It evaluates the maturity, adoption and future direction for technologies and trends and helps us to illustrate some technological challenges. In particular, the Hype cycle from 2013 highlights the evolving relationships between humans and machines. According to this research, Predictive Analytics technologies already reached their plateau of productivity phase and are currently becoming the mainstream technology. Complex-Event Processing and Content Analytics technologies that also pave the road to context-aware ACM are currently on their peak of inflated expectations phase, meaning that the value of these technologies is not yet correctly estimated and their reputation is grounded on both success and failure stories. According to Gartner, both Content Analytics and CEP technologies will reach their maturity (the plateau) in 5 to 10 years (Figure 3).

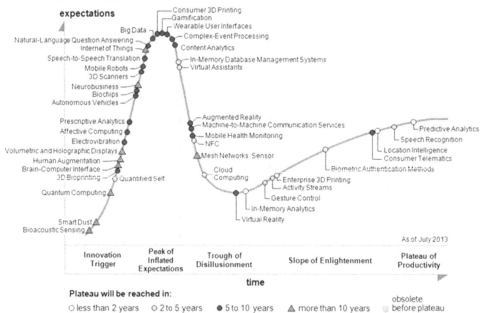

Figure 3: Gartner's Hype Cycle for emerging technologies in 2013.

The passage from the purely theoretical Case Navigation System described in this article to a concrete system that deals with a real life example presents a whole set of new challenges. We highlight just two of them:

- To **select the right level of granularity**, we have to identify relevant internal and contextual parameters that will affect the produced recommendations and determine case scenarios. This task is not easy even for a professional case manager with years of experience. The main risk is to

---

[2] Source: Gartner, August 2013 http://www.gartner.com/newsroom/id/2575515

get the system that is either too naïve (abstracts away too many parameters and produces only trivial recommendations) or too complex (produces scenarios and recommendations impossible to decipher or validate).

- To **specify and further improve the system logic**, we have to collect a substantial amount of data on case management history (past cases). Unfortunately, organizations often do not collect such history. Even if they do - very rarely they keep trace in a standard format that can be easily re-used/understood.

In this paper, we presented the concept of Case Navigation System, which is grounded on academic research of our group. Our idea is to extend the capabilities of ACM supporting systems of today and to transform them from useful assistants to experienced guides and reliable advisors. Though a perspective of having fully automated case management sounds like science fiction and we are still far from inventing HAL 9000, some exciting functionalities such as context-aware scenario prediction and evaluation can be envisioned.

5. REFERENCES

(Bates 2012) Bates, J.: John Bates of Progress explains how complex event processing works and how it can simplify the use of algorithms for finding and capturing trading opportunities, Fix Global Trading, retrieved May 14, 2012

(Bettini 2010) Bettini, C., Brdiczka, O., Henricksen K., Indulska, J., Nicklas, D., Ranganathan, A., Riboni, D.: A survey of context modelling and reasoning techniques, Pervasive and Mobile Computing, vol. 6, issue 2, pp. 161-180 (2010)

(Birkhoff 1940) Birkhoff, G.: Lattice Theory, First Edition, Amer. Math. Soc. Pub. 25, Providence, R. I. (1940).

(Clarke 1996) Clarke, Edmund M., and Jeannette M. Wing. "Formal methods: State of the art and future directions." ACM Computing Surveys (CSUR) 28.4 (1996): 626-643.(Luckham 2012) Luckham, D. C. Event Processing for Business: Organizing the Real-Time Enterprise. Hoboken, New Jersey: John Wiley & Sons, Inc.,. (2012). p. 3. ISBN 978-0-470-53485-4.

(IMDB 1968) 2001: A Space Odyssey (1968), directed by Stanley Kubrick. IMDB: http://www.imdb.com/title/tt0062622/?ref_=fn_al_tt_1

(Janiesch 2011) C. Janiesch, M. Matzner and O. Müller: A Blueprint for Event-Driven Business Activity Management, Lecture Notes in Computer Science, 2011, Volume 6896/2011, 17-28, doi:10.1007/978-3-642-23059-2_4

(Luckham 2011) Luckham, David C. Event processing for business: organizing the real-time enterprise. Wiley. com, 2011.

(Melo 2013) Melo, C.A., Le-Grand, B., Aufaure, M. (2013) Browsing Large Concept Lattices through Tree Extraction and Reduction Methods, in International Journal of Intelligent Information Technologies (IJIIT).

(OMG 2009) Object Management Group, Case Management Process Modeling (CMPM) Re-quest For Proposal: Bmi/2009-09-23

(Vanrompay 2011) Vanrompay, Y. & Berbers, Y. Efficient Context Prediction for Decision Making in Pervasive Health Care Environments: A Case Study, In: Supporting Real Time Decision-Making, Annals of Information Systems, vol. 13, 2011, Springer, 303-317

6. OTHER RESOURCES:

(Arcangeli 2012) Arcangeli, J.-P.; Bouzeghoub, A.; Camps, V.; Canut, M.-F.; Chabridon, S.; Conan, D.; Desprats, T.; Laborde, R.; Lavinal, E.; Leriche, S.; Maurel, H.; Péninou, A.; Taconet, C. & Zaraté, P. "INCOME – Multi-scale Context Management for the Internet of Things". In: Paternò, F.; Ruyter, B.; Markopoulos, P.; Santoro, C.; Loenen, E. & Luyten, K. (Eds.), Ambient Intelligence, Lecture Notes in Computer Science, vol. 7683, 2012, Springer, 338-347

(Bider 2013) Bider, I., Johannesson, P., Perjons, E.: Do workflow-based systems satisfy the demands of the agile enterprise of the future? In: Rosa, M.L., Soffer, P. (eds.), Business Process Management Workshops (BPM 2012), Lecture Notes in Business Information Processing, vol. 132, pp.59-64,., Springer (2013)

(Kirsch-Pinhero 2013) Kirsch-Pinheiro, M., Rychkova, I. (2013). Dynamic Context Modeling for Agile Case Management 2nd International Workshop on Adaptive Case Management and other non-workflow approaches to BPM (AdaptiveCM 2013), OnTheMove Federated Workshops, Graz, Austria, 9-13 September 2013, to appear.

(Rychkova 2013a) Rychkova, I., Kirsch-Pinheiro, M., & Le Grand, B. (2013). Context-Aware Agile Business Process Engine: Foundations and Architecture. In Enterprise, Business-Process and Information Systems Modeling (pp. 32-47). Springer Berlin Heidelberg.

(Rychkova 2013b) Rychkova, I.: Exploring the Alloy Operational Semantics for Case Management Process Modeling. In proceedings of IEEE 7th International Conference on Research Challenges in Information Science (RCIS'13) ISBN ISBN #978-1-4673-2914-9

(Swenson 2010) Keith D. Swenson. Mastering The Unpredictable: How Adaptive Case Management Will Revolutionize The Way that Knowledge Workers Get Things Done. Meghan-Kiffer Press, 2010.

Identity Management via ACM

Keith Harrison-Broninski, Role Modellers, UK

INTRODUCTION

Despite the current fast pace of innovation in Identity Management, new technologies still provide little support for securing the primary occupation of most knowledge workers - collaboration with colleagues, especially those who work for different organizations. If an organization is going to grant access to business-critical resources, it needs to know **why** access is needed and **what will be done** with those resources. This means understanding the work item that has caused the person to request access – i.e., the business process context in which access is being granted:

- The **Activities** the person is carrying out using the resource;
- The **Roles** they have been assigned, to which the Activities belong;
- The **Plans** (projects, programmes, processes, initiatives or ventures) of which the Roles form a part.

This paper discusses an ACM technique that not only enhances traditional Role-Based Access Control for use with collaborative work spanning multiple organizations, but also solves a related challenge into the bargain. Increasingly, business systems are used to send messages, by email and other means, often containing sensitive content. The sender may be known, but what about the recipients? The ACM technique presented streamlines and improves collaborative work across multiple organizations in such a way that not only the sender but also the recipients of any message are automatically authenticated, authorized and audited.

PACE OF CHANGE IN IDENTITY MANAGEMENT

In the last decade, Identity Management (IM) has matured yet remained - for many organizations – as bewildering as ever. Even setting aside technologies and considering only standards, are you confident that your IT department properly understands the relationship between, limitations of, and current direction of OpenID, OAuth, UMA, Open Social, Information Cards, XRDS, SAML, and WS-Trust?

Security professionals are well aware that their field is in rapid flux. For example, the semi-annual Internet Identity Workshop, which focuses on "the use of identity management approaches based on open standards that are privacy protecting", deals with the pace of change by adopting a unique format (www.internetidentityworkshop.com/blog):

> After the brief introduction on the first day, there are no formal presentations, no keynotes and no panels. After introductions we start with a blank wall and, in less than an hour, with a facilitator guiding the process attendees create a full day, multi-track conference agenda that is relevant and inspiring to everyone there. All are welcome to put forward presentations and propose conversations.
>
> We do this in part because the field is moving so rapidly that it doesn't make sense to predetermine the presentation schedule months before the event.

In this paper, I'm not going to try and navigate the shifting sands of IM in detail. Rather, I will take a very high-level view in order to discuss a limitation of **all** current approaches to IM. I will argue that typical IM implementations do not do enough to support the primary occupation of most knowledge workers—collaboration with colleagues. I will explain why this is an important problem, and show how to supplement any IM system in order to fill the gap.

WHAT IS DIGITAL IDENTITY?

Let's start by looking at the commonly accepted definition of digital identity, as stated by Kim Cameron in his seminal paper, "The Laws of Identity" [Cameron 2005]:

> We will begin by defining a digital identity as *a set of claims made by one digital subject about itself or another digital subject.*

Cameron goes on to provide some illustrative examples of this definition:

- *A claim could just convey an identifier - for example, that the subject's student number is 490-525, or that the subject's Windows name is REDMOND\kcameron. This is the way many existing identity systems work.*
- *Another claim might assert that a subject knows a given key – and should be able to demonstrate this fact.*
- *A set of claims might convey personally identifying information – name, address, date of birth and citizenship, for example.*
- *A claim might simply propose that a subject is part of a certain group – for example, that she has an age less than 16.*
- *And a claim might state that a subject has a certain capability – for example to place orders up to a certain limit, or modify a given file.*

The objective of IM as a discipline is to provide technical infrastructure for managing such claims. An overview of some aspects of the current state of the art is provided in a helpful diagram by Eve Maler [Maler 2012]:

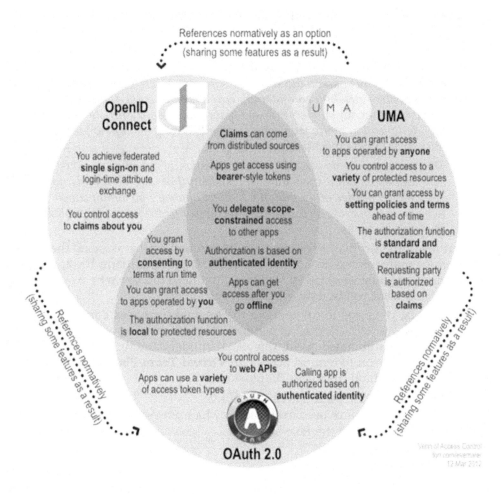

Figure 1: Venn diagram of access control for the API economy

This diagram is high-level, but not high-level enough. It is still a technologist's view, which tells us nothing about the nature of the claims that are being managed.

This is deliberate, of course – IM is agnostic of claim contents, and can be used to manage claims of any kind. As Bob Blakley points out [Blakley 2007]:

> *In discussions of digital identity one often sees "identity" defined as "a collection of attributes" or "a collection of claims" or "partial identity". The question naturally arises, "attributes of what?" or "claims about what?" or "partial identity of what?" These questions have no clear-cut answers. The answer "a subject" is too vague; the answer "a person" leads to arguments about how one distinguishes a natural person from a legal/juridical person, and perhaps even from a non-person; there may also be arguments about whether multiple persons can inhabit the same body, either at the same time or sequentially. And the answer "a human body" creates confusion about matters of intent and continuity of memory, which are important when making decisions about reward and punishment.*

This is heavy stuff – too heavy for the IDM industry, which deals with the issue like Monty Python's Brave Sir Robin, by bravely running away [Blakley 2007]:

> *In most practical cases it simply does not matter whether persons have immutable core identities; it is usually sufficient to answer an easier question: "Is this person the same person who did 'X' in the past?" While the (possible) lack of a core identity can create a small amount of doubt about whether our suspect previously did 'X', the evidence for or against the identification of the suspect is normally strong enough to justify confidence in the identification.*

> *This paper takes no position on the question of whether persons have core identities, but it does take the position that core identity is not observable by parties other than the subject himself – so identification systems need to operate on the basis of recognizing attributes or establishing the truth of claims.*

This cutting of the Gordian knot may suit IM researchers by reducing their scope to something more manageable, but is unhelpful for organizations. If you are going to grant access to business-critical resources, you need to know **why** you are granting access and **what** will be done with those resources.

In other words, you need to understand the **business process context** in which access is being granted – and if, as is usual, you are granting access to a person rather than to an automated agent, this means understanding the work item that has caused the person to request access. In **Virtual Team Planning** (**VTP**) terms, you need to understand [Harrison-Broninski 2013]:

- The **Activity** the person is carrying out;
- The **Role** they have been assigned, to which the Activity belongs;
- The **Plan** to which the Role belongs.

GRANTING ACCESS TO ROLES

The key element of identity here is the Role. In a workplace context, someone requests access to a resource not because of who they are (**Jane Smith**) but rather because they have been asked to play a Role in a Plan (**Training Manager** in **Dementia Friendly Communities Programme 2013**) and hence to need to do a specific Activity (**Review Workforce Training Needs**). It is only on being assigned to the Training Manager Role that Jane needs to review the documents – and if she is re-assigned, goes on leave, or is too busy, someone else will require access to the documents in her place.

Roles tell us how to think properly about confidentiality - something we rarely do, and something that is not encouraged by current approaches to IM. We only need to consider how the circulation of paper documents was traditionally controlled to understand the lack of thought that has carried through into current IM.

The classic workplace approach to safeguarding the contents of a document is to use a protective marking – to write RESTRICTED, COMMERCIAL IN CONFIDENCE or CONFIDENTIAL AND PROPRIETARY TO XYZ CORPORATION somewhere on each page. However, in most cases this is an almost meaningless gesture, providing little guidance as to who is empowered to view the document – and to who will actually get to see it.

In practice, the copy list of a document is generally used mainly to determine who gets it initially. Each recipient may then need to copy it to others in their company, project or team in order to carry out the actions that arise from the document. Subordinates may be delegated tasks that require use of the document, or may read it while looking through files out of interest. Excerpts may be taken and sent to suppliers, copied to managers, or used in status reports. Moreover, there are people who see the document not as a result of any direct business need, but as part of processing it on behalf of others—system administration staff, proofreaders, secretaries, and so on.

Executives may not wish to admit it publicly, but this spread of information is almost impossible to manage. Protective markings provide no basis for structured control, since they deal only with the first of the "3 A's" of security (Authentication, Authorization and Accounting) – yet protective markings are effectively the foundation of modern IM systems, which are generally used to handle "claims" such as "Jane Smith is currently a member of the Business Improvement Team". What we really need to know is **why** Jane wants to see the document, and **what** she intends to do with it – claims with business meaning, which can be verified after the fact.

To provide such information, it is necessary to appreciate that it is not the document that should carry the marking. A single document may be used in different ways at different times by different people. Further, the usages of a document will change over the life of a document – they cannot be predicted and set in stone at the time of writing. To **authorize** and **account** for the usages of an information item, access must be controlled by defining usages that associate the document with specific Activities in specific Roles in specific Plans.

RBAC IS BACK

The use of Roles as a guiding principle for security policy creation has a long and venerable history. Ross Anderson, in his authoritative survey of computer system security techniques, wrote [Anderson 2001]:

> The policy model getting the most attention at present from researchers is role-based access control (RBAC), introduced by David Ferraiolo and Richard Kuhn ... This sets out to provide a more general framework for mandatory access control than [Bell-LaPadula] in which access decisions don't depend on users' names but on the functions they are currently performing within the organization. Transactions that may be performed by holders of a given role are specified, then mechanisms for granting membership of a role (including delegation). Roles, or groups, had for years been the mechanism used in practice in organizations such as banks to manage access control; the RBAC model starts to formalize this. It can deal with integrity issues as well as confidentiality, by allowing role membership (and thus access rights) to be revised when certain programs are invoked. Thus, for example, a process calling untrusted software that had been downloaded from the Net might lose the role membership required to write to sensitive system files.

However, it is not enough to define a Role using the sort of text attributes that Anderson suggests – membership of a group, basically – since "Roles" thus defined have no process context. The fundamental nature of a Role in the modern, flexible, distributed workplace is as *process participant*. Hence a Role definition for IM purposes must include essential aspects of collaborative process management, such as:

- Goals
- Responsibilities
- Information resources
- Structured, purposeful communication channels with colleagues

- Well-defined Activities, including the ability to start and manage other Plans
- A means to manage the status of Deliverables.

Critically, it is necessary to support the dynamic nature of a business process, which means that a Role must not only be able to modify the structure and contents of its own information resources, but also to adapt to circumstances by changing its own behavior and that of others.

Further, there are serious security questions related to *delegation of authority* that can only be solved via a process-based implementation of Roles. It is common for one process participant to offload a particular piece of work to another, perhaps adding a new person to the process specifically for this purpose. With process support for Roles, this can be done either by creating a new Role to which work is passed, or by re-assigning the current Role to a new person, or by starting a sub-Plan involving the new person, or by various other means.

Finally, people typically collaborate with colleagues in different teams or organizations, which means that participants in a single Plan may use different systems to do so. In other words, the Plan must live in several places at once, and part of the function of an IM system is to manage this. A Plan that is distributed in this way cannot be managed using a process system that requires all process participants to login to a central server – rather, different people will use different process systems, which talk to each other in order to synchronize the copies of the Plan held by the different participants. Some participants may never even login to a process management system at all, preferring to use simpler messaging technology such as email to collaborate with colleagues – yet this must also be handled transparently.

To handle Roles in this way, you need a VTP system – and it is only by the integration of VTP and IM technology that access to information resources in the workplace can be properly secured.

THE IDENTITY METASYSTEM

The danger to organizational security is only increased by the new generation of IM systems, which aim to create a fully-fledged "Identity Metasystem" [Cameron 2006]:

- A way to represent identities using **claims**. Claims are carried in security tokens, as per WS-Security[1].
- A means for identity providers, relying parties, and subjects to **negotiate**. Dynamically negotiating the claims to be delivered and the security token format used enables the Identity Metasystem to carry any format of token and any kinds of claims needed for a digital identity interaction. Negotiation occurs using WS-SecurityPolicy[2] statements exchanged using WS-MetadataExchange[3].
- An **encapsulating protocol** to obtain claims and requirements. The WS-Trust[4] and WS-Federation[5] protocols are used to carry requests for security tokens and responses containing those tokens.

---

[1] http://en.wikipedia.org/wiki/WS-Security

[2] http://en.wikipedia.org/wiki/WS-SecurityPolicy

[3] http://en.wikipedia.org/wiki/WS-MetadataExchange

[4] http://en.wikipedia.org/wiki/WS-Trust

[5] http://en.wikipedia.org/wiki/WS-Federation

- A means to bridge technology and organizational boundaries using **claims transformation**. **Security Token Services (STSs)** as defined in WS-Trust[6] are used to transform claim contents and formats.
- A **consistent user experience** across multiple contexts, technologies, and operators. This is achieved via Identity Selector client software representing digital identities owned by users as visual **Information Cards**.

An all-encompassing Identity Metasystem may do more harm than good if the claims that it exchanges cannot be properly authorized or accounted for.

Physically, confidential information may be **stored** in operating system files or database records, but logically, it **belongs** to the Roles that need it. Only by providing access to information through the mediation of process Roles will organizations be able to properly authorize and account for that access. Without Roles, access can only be granted to a bewildering sea of names – and in the digital world, it is no longer possible to associate names with faces - as in Peter Steiner's famous cartoon from the New Yorker, showing two dogs sitting in front of a computer, with one saying to the other, "On the Internet, nobody knows you're a dog".

An enterprise infrastructure without an access control layer based on VTP Plans is shown in Figure 2:

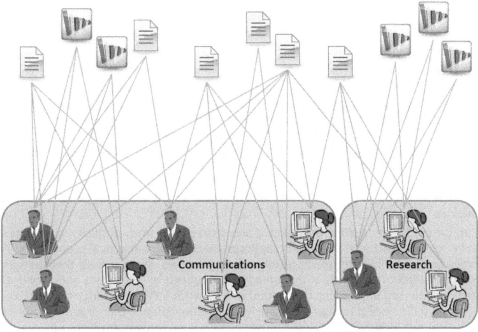

Figure 2: Identity "Management" without VTP Plans

Without some means of understanding why people need access to resources, and what they are doing with them, the situation is next to impossible to manage or audit. By contrast, Figure 3 shows how the picture simplifies if you introduce VTP Plans as an intermediate layer to facilitate authorization and accounting:

---

[6] http://en.wikipedia.org/wiki/WS-Trust

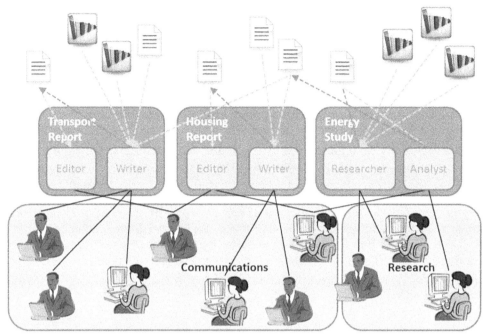

Figure 3: Identity Management with VTP Plans

Further, if access control is guided by Role assignment in VTP Plans, then sharing and delegation of access also falls under IM control. With Roles, data sharing becomes *conscious*, not accidental, and *tracked*, not invisible. This is not only because Roles mean something in a business context, but also because Roles exchange information via structured, purposeful communication channels. If a VTP system is used to manage workplace human interactions, messages are sent in context (by a **Role** as part of a **Stage** in a **Plan**) and automatically recorded for auditing. So not only is access authorized and accounted for, but also transfer of that access – which as we saw above, is a normal, fundamental part of the way that people use information.

Similarly, VTP Plans allow provision of access to people from multiple organizations to be managed without need for complex cross-boundary approval procedures. The organizational affiliation of each Role player becomes secondary to their assigned Role in a Plan of action that has already been agreed by all parties concerned. Organizations that implement IM in combination with VTP technology will be able to open up their systems to partners safely and manageably. Other organizations may only find out long after the fact that their data is no longer confidential – and still be unable to work out what happened.

SECURING EMAIL AND INSTANT MESSAGING

Finally, we are in a position to discuss the aspect of RBAC identified as the core subject of this paper, an aspect fundamental to the modern workplace: management of communications.

Most workplace messages are sent via email, with instant messaging increasingly an alternative option. Even if encryption is used for messaging, the volume of messages sent daily in most organizations makes it almost impossible to gain retrospective understanding of why people sent things to each other – a clear security risk, since it prevents meaningful audit.

However, once Roles are introduced to the security picture, it becomes possible to manage data sharing, even by email. This is because Roles exchange information via purposeful communication channels. If a VTP System is used to manage workplace collaboration, messages are not emailed by Alice to Bob and Charlie, but sent by the **Role** that Alice plays to the Roles assigned to colleagues in the relevant **Stage** (work stream) of a **Plan**.

Further, a VTP system unifies email and instant messaging – the user gains the ease of use and immediacy of instant messaging, but under the hood, all messages are transferred by email, and can be read using any normal email client. This enables encryption, ensures that all messages are automatically recorded for auditing in a context that is simple to understand, and makes it possible for people to choose how to send/receive messages – they can use email as usual, or the Web-based planning tool, just as they prefer.

In effect, the use of RBAC via Virtual Team Plans enables organizations to "secure the other end" – to manage the flow of information, not just internally but to and from partner organizations with who staff are collaborating. RBAC, implemented in this way, means that security does not stop with the message sender – it also applies to message recipients, automatically.

CONCLUSION

Virtual Team Plans allow provision of access to people from multiple organizations to be managed without need for complex cross-boundary approval procedures. The organizational affiliation of each Role player becomes secondary to their assigned Role in a Plan of action that has already been agreed by all parties concerned. Organizations that implement IM in combination with Virtual Team Planning will be able to share business information with partners safely and manageably.

In particular, RBAC makes sharing of business information conscious, not accidental, and tracked, not invisible. The first step in managing business communications is to understand them, which means putting them in process context. For long-term, collaborative work that spans multiple organizations, such processes can only be handled by treating them as Virtual Team Plans, and supporting them with a Virtual Team Planning system.

REFERENCES

(Anderson 2001) Ross Anderson. "Security Engineering: A Guide to Building Dependable Distributed Systems," Wiley Computer Publishing, 2001.

(Blakley 2007) Bob Blakley. "Current Conceptions Of IDM" in "At A Crossroads: 'Personhood' And Digital Identity In The Information Society", OECD Directorate for Science, Technology and Industry, 2007.

(Cameron 2005) Kim Cameron. "The Laws of Identity", Microsoft Corporation, 2005.

(Cameron 2006) Kim Cameron. "The Identity Metasystem", Microsoft Corporation, 2006.

(Harrison-Broninski 2013) Keith Harrison-Broninski. "Capturing Knowledge with Processes", published as bptrends.com "Human Processes" column November 2013 (www.bptrends.com/publicationfiles/11-05-2013%20COL-Human%20Process-Capturing%20Knowledge-%20Harrison-Broninski%20-Final%20%281%29.pdf).

(Jones 2005) Michael B. Jones. "Microsoft's Vision for an Identity Metasystem", Microsoft Corporation, 2005.

(Maler 2012) Eve Maler. "A New Venn of Access Control for the API Economy", Forrester Research, 2012.

Mastering Knowledge Flow, Aligning Social Networks, Knowledge Use and Process Design

Alberto Manuel, Process Sphere, Portugal

INTRODUCTION

We have been supporting our way of working and structuring organizational operations based on the increased processing capacity of information systems that created the illusion that the world is more stable, predictable as well as standardized.

Somehow, the human being continues to assume that it is better to sit on top of an ordered regime because it is much simpler to understand concepts, interactions, and our very existence, in a controlled manner. However we live in the world of uncertainty, and this implies a new attitude in the way we collaborate, how we design services, products, in addition to how we tackle the challenges in the face of volatility driven by external forces like social, mobile, cloud and internet of things. This implies constantly changing, making operations lean over and over again, in other words, *constant adaptation.*

Some say that adaptation has been always the "new norm" and the need for business transformation is a worn-out argument. I tend to concur with this point of view, but the difference is that today the pace of transformation is extremely fast.. I started my endeavour in Business Process Management, companies revisited customer-facing processes every year or every two years, like pre-programmed maintenance. Today, in some industries sectors like Telecom companies, it is usual to transform and flip business processes every three months, since it is necessary to change service and product offerings in innovative ways, re-engineering or implementing new paradigms, truly on end-to-end bases (from request fulfilment to customer billing and support).

What organizations turned out to be

Today, organizations consist of small- to large-scale technosocial service systems, defined as, orchestrations of information systems and people, whose dynamics and evolution are defined and driven by human behaviour [0].

The figure below is a Complaint Handling Process typically structured around this set of activities; Registering the Complaint, Handling the Complaint, Providing a Solution, and Closing the Complaint. This is supposedly very simple in terms of process structure and the sequence of process steps taken. Yet if you look at this image obtained through Process Mining discovery techniques, we conclude that this is a very complex process with increased effort of analysis. A complex system forms, therefore, a network or meshwork (spaghetti) that is defined in terms of its relationships and which can be described in terms of information processing. This characteristic unfolds two key features of complexity that today exist in business process execution: emergence and self-organizing adaptation [4].

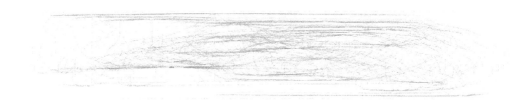

Figure 1 - Complaint handling process discovery using process mining techniques

In these new forms of complex systems, execution became knowledge oriented. This means that to perceive is to understand patterns; separating the signal from the noise. The signal is a quality that can be termed as emergent. How do these patterns of relationships occur between the components and thus become the focus for understanding the behaviour of process itself.

The systemic properties of a particular level like a complaint category related with product price or a service level agreement; dominant or exception process paths between two agents are called emergent properties, since they emerge at that particular level.

BUSINESS PROCESSES ANALYSIS MUST BE PREPARED FOR THE AGE OF COMPLEX SYSTEMS

As increasing diversity of execution possibilities driven by the fact that customers and other stakeholders have taken control of process execution and the exceptions are the most important part to analyse because they truly mean what is happening inside an organization, traditional analysis approaches cannot cope with such a rich environment.

For managers, the challenge is in understanding and designing such knowledge oriented processes that today are becoming standard, since defining and validating a structure is not enough. For knowledge workers the challenge is in making the most of their knowledge and developing their skills by putting them in service organizations.

Analysis characteristics of business processes should be expanded to:
- **Emergence**: agents (humans and systems) that belong to the network interact in an apparently random way. This is a feeling which is amplified if there are many agents and / or there are too many interactions that make patterns difficult to extract. Emergence is all about making important patterns emerge.
- **Adaptation**: enterprises, communities, exist confined in a particular environment where changes makes agents react.
- **Variety**: For an organization to be viable it must be capable of coping with the complexity of the environment in which it operates. Managing complexity is the essence of a manager's activity. Controlling a situation means being able to deal with its complexity, that is, its variety [1].

For that purpose, new analysis dimensions must be used. Knowledge type, process design pattern and social network configuration, must all be aligned in order to deliver value to the organization. If the process is rigid and the network is loosely coupled, high variation will occur, particularly if knowledge is tacit and not explicit (everyone performs the way they deem best, rather than in an optimized way of performing).

Knowledge type

Knowledge can be organized around four main domains as outlined below.

Domain	Codification	Abstraction	Diffusion
Ordered	High Explicit. Everything is documented.	High Abstract. Can be used in different situations	Low Restricted. The same actors perform.
Exploratory	Average Between explicit and tacit. Easily automatable	Average Abstract, but must be adapted to execution context	Average Open communication flows among a predefined set of actors
Complex	Average Typically tacit. The experience of the players plays an important role	Average Concrete. Applies only to a particular situation and requires great effort to adapt to other circumstances	Average Open communication flows between a set of actors that are invited to participate
Chaos	Low Tacit. It's the experience that counts.	Low Concrete. Only applies to a single or few situations	High Ubiquitous. Open communication channels

Figure 2 - Knowledge type evaluation framework - based on Knowledge Assets - Max H. Boisot

Process design configuration

Process Design can be organized around three main domains as outlined below.

Type	Model	Goals	Behavior
Structured	Rigid Specify exactly activity sequence (relay or step by step)	Fixed Achieve the same goal over and over again	Pre-defined It's not possible to change behavior if an unpredictable event occurs
Ad-hoc	Blended Composed of predefined activities, but with few degrees of execution freedom (e.g. guided by business rules)	Fixed Achieve the same goal over and over again	Partially defined Participants can change the behavior, but it usually depends on prior approval
Adaptive	Flexible Activities are defined on the fly, taking into consideration the goal to be achieved. Every process instance can be ultimately be unique	Changeable Goal changes according process instance challenge	No restrictions Behavior changes if any of process condition also changes (signal, goal, result)

Figure 3 – Process design evaluation framework

Social network configuration

Social networks typically present these patterns and typically have the following properties. The nodes can be made up of individuals, business functions, informational entities, companies. The links represent a multitude of possible relations, like similarities, relational roles, relation cognition or relational events (interactions and information flows) [5] meaning that it is possible to represent process execution under a complex system paradigm from different perspectives and points of view and identify what the emergent properties related to the way actors interact are. The existing connections will unveil the emergent patterns that are necessary in order to identify and understand behaviour from a social point of view (high coupling or loosely coupling between agents or group of agents).

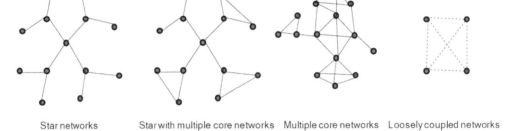

Star networks   Star with multiple core networks   Multiple core networks   Loosely coupled networks

Figure 4 : Network patterns types

Star networks	Star with multiple core networks	Multiple core networks	Loosely coupled networks
Characterized by being strong central and weak distributed	Characterized by being strong central and strong distributed	Characterized by being weak central and strong distributed.	Characterized by being weak central and weak distributed.

Figure 5: Properties of network configuration

DESIGNING THE NEXT WAVE OF BUSINESS PROCESSES

Bringing alignment among the presented dimensions is not an easy task and different approaches must be used to discover emergent properties as an alternative to performing process redesign or implementing a paradigm shift.

On network types

Most people often refer to social networks as places for expressing their beliefs on community networks like Facebook or subject expert groups like enterprise wikis. Although those are indeed important network types, they do not express the nature of organization operations because they do not record communication acts expressed on social activity.

Hence, I will concentrate only on *Coordination Networks*.

A Coordination Network is a network formed by agents related to each other by recorded coordination acts. Coordination acts are, for example, the interchange of emails, tasks as designed on enterprise systems or activity streams, just to provide some examples. The above definition is an adaptation of [2] because it does not include the importance of a coordination act that is related to the nature of work, rather the connection itself. The former is the important dimension related to business process management. Coordination acts are meant to be as defined in (adapted) [3] an act to be performed by one agent, directed to another agent that contains an intention (request, promise, question, assertion) and a proposition (something that is or could be the case in the social world). In the intention, the agent proclaims his/her social attitude with respect to the proposition. In the proposition, the agent reiterates the fact and the associated time the intention has expressed, which is recorded by the system, supporting the definition Coordination networks, whose configuration can ultimately be discovered, thus allowing for patterns to emerge.

Figure 6: Composition of a coordination act

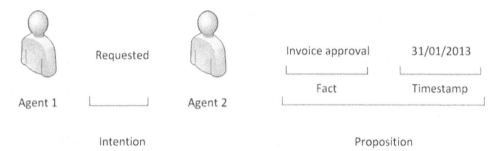

A REAL WORLD EXAMPLE OF HOW TO ALIGN THE THREE PERSPECTIVES

At the beginning of this paper we had the opportunity to look at a very fuzzy process, almost impossible to analyze using classic methods that handle complaints. The challenges of the organization were:

- Why is that every time agents build a solution for a particular complaint type that they start from a blank page?
- Which are the agents that, if they stop performing, the information flow will stop and the process will implode?
- Is the process design pattern the most appropriate way of dealing with exceptions?

Discovering knowledge

One of the patterns that emerged is during the creation of a solution to a customer, the business unit responsible for a particular category was blocked and instead recursively requested support from other business units with more knowledge in specific domains such as technical expertise or pricing, in order to construct the solution to resolve the complaint.

What transpired as a recurring pattern was that people did not know how to design the solution. It was not lack of access to information supporting the nature of service (service specification) formalized by contract (which was always available being stored in a document management system), but the lack of knowledge of how to compose a solution that would not only please the customer and avoid compensation payment, but prevent churn.

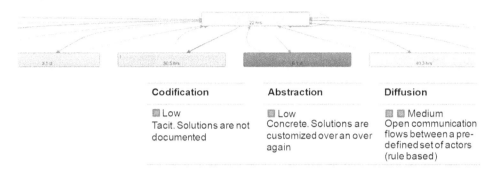

Codification	Abstraction	Diffusion
▣ Low Tacit. Solutions are not documented	▣ Low Concrete. Solutions are customized over an over again	▣ ▣ Medium Open communication flows between a pre-defined set of actors (rule based)

Figure 7 : Evaluating knowledge use trough pattern discovery using process mining

Another important point is that despite there being information systems and proper infrastructure to communicate, the act of getting support was somewhat random, meaning that agents did not know to how to request support and so sparked multiple requests. If the one in charge of handling the complaint wanted, he/she could search for other solutions provided in similar situations because these could be stored in the enterprise system, yet this feature was not used. On the other hand the network reach was limited by the rules set in the enterprise system that supported the process, a constraint that was identified during the analysis. Finally, the escalation rule that many process architects apply proved to be inefficient, only amplifying the problem, since the reason for the blockage was the lack of knowledge to provide the solution, not the availability of resources to perform it.

To overcome the problem, discussion forums were created where those responsible for the creation of the proposed solution could exchange their experiences and approaches and thus a knowledge base was built that was updated constantly on co-creation mode.

Unveiling different network structure

Social network analysis is not new. In fact, the first studies were done during the 1950s. Their refinement was centered around:

- **Degree distribution**: studying connection number around a node of the network;
- **Clustering**: groups with connection density larger than average;
- **Community discovery**: measuring alignment of connections in terms of organization hierarchy.

There is an immense list of techniques to analyse each one of the above dimensions, reflecting the high maturity level of each method, but the drawback is that SNA analysed on each dimension alone can induce managers in the wrong direction. For example, studying community discovery can be important because communities are a collection of individuals who are linked or related by some sort of relation. But carrying out the analysis without taking into consideration the content of the conversation (the coordination act) that drove the creation of the link is absolutely wrong, because the conversation is all about the way humans work.

Centrality is used to measure degree distribution. Centrality [2] is described as a process participant, business unit, group (a set of process participants or people) or an enterprise system (not forgetting the machines as part of that system) within the context of a social network. Centrality is also related with discovering the key players in social networks.

Some measures that can be used for centrality are:

- **Degree centrality**: calculate how many links a node has in terms of the remaining network nodes (commonly called network stars). Higher degree centrality means higher probability of receiving information (but does not mean driving information flow within the network).
- **Betweenness**: measures the degree to which a process participant controls information flow. Each participant acts as a broker. The higher the value, the higher the information flow traffic that moves from each node to every other node in the network. The importance of Betweenness in social network analysis is that nodes with higher values stop processing coordination acts and will block information flow from running properly.
- **Closeness**: measures how close a node is isolated in the network compared with other network modes. Nodes with low closeness are able to reach or be reached by most or all other nodes in the network, in other words, low closeness means a node is well-positioned for receiving information early when it has more value. Closeness measure must be supported on time dimension (see reference about the timestamp attribute on the coordination act exemplification), without the timestamp it, is useless.
- **Eigenvector centrality**: used to calculate node influence in the network. Higher scores means a node can influence (touch) many other important nodes.

In order to put it all together it is worth considering the following self-explanatory figure [6].

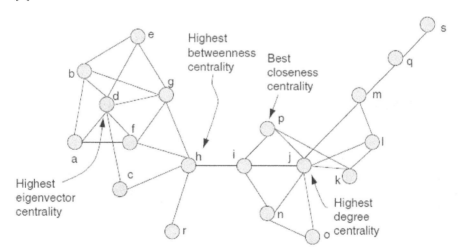

Figure 8: Diverse centrality measures and its meaning

Since SNA does not analyze the process type, only in terms of agent relation, there are some tradeoffs when using these measures. Eigenvector centrality is important in datacentric or adaptive processes, where the path is defined during process enactment, so it is necessary to create a team and involve others as the process progresses. Because the challenge was discovering whether agents stop processing information, what the consequences are was analyzed in the network configuration using betweenness.

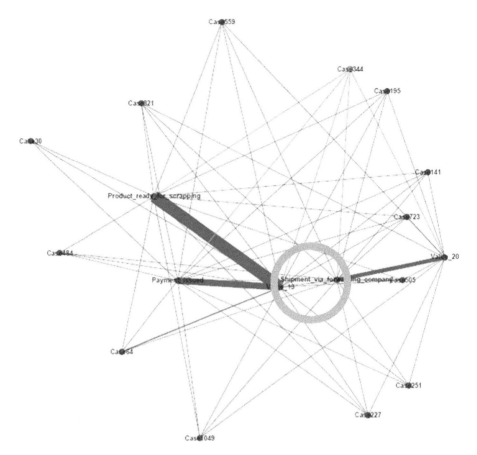

Figure 9: Network configuration using betweenness measure

In the network, there are three dominant paths (displayed with thick lines) where the action occurs and a fine line between the three vectors, meaning that if it is broken, knowledge will not flow. As presented during the discussion of the results, an escalation rule was in place, if an agent enters in idle mode. That rule was constructed to create a pool of resources that allegedly would take care of the cases that had exceeded the due date. Unfortunately, the pool was not constructed under a betweenness approach and latter was redesigned to maximize its value, increasing resilience to information confusion.

Process design patterns

This particular process was designed under a rule-based approach principle. While structured processes models define how things have to be done (i.e. in what order and under what conditions activities shall be executed), rule-based (constraint-based) process models focus on the what should be done by describing the activities that may be performed and the rules prohibiting undesired execution behaviour [7].

The challenge where the underlying principle as to what should be done was subverted to those who were able to perform at a particular stage, bringing a rigid approach to how work could be performed. Rule-based processes have in mind preventing (ultimately impeding) unsupported actions (like for example the agent that approves a compensation being the same that pays the compensation to the customer). Sadly the focus of the design was to route tasks based on responsibility to perform rather than the tasks that could be performed.

A redesign was put in place, keeping the basic sequence of managing a complaint (Register, Handle, Provide a Solution and Close), but instead of focussing on setting departments responsible for each process step, responsibility was allocated, taking into consideration betweenness measures, maximizing information flow, combined with knowledge externalization sessions carried out in internal forums.

CONCLUSIONS

Current business dynamics impose other ways of performing and organizing operations. We are entering into the experience of the real world enterprise approach where it is virtually impossible to manually analyze a process with such diversity present. Hence other approaches are necessary as execution is greatly driven by the capacity to transform data into information and then in knowledge. Step by step, processes and companies are headed toward knowledge-intensive work. That means that the universal principles for designing processes are not effective anymore, as also the same universal techniques are used to carry out an analysis. Finding emergent behaviour is the key to avoid crystallization of order.

References

(Boisot 1999) Max H. Boisot: Knowledge Assets: Securing Competitive Advantage in the Information Economy: Oxford University Press 1999 - ISBN-13: 9780198296072

[0] (Vespignani 2009) A. Vespignani: Predicting the behavior of techno-social systems; Science, vol. 325, no. 5939, pp. 425–428, Jul. 2009.

[1] (Rios, 2012) José Pérez Ríos: Design and Diagnosis for Sustainable Organizations; Springer; ISBN 9783642223174, 2012

[2] (Caldarelli Vespignani) Guido Caldarelli; Alessandro Vespignani: Large Scale Structure and Dynamics of Complex Networks; World Scientific Publishing; ISBN-139789812706645

[3] (Dietz, 2006) Jan Dietz: Enterprise Ontology; Springer; ISBN – 3540291695, 2006

[4] (Wolf; Holvoet, 2005) T. De Wolf and T. Holvoet: Emergence versus self-organisation: Different concepts but promising when combined; Engineering Self-Organising Systems, pp. 77–91, 2005

[5] (Borgatti, Everett, Johnson, 2013) Stephen P. Borgatti, Martin G. Everett and Jeffrey C Johnson: Analyzing Social Networks; Sage; ISBN 978-1-4462-4741-9, 2013

[6] (Arroyo, 2010) Daniel Ortiz-Arroyo: Discovering Sets of Key Players in Social Networks - Springer 2010

[7] (Reichert, Weber, 2012) Manfred Reichert, Barbara Weber: Enabling Flexibility in Process-Aware Information Systems: Challenges, Methods, Technologies; Springer; ISBN 978-3642304088

Real-World Award-Winning Case Studies

Axle Group Holdings Ltd., UK

Nominated by EmergeAdapt, United Kingdom

1. EXECUTIVE SUMMARY / ABSTRACT

In January 2012, Axle Group Holding, one of the UK's largest multi-channel tyre retailers, replaced four eCommerce systems along with a back-office platform to provide case workers with a tool to deliver customer service and post-order treatment. EmergeAdapt built the eCommerce systems and a new back-office case management platform, integrated to all four sites, and to a branch and warehouse system written in DataFlex. All systems were launched in December 2012.

Separately, and while engaged on the Axle project, EmergeAdapt was asked by a UK Claims Management Company to provide the same case management platform for the end-to-end management of circa one million claims. This solution allows 120 operators to manage case creation, through to customer contact and negotiation with the UK financial institutions defending the claims. The solution was launched in January 2013.

Both organisations are supported in production on a single multi-tenanted cloud platform, configuring their own case templates in order to deliver their unique service proposition.

2. OVERVIEW

EmergeAdapt had been looking for an opportunity to build an Adaptive Case Management platform in late 2011, with the aim of bringing enterprise process management to the mass, cloud market, while providing through abstraction, significant levels of end-user configurability. The company founders' experience in traditional on premise, customer-centric BPM led them to conclude that adaptive principles could provide longer-lived operational software solutions, with lower cost of ownership and higher degrees of end-user change.

At Axle, case management delivers a single point of reference for all customer orders coming from four of its eCommerce websites. Further to that, Axle wanted a platform that could grow with them as their business changed, supporting internal process across all lines of business. Case Management offered the promise of not only managing repetitive activities, but also providing flexibility for future, unforeseen process.

Meanwhile, CMC had been set up to industrialise claims processing, acting as a service provider to a range claim-book owners, or "work providers". CMC recognised the need for a case management tool which could evolve with the business. Claims processing had no precedent at CMC, and managing a process involving over 200 lending institutions with no industry standardisation would present multiple challenges. Being able to change the process under end-user control, without resorting to engineering was seen as desirable.

The main project challenges encountered were:

- Requirements capture was difficult at both organisations, and for different reasons. At CMC, the end-to-end claim process was not known at the outset and at the time of writing is still evolving. Ensuring that the platform could get the process off the ground early, while adapting quickly to change was critical.

- At Axle, due to commercial sensitivity, access to internal resource was restricted until very late in the development cycle, placing particular focus on establishing the correct task-oriented end-user experience.
- Building a new case management platform as a re-usable, generic product was a key objective, otherwise the platform would not achieve its goal of becoming an open-market offering. Each requirement was translated from being specific, into a generic requirement plus configuration.
- Ensuring the case management platform could support a broad range of process scenarios within any organisation, while giving the operational manager meaningful levels of control through configuration. For example, how to define a method for integration to external systems, through case template configuration.
- System rollout at Axle required a big bang approach, launching multiple eCommerce components and the case management platform simultaneously. Management of this change was pressurised especially when the volume of work passing through was significant and business critical

3. BUSINESS CONTEXT

Axle Group Holdings is the UK parent company of a number of brands: National Tyres and Autocare (with 220 high street branches plus internet presence), Tyre Shopper (internet), and Viking (wholesale). Axle also operates National Fleet, a service provider to company car fleet administrators.

Axle came to the end of 2011 with a renewed strategy of investment in IT to better serve the growth needs of their business. Incumbent technology was nearing end-of-life and Axle set a 12-month period for the complete replacement of key customer facing and operational systems, with new strategic platforms.

CMC was new to the volume claims market in 2012, and was created from the ground up, with no incumbent resource, process or technology. CMC had signed contracts for the delivery of the service and needed to rapidly create a solution which would support operations.

4. THE KEY INNOVATIONS

Innovations were made across a number of areas:

4.1. Case template definition

Axle and CMC system administrators gain the ability to define and rollout their own case templates, abstracted to the level of the business analyst or operational manager - data model, states, tasks, relationships and permissions. Templating has encouraged business-led change and reduced reliance on technical resource to build and maintain.

Schema configuration offers a YAML-model for entities and fields and allows configuration of entities, fields, calculated fields and external data sources:

Figure 1: Case template definition - Schema

At Axle, the schema contains the typical entities of an order including customer, order line items, fitting appointment (time and location), payment details. At CMC the claim (aka "matter") schema contains information such as the client, work provider, defendant, settlement and credit agreement information.

Configuring *case states* enables the organisation to define key milestones for different case templates and allows the end-user to reflect real world abstraction directly into their operational system:

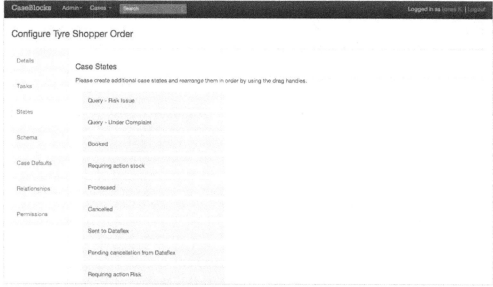

Figure 2: Case template definition - States of an eCommerce order

Configuration of *tasks* allows manual or automation tasks to be defined. Manual tasks act as guidance for case workers and can be added at runtime into case instances without affecting the underlying template.

Automation tasks take advantage of a bespoke scripting language to perform actions such as calling an external service, or updating case data. The scripting language is aimed at a spreadsheet user familiar with formula manipulation. A document model within the case gives access to all case instance attributes within a script:

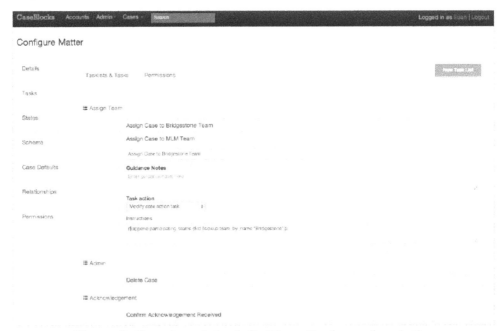

Figure 3: Case template definition - Tasks and scripting

Both types of tasks are presented as a task list within each case instance, which also depicts the status of each task and the participants. This has allowed Axle to create a comprehensive suite of tasks which cover all possible order treatment processes, including submitting a newly created order to the in-house ERP system:

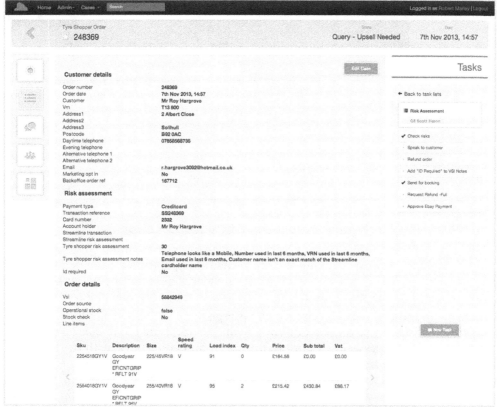

Figure 4: A live case: data, tasks, and participants

4.2. Management of work

Each case template is represented with a single work queue for cases, the 'All' queue. Every case instance appears in this queue.

Through the use of permission-based "buckets", management can create virtual queues based on queries on the All queue. This allows Axle to create work folders for different stock types, risk issues, stock unavailability and exceptions generated from the fulfilment system.

Being able to visualise orders across the full range of states and case behaviours has allowed Axle to improve their deployment of case workers. For example, during a recent failure by the online payment gateway Worldpay, eCommerce payments were not processed for new orders, resulting in customers thinking they hadn't bought any tyres, but Worldpay had actually taken payment. Management immediately setup buckets for these orders and created a team to investigate each payment before contacting the customer to ensure safe processing. Once the issue was cleared, the bucket and the team stood down.

Using a similar approach, CMC can track all claims and their status. At the beginning of the claim process, the client must provide physical signed authorisation on a number of documents before CMC can act on their behalf. Understanding which of these "client packs" are awaiting return by post is key to ensuring process efficiency.

Figure 5: Buckets: CMC's 'Matter' Case

CMC management makes use of bucket *alarms* to react to build up of cases in a particular state. For every business critical case state, alarms are defined to reflect the different SLA's agreed with each work provider. These can be progressive and provide alerts to different management levels within the organisation.

There are mandated periods once a claim is registered with the defendant, so making sure the business can react at both a volume and individual case level is fundamental to the service. For example, once a claim is registered with the lender, if no decision has been made within 8 weeks, the claimant, and CMC on their behalf, can lodge a complaint with the UK's Financial Ombudsman Service. That complaint process can also be administered by the case management platform and be associated with the relevant claim for future auditing.

4.3. Business

CMC serves two customers – the work provider, and the claimant. On their behalf, CMC pursues the defendant, typically a financial services company. There is a range of participants in the end-to-end process:

- CMC management directing and governing, with full system privileges
- CMC case workers who can view and modify cases, but can't export or import data from the system
- Agency-sourced case workers with 'view only' access to sections of the case data model and tasks
- The work provider, providing of large volume of claim case work, aka the claim 'book'
- The claim defendant

While the defendant would not be permitted onto the system given the adversarial nature of the process, all other parties are brought together collaboratively inside each case instance. Each user is created and assigned to a team, or multiple teams, and each team is given a range of permissions within the case template -

ranging from full permissions to create, modify and import/export, down to view-only privileges.

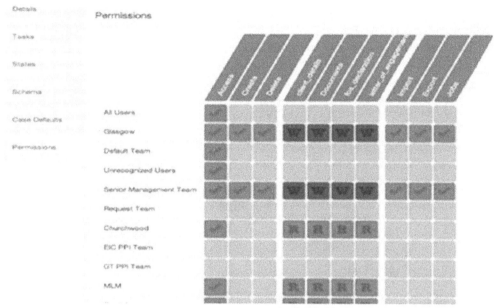

Figure 7: Teams & permissions

In this way, CMC is able to extend system participation to its work providers - this level of transparency has led to increased trust and stronger business relationships, and frees up internal resource when the work provider wishes to investigate individual claims.

Each work provider is prevented from seeing the other's claims through the same permissions mechanism.

4.4. Case handling

At Axle, case work was previously supported by two separate systems, one for retail orders, and the other for wholesale orders. These were functional applications which required engineering to change. The new case management platform consolidated all order types onto a single platform.

Axle's *order* case template was initially created during joint workshops between the delivery team and the client. This covered data, tasks, teams and permissions for the two mains teams who support the end-to-end process.

The *procurement* team is responsible for treating order exceptions - the 'normal' route for an order is to be submitted straight through to the branch and warehouse systems by the platform. Reasons for exceptions include stock unavailability, risk or payment problems.

The *finance* team is a second-line team responsible for processing any post-order financial transactions such as refunds and goodwill gestures. While front-line case workers are permitted to request a financial adjustment, they are not allowed to execute that task. The refund process itself is a manual task in the platform, and by a similar permission model, it is protected from misuse.

By configuring a bucket alarm, an email alert informs the finance team whenever an order requiring processing appears.

At CMC, the case template was initially created with just the schema, some basic states and no tasks. This allowed claim books to be imported and the first step in the process of gaining the client's authorisation to begin.

Over time, the CMC team learned more about the process from engagement with their work providers, the defendants and the regularity authorities. Changes to the case template were made incrementally at this stage.

For example, the case state of "Acknowledgement Letter Received" was initially created to mark the point when CMC confirms it has received a letter from the claimant. It was discovered that this status wasn't sufficient because letters were being received which contained issues needing resolution.

Management, at the request of the case workers, created an additional status of "Acknowledgement Letter Received - With Issue". Additional manual tasks were then created around this new state to help track these claims.

4.5. Organisation and social

For Axle, the case workers overall job description hasn't altered significantly. However, management is now able to set up teams quickly to deal with individual exception types. This has changed the culture of case workers cherry picking 'easy' work, which was common with the previous system.

5. HURDLES OVERCOME

The biggest technical challenge to conquer at Axle was complexity. Having to understand their requirements, to design and build a generic case management application, and then configure it for production, while building four eCommerce sites, with a simultaneous go-live ... this involved considerable effort from the entire team.

5.1. Management

The management of the delivery team, which grew to 12 at the peak, was challenging. A Scrum model, based on 2-week iterations, with multiple product backlogs was adopted. This became difficult to manage and led to team frustration and demotivation - lack of clarity of purpose being cited as the main reason - team members were working across multiple backlogs and tracking individual activity and dependencies across tasks became error prone.

Subsequently, the team adopted a Kanban-style model based on a single work stream, with features drawn from multiple areas. This has led to improved quality and team productivity.

5.2. Business

At Axle, time with end-users was limited, so the delivery team took audio & video recordings of case workers using the existing systems. These proved invaluable for communicating to Axle management deficiencies in the current way of working, and as justification for approaching the solution from a process-led perspective.

In one example a customer was phoned and taken through a 5-minute substitution sell process, only for the customer to inform the case worker at the end of the call that he had already been called and gone through this process one hour previously. This highlighted the need to present a clear view of case history easily accessible to the case worker and resulted in visual timeline which is intrinsic to all case instances, across all templates.

5.3. Organisation adoption

At both organisations, management mandated end-user adoption.

It had been agreed with Axle up front that a 'minimum viable product' approach was acceptable given the hard deadline of 31 December 2012, and this did have an impact on the case worker. Not initially having all of the system features which had been built into the previous systems over a period of years was frustrating for them and required work-arounds and manual processing for a period of time.

By a continual rollout of new features for three months after go-live, management and case worker confidence was regained and the benefits of the new system were found. This period was particularly challenging professionally and emotionally for both organisations, but the end result has now been warmly accepted.

Platform features have also been adopted in ways different from expectation. For example, case tasks have a notes facility which allows case workers to capture comments about individual tasks. Also, each case has a *conversations* feature which has a similar purpose, but for the case as a whole.

At Axle the conversations feature has been almost universally ignored in favour of task notes. While at CMC, case conversations have been preferred. In this way, the case management platform offers loosely coupled tools, in the confidence that the case worker will deploy which ones are best in any given scenario.

6. BENEFITS

6.1. Cost savings / time reductions

For Axle, moving their existing operational platform to the cloud has resulted in savings attributable to circa US$100k annually in terms of application and hardware support, and resource. It is too early to quantify other operational efficiencies.

For CMC, their cost savings translated into an investment in a new system. A per-case fee was agreed, which constitutes approximately 0.3% of the average revenue generated on a claim.

6.2. Increased revenues

The total solution for Axle has supported revenue at the same level as before, although the case management platform only manages orders that are generated from eCommerce sites outside of its control and subject to economic factors such as product pricing and search engine optimisation. US$4m of orders is processed every month by the platform.

For CMC, the solution will allow them to process one million claims over a period of 18 months, from a zero base at the start of the project.

6.3. Quality improvements

At Axle, they are able to identify training issues, by creating ad hoc buckets to represent orders in a particular state. For example the case worker can restructure the order by adding/removing line items, sourcing stock from 2nd line suppliers, and changing fitting appointments– and at this point a bucket can be created showing orders that have not been well formed, and alert managers to training needs.

The automated timeline stream of case events shows all data changes, timings, status changes and collaboration from other case workers. In previous systems at Axle, much of this was captured in a notes area and relied upon the end-user to capture all key activities. By automating and presenting case events in a standard format, end users have one source of truth about the case. This has resulted in greater consistency in the way case workers interpret and follow up case work, reduced unnecessary dialog with the customer and improved internal communication.

At CMC, the platform provides accurate real-time summary information across all claims, correlated in multiple dimensions. For example, summarising the total financial value of all claim books reduces the manual effort in collating that information for internal management and work providers.

7. BEST PRACTICES, LEARNING POINTS AND PITFALLS

7.1. Best practices

✓ *Change slowly – create a case template and trial among a small number of users, before extending to the rest of the community once it has matured.*

✓ *Add more case templates to extend the system function over time.*

✓ *Don't measure initially – stabilise the process first, then start to learn by using metrics and alarms on work queues.*

✓ *Assume that the first iteration of a feature in the solution will be improved, so form a process around capturing user feedback and feed back into the core platform – agile methods facilitate a rapid turnaround model.*

✓ *Understand the business change required to adopt a case management platform internally and support it with knowledge sharing.*

✓ *User-centric design can result in a more intuitive solution. Time spent with case workers will allow the designer to make strategic choices over interface design and navigation, rather than an engineering-led, functional approach.*

✓ *Big bang rollouts should be avoided wherever possible. If there is no choice, then prepare the organisation for the worst case scenario and have a fall back plan should things go wrong. At Axle, because certain features were not fully functional immediately, the operational teams were put under significant pressure to continually come up with mitigation strategies.*

7.1. Pitfalls

✗ *Creating features which are better implemented outside the core platform or where more specialised solutions are readily available on the market, results in dilution in the cohesion of the core platform. Integrate uniqueness out to services or 3rd party applications to minimise the effect.*

✗ *The platform provides different ways of solving the same problem – it is down to the ability of the configurator who will require knowledge of the operational process, steps, stages, business rules and team behaviour. Make sure that sufficient skill is present in the team performing the configuration otherwise task, and status proliferation will result in a bloated application*

✗ *Re-engineering process or system features, even in a small way can have a big impact on case workers and influence adoption of the system as a whole. The journey should have everyone on board from the outset.*

8. COMPETITIVE ADVANTAGES

CMC has a case management platform which allows them to deliver against SLAs agreed with their work providers, and takes account of the governance process imposed by the UK Ministry of Justice and the UK Financial Ombudsman Service.

Furthermore, the benefits of transparency offered by socialising case work with the work providers has further added to their reputation and rise in the marketplace. To the extent that in the specific sector they are operating, CMC is the largest service provider and will manage a number of claims 10x higher than their closest competitor.

At Axle, the initial strategy of establishing the core platform has recently been completed. Competitive advantage will only be realised by further improvements in the next phase of the project. The ultimate aim is to improve profitability by reducing costs relating to systems and process, allowing them to become more price competitive in what is a commodity market.

From the vendor's perspective, the case management platform created will allow them to compete on the global market place against established cloud case management suppliers.

9. TECHNOLOGY

The case management platform's technology stack is MySQL, MongoDB, Ruby on Rails, ember.js, HTML5, CSS3. All components are hosted on Amazon Web Services & OpsWorks:

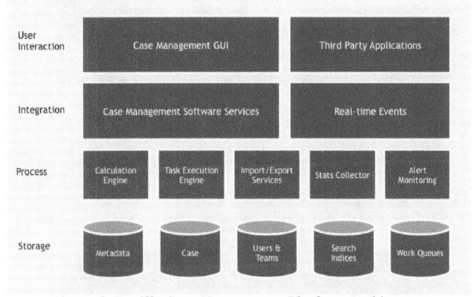

Figure 8: Vanilla Case Management Platform Architecture

Axle's deployment architecture is

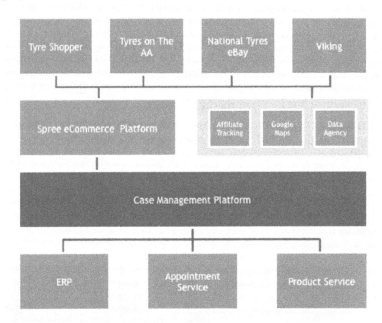

Figure 9: Case Management Deployment for Axle

CMC's deployment architecture is:

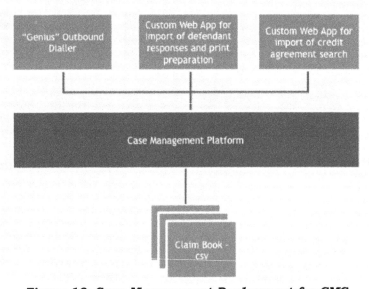

Figure 10: Case Management Deployment for CMC

The benefits accruing from the technology infrastructure and features vary according to the end-user:

(a) Technology benefits for Axle

- Building the case management platform as cloud application meant no on-premise hardware or dedicated support staff. This is estimated to save US$100k per annum in operating costs

- Time to configure and deploy a new case template such as a complaint is reduced to hours. This has allowed Axle to decommission a bespoke internal complaints system and allow them to relate a complaint directly to a customer order, which was performed manually in the past.
- Incremental change to the process, such as changing the data model in a case template or changing the tasks or permissions, can be performed by the end-user.
- The platform's permissions feature allows Axle to target specific areas of case work, such as financial processes, at the appropriate internal team. This had not been possible in the previously.
- Axle can quickly react to build-up of case work in different states, using alarms, for example if the bucket containing 'orders requiring stock' increases above ten over the period of an hour, then they can quickly allocate people to that work.
- The calculation engine allows a case worker to immediately recalculate an order after any changes post initial submission, this reduces chance of human error

(b) Technology benefits for CMC

- CMC is able to add users quickly and simply, and can include temporary agency staff with minimal privileges using permissions, e.g. not permitting them to export data from a bucket.
- The platform's API (case create / update / search) allows CMC to create custom applications which perform tasks too specialised for the case management platform. For example, preparing client packs for an external printing bureau and adding claimant credit search information to the case from a bulk HTML report
- The API also allows an on-premise dialler to call into the platform with case updates, based on telephone dialogue with the claimant.
- Performance and scalability is achieved using MySql in combination with MongoDB and Elasticsearch in the core platform. CMC has circa 750,000 separate claims cases under management in the platform and has allowed the user community to peak to over 100 users without additional infrastructure costs.

(c) Technology benefits for EmergeAdapt

- The platform is multi-tenanted - built into the application's data model and not using virtualisation. On-boarding new clients is quick as a consequence.
- The platform's open source software stack makes it inexpensive to develop and support.
- The user interface has been designed for a cloud subscriber where learning time has to be minimal. By focussing on user-centric design, the platform is functionally less dense than traditional corporate applications, with each screen highly focussed on the task in hand. This has resulted in almost zero training time for new users
- Data export and import mapped onto case template schemas allows the end-user to move their key data into and out of the system easily. This makes the platform attractive to companies where data migration is important.

10. THE TECHNOLOGY AND SERVICE PROVIDERS

Vendor: EmergeAdapt was set up in 2011 with the strategy of building "Case-Blocks" as a cloud/SaaS ACM platform. The product was built with Axle as the first tenant, and rolled out to CMC as the second tenant. EmergeAdapt built the product during 2012. Both solutions were launched in January 2013. All components in this case study were built by a multi-disciplinary team of eight people over a period of twelve months.

CaseBlocks will be launched as a general purpose tool to the global subscriber market in Q4 2013. It is intended as an ACM product for general consumer or service provider markets, and contains no domain-specific features, instead, focusing on the provision of cloud-based tools for the definition of all end-user case logic.

Contact: www.emergeadapt.com & www.caseblocks.com

CargoNet AS, Norway

Nominated by Computas AS, Norway

1. Executive Summary / Abstract

CargoNet AS is the primary Norwegian freight train operator, and GTS (Goods Transport System) is their system for logistics handling. GTS adaptively unifies contributions from knowledge workers across the organization, from marketing and sales to train configuration and composition, scheduling, real-time monitoring, handling of dangerous goods, truck operations and container quality assurance. It is an ACM system, multiplying as an ERP solution.

GTS is a mission-critical system used by most employees involved in the primary value chain, fully integrated with CargoNet's Internet customer portal. Since going online in 2002, GTS has been gradually enhanced in terms of end-user functionality.

GTS uses case folders with built-in task support—referred to as work folders in similar ACM solutions. Each work folder represents either a particular freight train "flight" or a freight train carriage / container booking. Work folders provide access to worklists, giving users active and dynamic task support while ensuring compliance with business rules and statutory regulations. Work folders are augmented with integrated tools for detailed scheduling and train / container composition, providing an elegant mixture of auto-generated and manual plans.

Showcasing a non-traditional application of case management technologies, the GTS architecture is information centric. A range of tasks and tools operate on shared work folder contents. The integrated customer portal for placing orders contributes to the contents of work folders. A ruggedized mobile client is deployed in cargo handling trucks, used for container reception, placement and depot management. Another mobile client handles container damage assessment.

2. Overview

CargoNet AS was formed as a result of splitting the Norwegian State Railways (NSB) into a passenger company and a freight company. In 2002, CargoNet also took over the Swedish company RailCombi AB from the Swedish freight company Green Cargo. In 2011 CargoNet had a turnover of NOK 1.452 billion, with a staff of around 550.

CargoNet is Scandinavia's leading railway company for the transportation of containers, swap bodies and trailers. The company operates more than 190 trains carrying containers and trailers between the largest terminals and cities in Norway, in addition to a large number of "system trains" for major industrial companies. Road transportation is the main alternative to CargoNet - in 2012, CargoNet relieved Norwegian roads of more than 590 articulated lorries daily.

CargoNet's primary tool for logistics handling, GTS, uses adaptive case management technologies in an innovative manner by handling trains and cargo orders as "cases". Every such case has a corresponding case folder that provides access to a worklist with adaptive task support for the tasks pertaining to the relevant train or order.

In addition to active task support, CargoNet also offers tool support that interacts with task support, enabled by a shared information platform. Tool support is offered for planning across several cases—both order cases and train cases—while task support provides compliance control, ensuring that all requirements are met.

Worklists—as collections of tasks—also serve as a shared cooperative environment across users, railway stations, trains and orders offering alternative access to impending tasks. This basic configuration of GTS provides for adaptability, in a setting where changes are the name of the game, and not just unwelcome "exceptions".

The shared information platform has also enabled the inclusion of new mobile clients closing the gap between "field work" and "office work", enabling capture of valuable operational data at its source, with high data quality.

3. BUSINESS CONTEXT

Shuttle trains carry trailers, swap bodies and containers from 20 to 45 feet as well as tanks. CargoNet carries freight for industry and commerce in an efficient shuttle net of intermodal terminals in Norway and to/from the Continental Europe. The core business is intermodal rail-based transport

CargoNet operates a shuttle network of 12 intermodal terminals in and between Norway and Sweden. Reliable access to strategic intermodal terminals in Europe is taking care of through cooperation with Real Rail in Sweden, Hupac in Switzerland and KombiVerkehr in Germany.

The GTS project started in 2000. The new system replaced a legacy system. Two important concerns were, firstly, to change the focus from train production to order based production, moving the attention from physical trains to customer needs, and secondly to obtain a more flexible IT-enabled production system.

Train freight operations are subjected to strict conditions. Important physical issues must be considered, such as brake limits, tractive power, weight, and length.

Most of the railway network in Norway is single track, and if a train is not on schedule, it will be downgraded. Hence, a five-minute delay at the starting point may grow to several hours delay at the destination. It is therefore important that trains depart from every station precisely on time. To operate as cost-effectively as possible, CargoNet needs a good real-time planning system supporting work right up to last minute checks before departure.

External events affecting transport occur all the time; containers do not arrive at the starting point on time, they are damaged, or they do not arrive at all. A wagon or a locomotive may be out of order. A train may have an accident, there may be too much snow on the line, the signal system does not function, or the power cable may have fallen down. An operating environment like this requires IT systems that can adapt—quickly and easily.

4. THE KEY INNOVATIONS

Case folders—the train and order case folder

GTS supports two different case types—booking orders and trains. The case folder for booking orders contain information about freight for one or more containers or wagons that may be conveyed in different ways, involving many trains. The case folder for trains contains information about the train and its distances, involving the transportation of containers and wagons, based on a set of booking orders. Each case type has its own set of task templates.

The two case folders interact closely, in a many-to-many relationship. Each order is fulfilled by transportation on one or more trains, whereas each train is made up from many orders. Below is a bird's eye view of the train freight process, showing how the beginning and the end of the process (square boxes) is handled from the order perspective, whereas the middle is handled from the train perspective.

Figure 1: Bird's eye view of the train freight process

Adaptive task support

Instead of trying to support linear and static "end-to-end" processes, GTS is based on supporting well-defined process snippets known as *task templates*. These are instantiated and recombined by events, rules and human judgment. Tasks operate on a shared data model of the particular case, and as a side effect they update and modify the data model and the documents of the case folder.

A task template consists of a set of steps as a general "recipe" for task performance. These steps are subject to several conditions, defined using predicates and rules, which make it possible to derive a contextualized task template as a unique recipe for a particular instance, always reflecting its state and data.

This contextualized task template is the basis for offering active task support to the user. The user selects and executes permitted steps, based on personal, professional judgment. Step conditions specify pre- and post-conditions in addition to repeat-conditions (step can be repeated), include-conditions (step is made available dependent on context) and mandatory-conditions (step must be performed); the interplay between these conditions result in a relevant offering of actions to the user. Each such step may utilize any functionality offered by the system, and may include a user interface component for operating on relevant case data.

The interaction between task support and tool support

An order case folder starts by the placement of an order. It continues by the planning of which trains the containers or wagons are to travel with. This planning may take place in several rounds, and be subjected to change, either because of something under control of the customer, or of something under the control of CargoNet. This part of the process is handled through tasks with task templates in the context of the order case folder, obeying the capacity conditions for each train involved.

When the time of the train departure comes close, the actual build-up of the train must take place. This is an operation focusing on a train, involving many orders, both for the wagons and the containers involved. It is useful to be able to move quickly from train to train. Since this functionality has to be performed repeatedly, be available at any time, is needed across orders, and also more or less, across trains, this is performed by means of a tool rather than through tasks with task support. This functionality is logically single step, performed an unknown number of times, and there is no completion status other than the checkout and departure of the train.

Also, the functionality for depot control functionality is handled as a tool.

Train production, checkout, check-in and unloading of containers, are operations performed by means of tasks in the context of the train. These operations are subject to severe compliance control, and must be performed according to specific fulfillment conditions for each train and station.

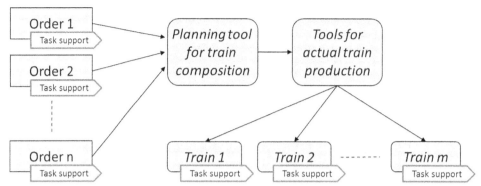

Figure 2 Case folders with task support and tools

Worklists for different perspectives

Case work folders, railway stations and users all have worklists.

Each case work folder maintains a continuously updated overview of all tasks pertaining to the case at hand—a train or an order. The user may set a desired time interval, to see which tasks are due inside that period. For each task it is indicated who is responsible. The same task may simultaneously sit in other worklists, enabling easy collaboration.

For the railway station, the worklist keeps track of the incoming trains and the tasks connected to handling the arrival of trains and, in case the station is an intermediate stop for the train, the following departure.

For a user, the worklist represents the personal inbox-component of their electronic workbench. A personal worklist contains the user's own planned and ongoing tasks.

Both the station worklists and the user worklists display information about which case folder the task is connected to. It is possible to navigate from the task directly to the case folder.

Changes are the name of the game

With the earlier system that GTS replaced, much work was spent handling train events or changes in plans due to containers not arriving at the terminals in time. This was generally attributed to error or faulty handling. At the start of the project, there was consequently a lot of attention to how to achieve good and efficient error handling. The project has managed to shift the focus from error handling to making an adaptive system that supports changes to plans as part of the normal procedure.

Adapting to mobile clients

Since GTS is based on one common information platform in a data centric architecture, adding more clients has been unproblematic. GTS has been expanded with a web client for customer self-service, a ruggedized mobile touch client for the terminal trucks and lifts, and a smart phone client for damage documentation.

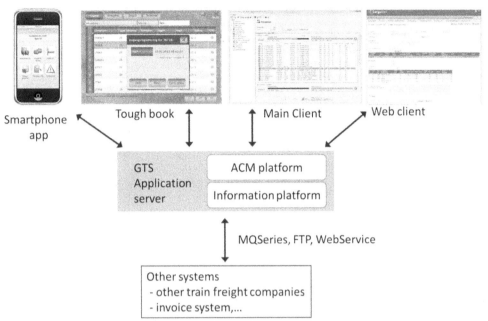

Figure 3: Overview of GTS with its different clients

4.1 Business

GTS has a web portal for customers. This enables large customers to place their orders and specify information about dangerous goods and other details and to monitor the freight from start to delivery.

The information initiates an order case, ready made with all relevant information. This increases the efficiency both for the customer and for CargoNet. The customer can ensure the order is correctly placed, and receive information on progress. CargoNet customers execute parts of the order registration process themselves, with a resulting decrease in the need for order registration at the customer center.

The customer portal also provides information about container presence in the container depot, available capacity in planned trains, as well as tracking and tracing of containers. This information is useful for the customer's transport capacity planning.

GTS' prime purpose is to record and manage a physical reality, and it is a great benefit if the recording can take place as close as possible to the physical events. GTS comprises a ruggedized mobile client with touch functionality, a "tough-book".

Figure 4: Placing an order in the CargoNet web portal

Figure 5: CargoNet Mobile Client, a mobile "tough-book" touch client to record container terminal events

All containers coming from the road are received at a station gate terminal. Terminal trucks and lifts are equipped with a GTS tough-book. The tough-book is used by terminal workers for directly registering the arrival, storage in container depot and placement on train. This ensures more accurate and continuously updated information in the system than before, when this information had to travel manually to the terminal office to be entered into the system.

GTS also has a mobile app for damage recording. A container will not be allowed beyond the gate unless it is in sufficiently good condition to be placed on a train. Even so, it may have minor damages that CargoNet needs to document, in order not to be held liable after delivery. The mobile app records damage to a container in context of the transport order. It utilizes the information in the case folder, enables textual and photographic documentation of the damage, and a damage report may later be printed from the main GTS client.

4.2 Case Handling

Task library and context information

GTS contains a task library, with a template for each task type. The template consists of a set of steps, each with conditions for when they are to be included, whether they are mandatory, or repeatable, if other steps are required to be fulfilled before they may be invoked, conditions for fulfillment and actions to be performed. The functionality needed to perform the step is brought to the user when invoking the step, as part of GTS-supported activities.

In many cases, the task must have a context in order to make sense. In GTS, it is not possible to start a context-dependent task unless this context is given at the time of task startup. When such tasks are not part of an emergent flow with a set context, they may be started from the task library in the GTS workbench. Alternatively, specific task types are directly accessible from buttons in GUI components where the needed context is available, for instance in a case folder.

When a task is started from the task library and requires the creation of a new case folder, this information is available in the task library, and such an object will be created and connected to the task when the task is created.

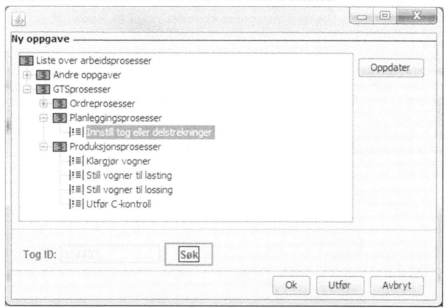

Figure 6: Task library; filtered for tasks available when a train is selected

Case folders—for orders and for trains

All freight items, be it containers, swap bodies or wagons, are handled through the placement of an order. Each placed order constitutes a case, and will handle the transportation of a set of containers or a set of wagons. An order may be repetitive, so that it may for instance be an order for a number of containers every Tuesday and Thursday for three months. Small changes may be made to each occurrence of such a repetitive order. Invoice information is automatically sent to the CargoNet invoice system, based on the information in the order case folder.

Figure 7: Order case folder with worklist and task support

Every train also constitutes a case. A train may have one or more distances, depending on the number of stops. Each distance must be planned with respect to train composition. The planning goes from less specific to fully specific, starting with restrictions for length and weight, via types of wagons and containers to specific wagons physically placed together where it is permissible to place specific containers. In all stages, the system applies complex rules to reason about brakes, weights, and which wagons can take what sort of load.

As stated previously, the two case types "train" and "order" interact. All wagons and containers that are transported by train occur both (a) in one or more order case folders and (b) in one or more train case folders. If a train is delayed or exposed to an event that requires changes in the transportation plan, the train case contains a task to send information to all involved customers. This task will use information about the customer and from the order cases to ensure compliance with the preference of the customer for this particular order.

Figure 8 screenshot with text:

Togmappe 5804 15.01.2013

TOGNUMMER: 5804   Rutemessig avgangstid: 15.01.2013 11:00   Rutemessig ankomst: 15.01.2013 21:17
Operatør: CN   Utgangsstasjon: GANDDAL   Endestasjon: ALNABRU

TogInfo | Belegg | Arbeidsliste | Historisk arbeidsliste

Status
Produksjonsstatus: Ikke i produksjon   På strekningen:
Forsinkelse (min):   Siste kommentar:
Ankomst: Avgang:

Ruteinformasjon

Fra stasjon	Til stasjon	Avgangstid	Max vekt	Max lengde	Aktivitet	Merknad
GANDDAL	KRISTIANSAND	11:00	750	415	Innsett	
KRISTIANSAND	ALNABRU	14:46	750	500	Inn/utsett	

Merknad:

Resend EDI til operatør... | Send melding til Amtrix... | Forhåndsvis melding til Amtrix | Vis togrute...

Ny oppgave for tog og delstrekning

Sett sammen tog | Motta tog | Vis R206 | Vis R207

Motta containere | Ta containere av vogn | Ekstraordinær innsett/utsett | Informer kunder om hendelse

Figure 8: Train case folder with designated task buttons for distance functions

Planning a train—tools for planning across orders

CargoNet employees must plan and produce the transportation. The first part of the planning takes place by means of task support connected to the order case, and involves planning which train(s) the container or wagon is to be part of. All the wagons or containers in the same case folder need not travel by the same train. If, later on, the planned transportation cannot be carried through, either in full or in parts, the case manager may create a task to change the plans. All parts of the plan may be changed, unless they have already been started.

The planning of the making-up of the train takes place in a dedicated tool. This tool handles both wagons and containers, and functions both for unspecified and specified carriers. The output is only a plan, and does not yet contain information about where these carriers are physically at any point in time.

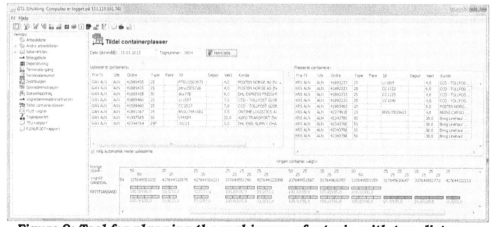

Figure 9: Tool for planning the making-up of a train with two distances

Interacting with the physical world—terminal work and train production

For the registration of the physical position of wagons, containers and the make-up of the train, there are both tough-book and main client tools as well as task support in the train case folder.

Figure 10 Tool in tough-book to place container on train

The train case folder also contains tasks to ensure that the train is fully made up, and that everything is in order before the train is cleared to leave. The train case folder is automatically created from the train timetable, with a worklist containing all those tasks that logically follow from the timetable. Moreover, the train case folder contains functionality to add new tasks in case of deviations from the original plan, such as adding an extra stop on the fly, and informing customers of changes. In addition to this, a tool for generating train capacity reports is used to reserve last minute remaining capacity before train departure.

The train as an adaptive relay baton

The train case folder is initiated with a complete set of tasks for all operations necessary for the standard production of the train flight. As the train checkout task is executed, the train's tasks for the next station are added to the worklist of that station. Thus under normal conditions, the train functions as a relay baton of tasks.

In case of deviation due to external events or human decisions, it will be necessary to change the train plan accordingly. The GTS train folder supports the creation of the appropriate tasks. This includes tasks for introducing extra intermediate stops, changing the train configuration and alerting customers.

The smartphone as a data registration tool

GTS includes a smartphone app to document and handle damages to containers. Containers that are not fit to be transported on train are rejected at the gate. The app utilizes data from the order folders, and offer functionality to add pictures taken with the phone to the documentation registered in the app entry forms.

Figure 11 Screenshots from smartphone container damage assessment app

4.3 Organization & Social

The innovative use of process support technologies in GTS has resulted in a very robust system with sufficient adaptability for actually dealing with a world where change is the name of the game. This innovative use consists of the following elements: adaptive task support, role-based task library, use of trains and orders as cases, worklists across trains, stations, orders and users, use of task support also for "fixing problems", all enabled by the shared information platform.

Instead of detecting and responding to "errors", GTS enables CargoNet to adapt to changes in its business environment in a flexible manner.

The inclusion of new mobile technologies (the tough-book container management client used in trucks and lifts at the terminals, as well as the smartphone container damage assessment app) has resulted in much better work support for the cargo terminal workers. They are now able to capture data at the source in real-time, instead of having data entered back at the office. This also results in higher data quality.

5. HURDLES OVERCOME

Management

GTS has met many challenges during the time it has been operative. The first was when CargoNet took over the Swedish RailCombi AB. RailCombi had a container operation system of its own, but it was decided to use GTS in Sweden as well. The main reasons were the benefits of using the same system throughout the company and to be integrated in the common information platform.

At several points in time, management has wanted to replace GTS with commercial off-the-shelf product(s). Each time, however, it has been decided that the shelf-ware candidate could not meet the needs. These products were meant for container transport on cars, not trains, and it turned out that the cost of adapting them to the needs of railway transport made them unsuitable.

Business

GTS is an ACM system that is adaptive not only in the flexible support offered to knowledge workers; it is also adaptive in the sense that the application itself was conceived as a "built-to-change" solution that can adapt to a drastically developing business environment, surviving several generations of older underlying technologies. Over the last decade, GTS has adapted to significant environmental and organizational changes, and it is expected to continue to do so. This business adaptability is partly due to the use of an ACM framework supporting declarative knowledge representations, and partly to the data centric architecture. As an enterprise ACM, this adaptability has enabled responsiveness to new technologies, such as the integration of the ruggedized mobile client in trucks and mobile solutions for container damage assessment. GTS has been operational for more than ten years, and all this time the system has been subject to continual improvement in close collaboration with the system vendor.

Organization Adoption

GTS utilizes a combination of task support, or adaptive process snippets, in combination with user oriented tools. The shared information platform of planning and production tools, order portal and tools used at the terminal enables each user group to concentrate on their relevant information. This information will always be up-to-date and integrated with the information relevant to other user groups. They are all both producers and consumers of information.

The tools are mainly used to handle situations where carriers from many orders must be planned or produced simultaneously. GTS is used outside at the terminal with the carriers as they arrive and are placed in depot or on train. The fact that GTS is present where the physical work takes place is favorable for user acceptance.

As IT technology has matured, GTS has been extended with mobile, "tough-book" terminals on the trucks and lifts, so that data capture can take place at the source, where the actual physical work is performed. With the arrival of multi-functional mobile phones, GTS has been extended with a mobile app to record container damage. Earlier, data recording had to be performed twice, once in the field and once in the office afterwards—and lapses would occur. Addressing such daily frustrations has contributed to staff acceptance.

6. BENEFITS

6.1 Cost Savings / Time Reductions

GTS has played an important role in transforming CargoNet from "train production" to order-based intermodal transportation. CargoNet of today is a flexible business organization that is able to adapt to continual changes in its environment, handling changes as normal business activity instead of trying to deal with them as "error handling" within or outside of the support system.

As an integral part of a major business restructuring operation, it is hard to quantify the benefits due to the GTS system as such. There can be little doubt, however, that the planning support in GTS has led to better transport capacity utilization. In Norway, it is a political goal to move transport off the roads and onto trains and ships. GTS plays an important role here in utilizing available railway capacity.

The use of mobile clients, bridging the gap between "office work" and "field work", has increased efficiency at the transport terminals, supporting physical work where it actually takes place, and capturing data at the source.

6.2 Increased Revenues

Norway's largely single-track railway network limits the effect that GTS can have on CargoNet's topline. The tightest bottleneck determines the maximum traffic volume, and no train can be longer than the platforms and the shortest sidetrack available en route for passing trains. The revenue benefit of GTS lies mainly in ensuring full use of available railway network capacity, and finding optimal solutions more efficiently.

6.3 Quality Improvements

The use of active task support in the manner described here makes it possible to build support for the compliance aspect of work performance, i.e. the work support system can be designed to ensure that work is performed according to "business rules", be they government regulations or internal best practice requirements.

The new planning tools help reduce complexity and produce plans of better quality and with better resource utilization than manual planning. These plans also have the potential to dealing better with hazardous goods through built in checkpoints in the task support.

Finally, the use of mobile clients over the shared information platform results in better data quality with data captured at its source and immediately being made available in the system.

7. BEST PRACTICES, LEARNING POINTS AND PITFALLS

7.1 Best Practices and Learning Points

- ✓ A "case" may be anything that needs to be managed and controlled throughout its lifecycle. The cases in GTS are not similar to cases in traditional "public sector" case management systems - they reflect trains and orders. Nevertheless, they do correspond to "the stuff that must be adaptively handled" as part of the daily work performance.
- ✓ An ACM as a data-driven application is beneficial for providing active task support, but also for providing tool support where tools are given access to the same underlying information platform.
- ✓ Choose active task support to offer system functionality in a specific context, or when you need to control data quality, or when there is a possibility of emergent workflow realized by tasks creating new tasks.
- ✓ Choose a tool approach for supporting complicated "mass-production" across several cases, or for efficient information retrieval/lookup.
- ✓ The data-centric approach to ACM applications is beneficial for horizontal extensions, making data available in the field and enabling data collection at the source using mobile devices.
- ✓ Adaptivity is along at least two orthogonal dimensions—end user flexibility in planning and performing work, but also organizational flexibility in adapting to business logic and environmental changes. Both are equally important. Enterprise ACMs built-to-change benefit from a data-centric architecture.

7.2 Pitfalls

- ✗ Avoid intermediaries between the customer's subject matter experts and the development team.
- ✗ Find the right balance between bleeding edge technologies and future technical debt for a core business application with a presumed long lifecycle.

8. Competitive Advantages

CargoNet has during the time GTS has been its central and most business critical system, met great changes in the conditions for its operation. At the start, CargoNet was a subsidiary of a company with monopoly on Norwegian railway. Then CargoNet entered a more globalized world by starting to operate also in Sweden. On the other hand, the Norwegian railways were opened for competition. CargoNet is still the main train freight operator on Norwegian rail.

CargoNet's real competitor in Norway is container transport on roads. GTS is an important factor in keeping CargoNet efficient and on top of its operations.

9. Technology

The task templates, worklists and task support functionality and engine, rule engine, work folders, xml terminologies and code- and relations framework were implemented using a complete ACM framework developed and used for process oriented business applications during the past 15 years. In GTS, this ACM framework was used in its Java Platform Enterprise Edition version.

10. The Technology and Service Providers

Computas AS is an employee-owned Norwegian IT consulting company with around 220 consultants, which provides services and solutions for business processes and co-work. Computas AS has delivered numerous work process support applications to the Norwegian public sector and private enterprises, based on the ACM framework FrameSolutions™.

FrameSolutions™ currently has more than 100 000 users, and handles an annual cash flow of around 50 billion NOK. IT solutions based on FrameSolutions ™ provide work process support and task support resulting in higher efficiency and quality in organizational processes. FrameSolutions™ is a framework for realizing bespoke process-centered case management solutions.

Assembled and authored by Helle Frisak Sem, Steinar Carlsen, Gunnar John Coll, Håvard Holje, Eli Landro, Heidi Mork and Thomas Bech Pettersen, Computas AS.

Department of Transport, South Africa
Nominated by EMC Corporation, United States

1. EXECUTIVE SUMMARY / ABSTRACT

The Department of Transport, based in Pretoria with offices in Cape Town, oversees all modes of transportation in South Africa. The Department is organized into branches responsible for civil aviation, maritime, motor vehicles, passenger and freight rail, and other means of public transport.

While many of the Department's processes followed a case management pattern of work, both internal and external, these processes were manual and time-consuming. Externally, constituents submit queries or apply to the Department for licensing. Internally, employees respond to requests from Parliament and the Cabinet, and submit requests and issue memos that must be reviewed and approved at higher levels of the organization.

Previous to implementing a case management solution, each branch in the Department had developed its own processes, and individual employees had their own methods of managing documents and records. As a consequence, documents were frequently lost, workflows were unacceptably slow, process steps were impossible to track and trace, and service targets remained unmet. What's more, the Department struggled to comply with regulations for information management and access.

The answer was to implement a case management solution for Department-wide document capture, case management, analytics and reporting, and continuous improvement. Integral to the solution was enterprise capture software to digitize relevant documents and serve as an on-ramp to case management. The objective was to enable a centralized, highly visible set of automated processes that allow for flexibility should people need to interact and help make a decision, resolve exceptions or adapt the system to changing business needs. This system would also have the ability to collect and maintain all relevant information and documents in context and maintain complete and accurate records to ensure regulatory compliance.

As a result, the Department is now able to avoid costs of manual and broken processes, better manage case workflows, ensure accountability in all case-related activities, comply with relevant regulations and guidelines, and deliver significantly higher levels of service to all stakeholders.

2. OVERVIEW

The Department of Transport is a government entity that oversees all modes of transportation throughout the Republic of South Africa. Its mandates include the development of integrated and efficient transport systems through policies, regulations and implementable models that support broader government strategies for economic and social development. In particular, the Department is tasked with promoting reliable, safe and affordable modes of transportation, stimulating innovation in the transport sector, and ensuring transparency, accessibility and accountability in all its operations.

The Department sees its role as integral to South Africa's economy. "Transport and its related services [are] a catalyst for economic growth, and direct and indirect job creation in South Africa," states the government's official website. With that in mind, the government increased transport-infrastructure spending to $7.3 billion USD in 2012 and plans to raise it to US$8.9 billion in 2014.

The Department is organized into five branches responsible for civil aviation, maritime, motor vehicles, passenger and freight rail, and other means of public transport. Within those branches are 12 separate agencies, each of which manages its own initiatives and processes for supporting the Department's mission.

The agency's 600 employees engage in various aspects of case management. External case management involves the acceptance of queries and applications and the issuance of certifications and licenses for everything from taxi operation to transport-related construction projects. It also includes queries, complaints and comments from the public related to all aspects of transport.

Internal case management covers everything from employee travel and procurement requests and approvals, to memos ordered by Department officials and issued by Department staff, to official information requests from the South African Parliament and Cabinet. In each situation, the case starts off following an approved workflow, moves through various stages of approval, and is securely preserved for future access and reference.

In some instances the case continues to follow a structured workflow. These are often simple requests such as approving a basic travel request that doesn't violate travel-policy rules or thresholds. For most cases, however, there can be multiple processes, stakeholders and interactions that take place in collaborations within the case management solution, face-to-face meetings, phone calls or e-mail exchanges, and these can't be predicted ahead of time.

The challenge the organization faced is that over time, each agency within each branch of the Department had developed its own processes for case and records management. Primary documents weren't always captured, workflows weren't always defined or complied with, cases and documents couldn't be tracked throughout the process, and records often weren't retained for later access.

As a consequence, processes were slow, information was inaccurate and the Department wasn't meeting service levels, either internally or externally. There was little or no visibility into where a given request was in the process, and there was no ability to measure success through metrics and reports, or to identify areas that needed to be improved. In addition, the Department was out of compliance with regulations for standardized file management and for public access to non-classified government information.

In response, the Department embarked on an organization-wide initiative to centralize and standardize all document capture, case management and records management, with the ability to track and trace cases and to ensure workflow compliance. Key to the effort was the implementation of a comprehensive, end-to-end software solution for document capture, case management, and records management. It was further supported by the procurement of new scanner, server and PC hardware.

The project reflected a government-wide push to migrate toward electronic government (eGovernment) services and IT-enabled processes. It was also implemented as part of the Department of Transport's "IT Hub" initiative, a broader effort, spearheaded by the Minister of Transport, to enhance the transport infrastructure with information and communications technology.

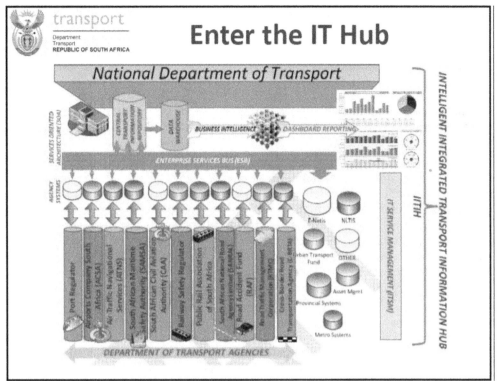

The Department of Transport South Africa's new case management system was implemented as part of a broader effort to enhance transport with information technology.

The primary objective of the project was to improve service levels, both internally and externally, to employees, other departments and public constituencies. Other goals included electronic capture of all documents, central storage and access of all cases and relevant documentation, standardization of processes across all Department agencies, and better compliance with government regulations.

Today, all 600 employees throughout the five branches of the Department of Transport take advantage of the new case management system. The Department can capture and manage documents in any format, and all authorized users have access to the information they need, whenever they need it. Manual, siloed processes are now fully automated, better decisions and outcomes involving people are being made, and workflows traverse seamlessly among agencies. Most important, Department staff, Parliament, the Cabinet and public constituencies all benefit from significantly faster and more accurate service.

3. BUSINESS CONTEXT

The Department of Transport South Africa comprises 12 agencies across five branches. Each agency had developed and implemented its own processes and workflows, retention policies and document standards. Some embraced technology, while others were completely paper-based, with manual data entry or re-keying required when forms were received.

Incoming or primary documents weren't always digitized or even captured. Individual employees might retain documents in their own files. There were no consistent ways of appending documents to a case. Workflows could become bottlenecked, with no way of tracking where a case was held up. Reviews and approvals of internal and external cases such as procurement requests, proposals, cost-benefits analyses and official information requests from Parliament or the Cabinet could take weeks.

"With a manual system, we did not have a method of ensuring that schedules could be met," explains Nonhlanhla Nyathikazi, Director of Business Systems for the Department. "Also, we did not have a solution that could properly and securely archive these materials. Because of that, and if we were audited, it could sometimes be difficult to prove that a response had been actioned within a timely fashion."

Certain branches of the Department had achieved some level of automation. But these content systems were siloed, and there was no way to track and trace documents across agencies. Version control was a particular problem. And there was no system for retaining and managing records. Because of the lack of process or case management, new employees had no way of knowing what steps had or hadn't been taken by their predecessors, no way of seeing whether any steps had been skipped, and no way of accessing critical documents. If a case got held up, there was no way of determining where the case was in the workflow, no way of knowing whether documentation had been lost, and no way of ensuring individual accountability.

As a consequence, service levels to employees, Department officials, Parliament and the Cabinet, and the general public were unacceptable. Likewise, the Department struggled to comply with government regulations for standardized file systems and prompt public access to non-classified government information.

Deficiencies in case management were part of a broader set of issues for the Department, which outlined its challenges as follows:

Business Problems

- Department interactions with citizens were incoherent and fragmented. As one example, passenger ticketing systems varied by transport mode and geography.
- Driver and vehicle licensing wasn't reliable, consistent and traceable.
- Goods at seaports and airports weren't processed promptly.
- Tolling facilities lacked effective systems for monitoring and revenue management.

IT Problems

- IT systems were siloed.
- The citizen and stakeholder experience was fragmented.
- There was no single service strategy.
- There was no single version of the truth.
- Procurement and sourcing were fragmented.
- Total cost of ownership was unacceptably high.

In response, the Department established a strategic vision that included the following core objectives:

- The Department will focus on integrated services, improving entire areas and functions rather than just individual services.
- The Department will emphasize collaboration across agency services and organizational boundaries.
- The Department will empower staff to deliver services when and where they're needed.

- The Department will deliver a better citizen experience through the application of information and communications technology.

4. THE KEY INNOVATIONS

4.1 Business

The Department started by implementing comprehensive, enterprise capture software to digitize all relevant documents. Enterprise capture served as an on-ramp to case management software, which was deployed next, as the captured documents would automatically create a new case and kick off the appropriate business processes. This allowed the department to manage all cases in a centralized, standardized way, across the organization's five branches and 12 agencies.

"The system not only helps to ensure that we get back to the public within required timeframes, but also files and tracks both the original documents and subsequent responses. If we are audited, the system provides the information that we need to prove our effectiveness," Nyathikazi explains.

What's more, the new case management system is streamlining processes at every level within the Department and beyond. "It is facilitating correspondence at even the highest government levels—for instance, between the Minister of Transport and other government ministers," Nyathikazi says.

4.2 Case Handling

The Department handles comments, complaints, proposals and applications related to every mode of transport in South Africa. Internally, it also manages travel and procurement requests, official memos, and queries from Parliament and the Cabinet.

In the past, those cases were handled in a manual or semi-automated fashion. There was no consistency across the Department's branches and agencies. There was no way to track workflows. And there was no consistent means of retaining and accessing records to ensure institutional memory.

The project team identified several key processes that followed a case management pattern and that needed to be automated. These included:

- External correspondence—Queries, complaints, proposals and licensing applications from the public
- Parliamentary memos—Queries and other correspondence from Parliament to the Minister of Transport, which must be replied to within a defined timeframe
- Cabinet memos—Queries and other correspondence from Cabinet-level officials
- Submissions—Procurement and travel requests

Today, cases are initiated electronically and automatically forwarded to the appropriate employees or public officials for review and approval. Guidance and timelines are incorporated into the workflow to indicate what the appropriate response options are and when a response is required. Notes, comments, addendums and signatures are appended to support the workflow and enable future audits.

Cases are tagged with keywords to facilitate search and retrieval. System managers can assign access rights with role-based security, ensuring that only authorized personnel can access specific documents.

"The system has completely changed the way that the Department manages vital memoranda and proposals," Nyanthikazi notes. "With the old manual system, almost no one complied with schedules. Today, 80 percent of document recipients comply with timeframe requirements."

4.3 Organization & Social

The impact on employees and the way they work has been dramatic. Now, as the Department receives or generates paper or electronic documents, the documents are scanned, relevant content and metadata is extracted, the information is validated for completeness and accuracy, and the documents are attached to the relevant case. Using skills-based employee profiles and sophisticated work queues, tasks and cases are routed to assigned employees to expedite the appropriate response, minimize misqueues—often the most costly portion of handling a case—and ensure that employee workload is balanced and employees aren't overloaded. Cases can also be easily delegated or escalated to others in the Department, should the needs in the case change or should input be required from others to make the most informed decisions.

Cases follow a Department-wide lifecycle from initiation through to resolution. Users can create a case, append relevant documentation, track its progress through approvals, understand where it resides in the workflow at any time, and retain records in a centralized, standardized fashion. This visibility extends across all five branches and 12 agencies of the Department.

All communications generated or exchanged within the Department, with the agencies or with constituents are tied back to the case. This allows case workers to have a "one-stop shop" for all relevant information in the context of a case. The new system also allows authorized users to assign retention policies to documents. This enables the Department to comply with strict regulations for records management and access.

Built-in content and process analytics enable users to track performance, drive to key performance indicators and thresholds, and visualize the results through role-based reports, charts and other graphical elements. Alerts and notifications keep users informed, for example, if the time for an approval is about to exceed a predefined threshold. A governance module allows for monitoring of the 12 agencies for financial reporting and to ensure compliance.

5. HURDLES OVERCOME

5.1 Management

Although the transformation was driven by the IT organization, the highest levels of the Department of Transport were involved from the beginning. The Director General and other senior managers contributed to planning and implementation to ensure that the project wasn't derailed for lack of executive sponsorship.

5.2 Business

The project team worked hard to ensure that the transformation wasn't perceived as an IT project or a technology initiative. To that end, it identified key users in every branch of the Department so that all stakeholders would be represented. Those users participated as steering-committee members and project-team members. They participated in working sessions and user-needs assessments to be sure their requirements were captured and reflected. The goal was not only to achieve buy-in but also to seed advocates for the project throughout the Department.

5.3 Organization Adoption

Ensuring that all 600 employees throughout the Department's 12 agencies would adopt the new system required focused training. All employees were required to attend two all-day training sessions. Training included hands-on practice sessions to ensure that all users had absorbed knowledge of how to use the system. In addition, employees who worked on a particular type of case were trained together, ensuring that they could ask questions relevant to that type of case and that there wasn't a training gap where some employees were trained and others weren't. This facilitated instant success, as it took several weeks to train everyone in the department.

For users who failed to attend classroom training, the IT department provided on-site training to ensure 100 percent compliance. After the new system was up and running, track-and-trace features, along with alerts and notifications, ensured accountability among all users.

6. BENEFITS

6.1 Cost Savings / Time Reductions

- The Department uses the new system to manage more than 70,000 cases per year—200 to 300 every business day.
- Response times for case management approvals and replies has dropped from weeks to days.
- Full visibility into cases, associated processes and bottlenecks, visual role-based reporting, and automatic notifications have contributed substantially to the reduction in response times. Timeframe compliance for case approvals and replies has increased from essentially zero to 80 percent.
- Case and document search and retrieval is virtually instantaneous.
- Employees don't waste time looking for lost or misfiled documents.
- Case management processes are significantly faster, so employees can handle more cases in the same amount of time.
- The Department can respond to public queries and issue licenses in a much more timely fashion.

6.2 Quality Improvements

- Case management processes are significantly more efficient and effective.
- All relevant documents entering or created in the Department are captured electronically, tagged and indexed, and stored in relevant electronic case folders.
- Documents are electronically appended to and associated with relevant cases.
- Documents are stored centrally to ensure proper security as well as access by authorized users.
- Cases are retained or disposed of according to retention policies as appropriate.
- All employees have access to the records they need and can understand where cases reside in the workflow.
- The Department monitors the performance of case managers to ensure accountability, as well as the entire organization for financial reporting and auditing.
- The Department has significantly improved service levels both internally and externally—to public constituencies and to other government bodies such as Parliament and the Cabinet.

- The Department now complies with regulations for standardized file systems and public access to non-classified government information.

7. BEST PRACTICES, LEARNING POINTS AND PITFALLS

7.1 Best Practices and Learning Points

✓ Even if a project is driven by the IT department, make sure it's perceived as a business project, not an IT project.

✓ Involve users from all functions in the organization to contribute to planning and gain buy-in.

✓ Work with business functions upfront to ensure that users become advocates for the project.

✓ Make sure users have the tools they need to make the project a success. For example, if you're deploying an enterprise-wide software solution, make sure user PCs are powerful enough to use the system, so users can't use that as an excuse to resist new processes.

✓ Make sure you deploy supporting technology and processes, such as document capture and retention, so all on-ramps and off-ramps are accounted for and the solution isn't constrained by gaps or limitations in your capabilities.

7.2 Pitfalls

✗ No matter how hard you work to develop advocates in various functions, some people will always resist technological and process change.

✗ For employees who refuse to attend classroom training, use video-based training or take the training right to their offices and train them there.

✗ Don't try to do everything at once. Even if you can implement the technology with a "Big Bang" approach, process transformation should be done in phases to show success early and often.

✗ Identify the most important process or the easiest process to transform, and start there. Then apply lessons learned to enable faster and smoother transformation of other processes.

8. COMPETITIVE ADVANTAGES

As a government agency, the Department of Transport doesn't compete in the marketplace the way a corporation would. However, the Department's new case management system does set it apart from other government agencies in South Africa. For starters, it's now better able to meet its mandates and deliver superior service to its constituencies.

The Department is also better positioned to comply with regulations for information storage and access. For example, it's now compliant with the National Archives Act and the government Minimum Information Security Standards (MISS), which set guidelines for how documents should be filed, retained, discarded and secured.

Interestingly, the Department of Trade and Industry is now using the same system for its own case management. Although the Department of Transport and the Department of Industry and Trade have unique needs and processes, the two entities meet regularly to share ideas, lessons learned and best practices for case management.

9. TECHNOLOGY

The Department of Transport South Africa invested in EMC Captiva for enterprise capture, EMC Documentum Platform for enterprise content management and records management, and EMC Documentum xCP for case management which all share a common, unified, repository. The Department also deployed new scanners, computer servers, PCs and other IT hardware to support the project.

EMC Documentum Platform provides the Department with organization-wide content management. It delivers a scalable and fault-tolerant architecture to manage and control access to the Department's information, provides version control, supports file/format transformation, and delivers a host of other library services. It also improves compliance through fine-grained authentication, authorization and auditing. EMC Documentum Platform also allows compliance officers to assign retention policies to cases and documents in a seamless and automated fashion, without requiring user or case-worker interaction.

EMC Captiva intelligently captures and transforms paper and electronic documents such as e-mail into electronic information that is exported and stored in appropriate case folders. Using automated workflow processes, EMC Documentum xCP routes cases to appropriate employees for approval or reply. All case handling, work-queue management, collaboration and monitoring via charts and reports takes place inside the EMC Documentum xCP user interface.

10. THE TECHNOLOGY AND SERVICE PROVIDERS

EMC Corporation is a global leader in enabling businesses and service providers to transform their operations and deliver IT as a service. The EMC Information Intelligence Group (IIG) transforms how organizations connect information with work. By delivering enterprise solutions and services, IIG provides content management, process and case management, pervasive governance, capture, customer communications, and secure file sync and share to allow people to collaborate and connect with the right information at the right time. Whether on-premise or in the cloud, IIG technologies simplify the complexity of managing and protecting an organization's most valuable asset: information.

Case management specialists from EMC South Africa and Faranani DocTec (http://doctec.co.za) helped with the deployment and implementation of the system. The excellent technical team provided a solution that fully addressed the department's requirements.

EMC products that were fundamental to the transformation project at the Department of Transport South Africa include:

- EMC Documentum xCP (http://www.emc.com/xcp)
- EMC Documentum Platform
- EMC Captiva

Directorate for the Construction of Facilities for EURO 2012, Ukraine

Nominated by PayDox Business Software, Russia

1. EXECUTIVE SUMMARY / ABSTRACT

Preparations for the 2012 UEFA European Football Championship "EURO-2012" required implementation of large-scale projects for construction and renovation of stadiums. These projects relied on information technology for flexibility in the management of a large number of business processes containing a lot of tasks, assignments, documents, and discussions. A key system requirement was to the ability to quickly respond to changing circumstances in the project. To meet this requirement all project management was carried out using the Adaptive Case Management (ACM) system.

2. OVERVIEW

A significantly large portion of work performed in large-scale construction projects is unstructured, requires discussion, assignment of tasks based on analysis of the current situation, and control of time lines in completion of tasks and assignments. These unstructured project activities cannot be supported by traditional BPM and require the appropriate ACM software tools.

The success of the ACM implementation project for EURO-2012 was measured by the quality of interaction between the customer, the contractor, and the organization working on the project. The "instant start" system was chosen to operate the project, and worked well with the tight construction schedule. It went into operation within one month.

Use of an ACM approach to the huge construction project management helped avoid bottlenecks. Prior to the implementation of the ACM system, key irreplaceable employee vacations would result in significant strain and work stoppages for remaining colleagues. The ACM system allows them to relax in peace during their vacations with all the current results of their corporate activities (tasks, contacts, documents, discussions) stored safely and accessible to the others.

Social business processes, prevailing in a modern office, are often "automated" through any means at hand – e-mail, forums and blogs. Plugged in office workers, equipped with IPhones and IPads are waiting for business-applications that provide familiar ease of use.

3. BUSINESS CONTEXT

A Ukrainian State Enterprise "Directorate for the construction of facilities for EURO 2012" was specifically established to manage construction of sports facilities. This organization became the General Customer of the project management system.

4. THE KEY INNOVATIONS

Geographically distributed project managers and employees got the opportunity to interact online for the coordination of work and reconciliation of documents (contracts, bills, drawings etc.) for each project. All assignments, discussions and documents for all construction objects were stored in the project history in appropriate case folders.

The project participants got the opportunity to manage not separate tasks and assignments, but cases – collections of tasks and assignments, connected with the execution of an entire business process.

All project information (thousands of documents, photographs, videos, drawings and other files) was stored in virtual case folders. Customers and project managers got the opportunity to track the current project state, outstanding and overdue tasks, actual daily photo and video of construction objects day-by-day directly in the ACM system.

4.1 Business

The project was implemented by companies:

- Ukrainian State Enterprise "Directorate for the construction of facilities for Euro 2012"
- IT-integrator INTSOL

Some of the Euro 2012 project management objects:

Lviv Arena stadium

Shakhtar stadium

4.2 Case Handling

Some project numbers:
- the number of users – 272
- the number of categories of documents – 50
- the number of construction projects – 20 (stadiums and other construction objects)

The users of the case management system are:
- construction engineers and foremen
- project analysts
- controllers
- architects
- economists
- top management

The key roles of the system are:
- case team members
- addressees
- assignees
- controllers
- case / task owners
- message authors

The case / task statuses are:
- open
- closed
- suspended
- cancelled
- inactive
- informational

The ACM system:
- does not require detailed inspection of business processes and programming with configurations for new business processes. New cases are formed by users with lists of tasks, which require completion These can be corrected and extended in the course of performance of the process
- supports a library of templates, where users can successfully drop completed cases in one click, so that later users can create a whole case on any topic based on the template, already containing all tasks, all implementers, all samples of documents and other files
- manages users within the case project team, give or revoke access to case tasks, files and messages, inform users of the need to begin work on a new task within the project
- supports discussions for any task in the case
- stores all information on a business process in a virtual folder – all documents, photographs, videos, drawings and other files
- manages cases – collections of tasks and assignments, connected with the execution of an entire business process (and can manage single human tasks and assignments as well)
- maintains control over rules, allowing for automatic activation of the case's next task once a task has been completed, send users reminders, etc.
- allows users to self-register and to register other e-mail accessible users

The ACM system provides the full functionality on desktop computers, laptops, and tablets (iPad and Android-based). Main features are available on the single screen.

4.3 Organization & Social

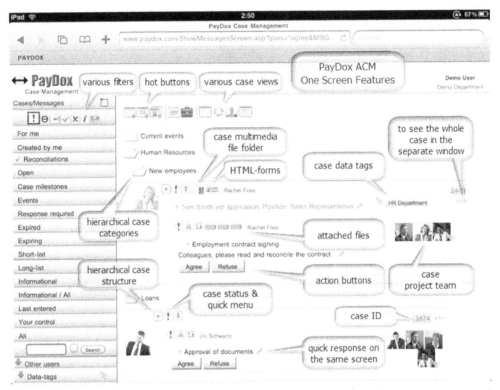

The adaptability and flexibility of ACM-based construction project management allowed customers to automate their business processes "as is", in a fashion that is familiar to employees, without engaging in a risky implementation process, without stressing staff, or breaking existing business processes to achieve a theoretically correct condition "to be". Possible "chaos", which in this case is automated, becomes qualitatively different – measurable and controlled. After implementation of ACM, business processes become transparent, it became possible to perfect them in practice, and not on paper – easily adjusting and improving case templates.

Successfully completed cases, containing valuable information on collaborative work performed by employees, are stored in a library of templates, slightly adjusted and cleaned up for universal application (all non-essential discussions and comments are deleted, only important assignments and control points are kept). After this is done, a new case on the same topic can be created with a single click. Then the process is repeated. As a result, for each subsequent project there is a convenient template with a list of tasks, assignments, participants, lists of implementers and document templates. The ever-increasing library of case templates composes corporate Knowledge Base, separated from concrete employees and stored in a digital format for corporate use.

5. HURDLES OVERCOME

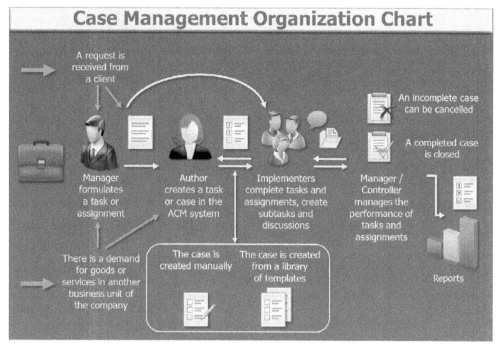

Key issues required a decision during the system implementation:
- Failure of timing during construction
- Changes to the project management team
- Territorial distribution of construction objects, and a large number of objects
- Adequacy of project management to the strict control of State authorities

Representation of all the necessary project information in the case form allowed to provide the transparent control over the execution of tasks and documents.

The use of standard role assignment feature allowed management to promptly replace staff in the project implementation process.

Internet access to the ACM server allowed geographically distributed employees to interact online inside each project.

6. BENEFITS
- The dramatic reduction of the number of overdue assignments and documents (from 80-100 per user to 10-15)
- Significant reduction of processing time of documents, orders and tasks.
- Optimization of collaboration among geographically distributed employees
- The number of oral ("telephone") assignments and tasks significantly decreased. The management of one-time and current tasks became computerized

7. BEST PRACTICES, LEARNING POINTS AND PITFALLS

7.1 Best Practices and Learning Points

✓ *There is no need to describe in detail the business processes, but it is extremely desirable to have a list of initial tasks, milestones and document templates*

✓ *A significantly large portion of work performed by teams of employees, in collaboration, is unstructured, requires discussion, assignment of tasks based on analysis of the current situation, and control of time lines in completion of tasks and assignments. These unstructured office processes cannot be supported by traditional BPM and require the appropriate collaboration software tools. It is very desirable to provide such tools to project participants.*

7.2 Pitfalls

✗ *Since unstructured projects do not have a strict performance algorithm (and have possibilities for unrestricted discussions), they require the use of metrics in order to achieve results in a reasonable time*

✗ *Avoid tasks having no responsible person or having several equal responsible persons*

8. COMPETITIVE ADVANTAGES

There were several main criteria used in assessing the chosen ACM. The criterion included the ability to collect, process, store, operationally use, and electronically reconcile a large number of tasks and documents. This included contracts, construction object descriptions, drawings, photo and video materials, and a diverse organizational documentation.

Sociality and simplicity – the key advantages of the system. Instead of complex descriptions of business processes, the entire project management revolves around checklists, lists of tasks which must be completed, documents, discussions and milestones. All the managing projects oriented on results, a process to achieve these results is adapted along the way.

9. TECHNOLOGY

The ACM system works as a web application serving unlimited users from a single web-server. Key issues:

- Free version can be downloaded, installed & run in minutes.
- No any initial settings. The system runs immediately after installation.
- Potential users can see and try ACM at the web-site in a couple of clicks, without registration.
- On-premise ACM server installation requires MS Windows, but users can access ACM system from computers of any type, including iPad and Android-based tablets using any web-browser such as MS Internet Explorer, Mozilla Firefox, Google Chrome, Apple Safari etc.
- Users can self-register and can register other e-mail accessible users
- A number of pre-defined case templates are already provided in the installation package (loan application processing, new job applicant tracking, order management, etc.)

10. THE TECHNOLOGY AND SERVICE PROVIDERS

The ACM system used in the project:

- PayDox Adaptive Case Management (PayDox ACM) www.paydox.com

IT - Integrator:

- INTSOL, Ukraine http://www.intsol.dn.ua/

Vendor:

- PayDox Business Software, Russia www.paydox.com

Fleet One, USA
Nominated by 4Spires, USA

1. EXECUTIVE SUMMARY / ABSTRACT

WEX Fleet One[1] is a midsized company that provides fuel cards and other financial services to private and governmental organizations with fleets of vehicles. The 9-person marketing department was struggling with managing their workload. They receive numerous requests from company management and colleagues in other departments for preparing marketing collateral, advertisements, exhibits at trade shows, marketing programs, etc. On an ongoing basis the department is typically working on 20 or more requests at a time.

Each request can be characterized as a "case" that requires coordinated and collaborative work from several knowledge workers in the department on a strict delivery deadline. For example, a relatively simple piece of promotional collateral requires interactive input and participation from copy-writer, layout, production, and distribution staff that must also collaborate with subject matter experts, product managers, corporate attorneys, accountants, and management reviewers. Each individual's obligations to complete the project must be tracked on a strict deadline. Each knowledge worker in the department is working on multiple requests at a time on various schedules; and so oversight of the whole workload, both by person and across the department, is critical to managing personal and departmental resources. Flexibility is key; individual obligations are initially mapped out in the context of the final delivery, but it rarely turns out exactly according to plan. A high degree of communication and collaboration among the team is needed to juggle changing schedules across multiple projects. In October 2012, Fleet One installed an innovative knowledge worker system that enabled the department to improve their coordination, efficiency, visibility, and governance over the activities in the department. Over the first 4 months the group handled over 250 requests with the new system. The system is producing a new class of granular performance data that is providing new insights into individual and group performance.

2. OVERVIEW

Due to the nature of the marketing department's activities and the high degree of interactivity between knowledge workers, **the fundamental challenge was to improve collaboration.** The head of the department, the Director of Marketing, can be considered the "case manager". In order to deliver each case on time she must ensure the successful coordination of work across several people in her department. The nature of these tasks requires a high degree of engagement and interactivity between knowledge workers which depends on an up-to-the-minute, shared understanding of "where do we stand" and "who's got the ball for the next action". This high degree of interactivity requires a balance between structure and flexibility.

Each work request the Director makes spawns a work-delivery "conversation" between her and the performer. The conversation follows a specific workflow sequence of four stages: Negotiation, Delivery, Acknowledgement, and Closed.

Negotiation Stage. The Director makes a specific request of an individual in her department (e.g. Can you get the ad developed by next Friday?). The request is

---

[1] Fleet One was acquired by Wright Express in 2012 and was rebranded to WEX Fleet One in 2013

entered in the new system using a simple form that also captures contextual information like customer, project name, and proposed budget hours. Any associated documents can be attached to the request. Because various performers will be involved in completing the work, she shares/broadcasts the request to other "Observers" who can then follow the conversation and add comments for the record.

The copy-writer/performer receives an email trigger that the request has been made, and a link in the email directs them to the system for entering a response. Once the performer has logged in to the system, the request shows up in the performer's "Due From Me" list. Upon opening the request, the performer is presented with four specific response options: Agree, Decline, Counter-Offer, or Comment (e.g. ask for more information). The performer selects one of the four responses to the request (e.g. Counter-Offer: I can't get it done by Friday, but I could by the following Tuesday. Will that be ok?). The two parties (requester and performer) conduct an explicit conversation, and the negotiation stage concludes with the performer making a clear agreement to deliver on an agreed date. This is a key differentiator from task and project management systems that "assign" work tasks without response or explicit commitment from the performer.

Delivery Stage. In this stage the performer is engaged in following through on their delivery agreement. The system supports and encourages ongoing dialog between all the parties (requester, performer, and observers) by enabling specific follow-on actions. For example, the requester can ask for progress reports, add comments, or, if necessary cancel the agreement. Performers, on the other hand, may report progress or request to amend the agreement as new issues or problems emerge along the way. Performers are also obliged to keep the requester up to date on the status of their agreement by indicating one of three states: "commitment is on track" (green); "commitment is in jeopardy" (yellow); or "commitment can no longer be met" (red). In this way the requester, and other observers, can be alerted in real time as to when breakdowns are occurring and not spend time on needless follow up. This stage concludes when the performer takes the action to "Deliver".

Acknowledgement Stage. The system sends an email to the requester signaling that a delivery has been made. The task is not complete until the requester/case manager is satisfied with the final product. Otherwise they have the action to "Request rework" which sends the task back to the performer. When the requester takes the action to "accept" the final delivery, the conversation moves to the "Closed" stage.

Closed Stage. Completed conversations are archived in a list view that enables sorting and retrieval according to a variety of criteria including requester, performer, due date, project, and customer. Each record includes a complete thread of the whole dialog from request through acceptance. This documentation enables granular review of who said what to whom and all the associated details and documents associated with the initial request. The commitment data enables new levels of governance and performance management insights. Archives can also be helpful in tracking compliance issues.

Beyond just tracking the dialog between participants, the whole work-delivery conversation is also shared/broadcast to other concerned parties. The system enables the Marketing Director to designate her supervisor as an "observer" for all the cases in her domain, thus enabling, for the first time, the entire workload of her department to be presented to her superior. This has replaced writing progress and status reports and has enabled a more granular discussion of issues and performance metrics with her superior. The Director can also designate observers in other departments outside of her own who have interest in the progress of the case.

The underlying technology enables all users of the system to be equally responsive through their mobile devices. All screens and features are available across the internet.

All communications surrounding each case are unified. All inputs and updates made in the system are sent immediately to each participant's email as well as their private group social media channel. Each action taken by every participant in the case is date-stamped and recorded in the case history along with associated commentary and supporting documents. The complete dialog thread is presented in the context of the case and archived for later review and analysis.

The second challenge was enabling flexibility while at the same time maintaining rigor and accountability. Since flexibility requires order, the system assures rigor in two ways. First is the requirement that each request must go through all four stages (negotiation – delivery – acknowledgement - closed). Second is the requirement that each request can have any number of observers, but only one performer who is accountable for delivery of the agreed outcome. Complex cases involving several people are handled through the use of any number of "supporting" requests. An essential requirement of the system was the ability to link together supporting requests. Successful completion of a "parent" request may depend on the performance of one or more "supporting" requests, but each has a specific individual performer. Request-to-supporting-request dependencies can be added at any time by the performer. This enables the tracking and oversight of the whole network of interdependent requests by case, by due date, by performer, by account, etc.

Beyond these two requirements (i.e., four-stage workflow and one accountable performer), the system must be extraordinarily flexible in terms of size, scope, and number of participants. Some requests last a couple days, while others last 3 months or more. Some involve one performer while others involve up to five supporting performers. While the same expertise is needed by each performer (e.g. copy-writer), each request is unique. Delivery dates are often extended, sometimes up to four or five times over the course of a case that took two months to close.

The third challenge was providing access to case histories and archiving. All participants in a case (Marketing Director, performers, and all observers) have any-time/anywhere access to the full case record including supporting documents. Access to records is limited to those participants based on satisfying login credentials and strict authentication/permission requirements. Closing a case can only be accomplished by the requester after they have received and accepted the performer's final delivery. Closed cases are archived and remain viewable by all participants in the case. Sort and retrieval capabilities are available across several criteria to enable contextual follow up, analysis, and compliance monitoring.

3. BUSINESS CONTEXT

Before the new system was implemented the marketing department used Outlook Tasks to track their work. Tasks were identified and assigned with due dates to various people in the department. The group had been using Outlook for several years. The Marketing Director, however, was dissatisfied with this solution and had been looking for over two years for an alternative system that would better support collaboration among her team.

4. THE KEY INNOVATIONS

4.1 Case Handling Business

The new system provided numerous innovations, but perhaps the most important was the ability to easily link requests to other requests. Supporting requests could be added onto "parent" requests at any time. Major requests are linked to a hierarchy of supporting requests. The manager can now see the entire project and all its dependencies in a single context. The manager can drill down the chain to view the details of any supporting request. A second innovation was the ability to attach files and documents that reside within the context of the work request.

Third, any number of "observers" can be added to a request tracking conversation. This provides all interested parties with up-to-the-minute status on issues as they emerge. For the first time, the Marketing Director is able to provide a comprehensive view to her superior of all the activity going on in her department.

Fourth, a series of dashboards enable users to quickly review and sort all requests "due from me" and "due from others." Another dashboard shows all active requests where the user is requester, performer, observer, or parent requester. This view enables a comprehensive and interactive view of all the tasks each user is involved in.

Once deliveries are made and accepted, the complete work conversation, including attachments, is saved in an easily accessible and sortable archive. Historical information and performance metrics can be mined from this data.

4.2 Business

The new system has changed the way the Marketing Director and her department engage with their customers and stakeholders. First of all, the Director began the practice of making her superior executive an observer on all the work tasks underway in her department. For the first time, she was able to enable her superior to view and participate directly in all the activities in her group. This led to richer conversations about her goals and the performance of the group.

The marketing group customers include colleagues in other departments across the company who request collateral, promotion, campaigns, etc. that the marketing department develops and delivers. In order to consolidate requests from these customers with the activities and responsibilities of the staff within her department, the Marketing Director began the practice of requiring that all requests of her department be composed, submitted, and negotiated with the same new system. Managers in other departments now make requests and negotiate clear delivery agreements with the Marketing Director who then, in turn, makes a series of linked, supporting requests to her staff in the same system. These customers can then monitor progress and participate directly in the work conversations.

4.3 Organization & Social

Collaboration among team members has improved. The system enforces a "managed conversation" that has added precision to the work dialog. The "one-way" task assignment process that was used formerly has been replaced with a "two-way" negotiation that results in a clear agreement to deliver on a certain date. The performer is now more involved in establishing achievable outcomes. Commitments are clarified as to who is accountable for what and who has the ball for the next action. Each person in the group has a personal work list that shows tasks "due from me" and "due from others."

Each performer is also expected to maintain an up-to-date indication of the status of meeting their individual commitments using simple color-coded icons. Green indicates they are on track to meet the agreed target date. Yellow means their commitment is in jeopardy. Red indicates that there has been a breakdown that will prevent the performer from meeting their agreed due date. This simple reporting both cuts down on needless check ups by the requester, and enables early identification of problem areas. Often these breakdowns are identified much earlier than in the past. When a performer changes the status, amendments to the original agreement, or new agreements, are made explicitly. The integration of task and relationship management requires more direct communication and has tended to build trust.

The new work management system is integrated with both the email and social media tools (Chatter in this case) everyone uses each day. Every entry, change, and update in the system is immediately sent to all participants in that work conversation (i.e. requesters, performers, observers, and parent requesters). Links in the emails bring the user directly to the relevant work request where the entire conversation thread is captured and presented in the context of the work request.

The new system has become the "center" of all marketing tasks. Everyone in the department uses it to submit and execute work commitments. It is now a standard part of the work cycle on each project.

5. HURDLES OVERCOME

Organization Adoption

The cost to acquire and install the new system was minimal so there was no significant hurdle to get management approval. Adoption was virtually immediate. Except for a department meeting to discuss the change in business practices, the system required no training regarding the user interface or functionality. The new tool was "plugged into" their current work environment. Within two weeks, the entire marketing department was "100% committed" to using the new system. The benefits gained by the system were apparent to both the department head and the individual staff members.

6. BENEFITS

6.1 Cost Savings / Time Reductions

The system has improved efficiency and reduced the amount of time the department spends on collaboration and execution. Handoffs are clearer. Visibility and reporting on work progress are much improved. The group has a better view of commitments and the various people involved in each commitment. Performance management and governance has improved. The group reports improvements in hitting their deadlines. With less time spent on coordination, the group reports more time is being spent on getting marketing results for the company.

6.2 Increased Revenues

Though the effect to increase revenues is indirect, the improvements in the quality of reporting and viewing the marketing funnel certainly save time and lead to more time spent bringing in leads and branding the company.

6.3 Quality Improvements

All users of the system (the Marketing Director, staff performers, her senior executive, and colleagues in other departments) have become more effective and efficient. Work agreements are explicit. Individual accountability is clear and visible to all. Dashboards enable better tracking of activities by performer, customer, account, etc. Coordination has improved which has resulted in time-savings. Over the initial four-month startup period, the marketing group has successfully handled over 250 differentiated, non-repeatable work tasks according to a standard process (request–agree-deliver–assess). Archives of completed tasks promote organization learning.

Senior management has improved visibility into the department workload and performance issues. Work relationships are improving.

7. BEST PRACTICES, LEARNING POINTS AND PITFALLS

7.1 Best Practices and Learning Points

✓ *New work norms should be discussed ahead of time. While the system appears to be just a simple work-tracking tool, its underlying behaviors and practices reflect significant changes in work norms.*

✓ *The idea of allowing staff people to "negotiate" work assignments may be a radical notion in some organizations. Getting the group comfortable with the new approach takes some getting used to.*

✓ *Yielding a level of "authority" over to staff people who are empowered to respond to work requests is the quid pro quo to achieving greater accountability and commitment to shared outcomes.*

✓ *The new system may work best in high-trust organization where sharing details about individual work performance is a reasonably comfortable practice.*

7.2 Pitfalls

✗ *The new practices and communication patterns encouraged by the system may be seen as incompatible with a command-and-control management style where assignments are more-or-less passed down as "orders".*

✗ *The success of the system will largely depend on the maturity and trust among members of the group. A certain level of trust is needed before individuals will feel comfortable exposing details of their individual work activities to others.*

8. COMPETITIVE ADVANTAGES

As mentioned above regarding increasing revenues, improvements to the company's competitive advantage are indirect but some advantage can be inferred.

9. TECHNOLOGY

The new work management system was implemented on top of the Force.com technology platform. All system users were already licensed to use the Saleforce.com CRM tool. The work tracking system described in this case study was identified, selected, and installed directly from the Salesforce AppExchange by Fleet One's system administrator without any assistance or support from the system vendor. The work-tracking system was downloaded, installed, and distributed to users in less than 15 minutes. The new application integrated seamlessly into the pre-existing menu structure and matched the user interface style of the existing Salesforce application, and so there was no training required. Users were up and running within 30 minutes of the installation.

10. THE TECHNOLOGY AND SERVICE PROVIDERS

The CommitKeeper (www.commitkeeper.com) work management/business execution system was provided by 4Spires (www.4spires.com). The product was installed directly from the Salesforce AppExchange without support from the vendor and automatically incorporated into each user's Salesforce application. The cost is $9 per user per month ($972 per year for the whole 9-person department in this case). 4Spires also offers a generic cloud version of the CommitKeeper system that requires only internet access and a browser (i.e. no underlying technology platform license). Other versions under development include a SharePoint version, mobile version on the Android platform, and an API for enabling quick incorporation of the conversation-tracking system into other complementary systems.

Info Edge India Ltd., India
Nominated by Newgen Software Technologies Limited

1. EXECUTIVE SUMMARY / ABSTRACT

Info Edge (India) Ltd. is India's leading online classifieds company with a strong portfolio of brands, experienced management team and a business model that is driven to further capitalize on its first phase of growth.

The company wanted a robust, scalable, enterprise class solution for Naukri.com, India's biggest jobsite and its flagship brand. They were looking for a solution to standardize five core processes namely resume writing, cover letter, application writing, and info-graphic resume and video resume script writing. The company faced challenges in handling the huge transactions related to their job applications. There was no proper *workflow* management in order to complete the transaction life cycle which resulted in loss of transactions some times. All the different types of requests needed to be processed and routed to the executives based on their skills metrics, experiences and availability. There was no real time communication. The client needed a bulk e-mailing feature to increase response time of Info Edge customers via emails (E.g Movement of transaction based on response received from customer via email)

Keen to plug this gap, the company decided to implement a solution for its strength in process definition, quick deployment cycle and flexibility. Newgen's solution was coined "Resumepedia". This solution consisted of its Business Process Management tool and Enterprise Content Management tool. It replaced the existing workflow solution and currently has more than 100 active users.

The client was able to attain the following benefits:
- Savings
  - Reduced Operational Costs
  - Improvement in average daily output
- Agility
  - Decreased Time-to-Market
  - Faster Response to Market Opportunity
- Differentiation
  - Improved Quality
  - Increased Customer Satisfaction
  - Greater Market Penetration
- Other key benefits
  - All transactional data is maintained in the repository
  - Increase response time of customers of Info Edge by real time communication with customers through email. Bulk emails are sent to the customers as a batch process

2. OVERVIEW

Info Edge (India) Limited wanted a robust, scalable, enterprise, class solution for Naukri.com jobseekers services branded as Naukri Fast Forward. They wanted to automate all 5 processes. The client was looking for a solution to overcome their present challenges in order to run the following processes:

- **Resume Writing:** A resume is a written document that lists candidate's work experience, skills, and educational background. It is used as a marketing tool for job seekers. In Resume Writing the categories are divided basis the work experience of Customer (Fresher, Entry, Mid, Sr.), sub categories are further made depending upon the SLA.(for eg: Normal, express, super express)
- **Cover Letter:** A cover letter is a document sent with your resume to provide additional information on your skills and experience
- **Application writing:** Application writing helps candidates to complete their applications for applying to various universities post obtaining their GRE/GMAT scores. The service offers various combinations for GRE and GMAT candidates including essays, statement of purpose, letter of recommendations, CV, etc. based on the number of institutes to which they are applying
- **Visual resume:** Is a graphical representation of a resume. An infographic resume enables a job seeker to better present his or her career history, education and skills
- **Video resume script writing**: Is a document containing the script that can be used by the job seeker to get his video resume developed.

The solution was expected to help Info Edge to phase out their current-workflow solution, in which they were facing certain issues hampering the efficiency of users and the process. The client wanted a solution that would route work and documents where they needed to go. However, this was a very conventional understanding of case management and the proposed its solution that has re-imagined case management to include the following:

- Re-thinking the old-style imaging/workflow – The solution performs many of the same imaging and workflow functions but has a different approach on how to - improve customer experience, enhance performance, empower employees, easily handle exceptions and support the dynamic work environment
- Focus on Change – The solution is designed to handle different types of cases, from those that follow a generic pattern and require specific action to those that have a unique completion path that is distinct from any other instance in the system
- Exception-Oriented – Users are empowered to handle exceptions in real-time. The case management solution helps the user to create a path or process for an exception on the fly thereby enabling him/her to handle the case dynamically. This eradicates the need to anticipate all possible exceptions and makes the user and process more efficient
- Support for a wide range of untamed processes – Organizations face the daunting task of handling processes that belies strict definition and keeps evolving over time based on the nature of work. Work is such a process is extremely dynamic and it becomes pertinent that the system adapts to the way employees work rather than employees having to adapt to the system.

Challenges:
- Lack of standardization in processes
- Single account manager handling all tasks resulting in sub-optimal efficiency increased stress levels
- Performance of existing application is very slow due to high volume of transactions
- Existing application is not very user friendly (GUI)
- Performance issues in the existing application resulting in loss of transaction some time

- Difficult to implement the SLAs for sub processes due to loosely coupled departments, no controlling parameter exist
- Difficult to maintain the repository of transactional data (They have to do manually on local drives)
- Sending bulk emails to customers as a batch process (in evening time). No real time communication

Some of the key benefits experienced by the client are:
- Reduction in turn-around-time
- Reduced operational costs
- Bulk emailing features are provided to the customers as a batch process
- Ensure tracking and monitoring of resource utilization
- Improved transparency
- Real time access to the experts skills
- Improved Quality
- Increased Customer Satisfaction

3. BUSINESS CONTEXT

With ever-increasing customers, Info Edge felt the need for a case management solution. The client was already using a BPM platform for 2 years. However the client was very dissatisfied by its performance as they were not able to track the transaction in the process flow. Also many times when documents were moving from one step to another they would get lost and could not be tracked. The client had also spent a lot of money on the earlier system without accruing expected ROI. All these reasons convinced the client that it needed to replace its BPM Solution. Earlier, cases were allocated based on a manual process and individualistic style, without having a clear picture of workload of each professional within the organization and across the location. Since the system was based on physical file movement, only one user could work at a time on the case.

Also the resumes created over the year were fragmented and not available centrally for access to the entire user community. Coupled with the above issues, customers had no visibility about the status of their cases unless they knew the individual executive more candidly.

With the advancement of technology, the client wanted to serve its customers via multiple channels like Sanitization desk, Pre-development chat (PDC) cello, Content design cell, Quality Audit Cell, Mail Management Cell, Application Writing cell, Cover letter cell etc.

The major challenges, faced by the resident BPM solution were:
- Performance of the application was very slow due to high volume of transactions
- There was isolation of departments/ work, no proper communication channels and intersection of SOPs
- Performance issues in the existing application resulting in loss of transaction some times
- Difficult to implement the SLAs for sub processes policies due to loosely coupled departments, no controlling parameter existed
- Difficult to maintain the repository of transactional data
- Absence of real-time communication with customers.
- Lack of complete process visibility/transparency in processes
- Poor resource utilization
- Higher process cycle time
- The client's traditional BPM and workflow products failed to provide run-time adaptability

4. THE KEY INNOVATIONS

4.1 Business

Info Edge wanted a full-featured case management system that would be tailored to meet the online classified company's specific needs and requirements, and to organize all their candidates' contact information and documents within a proven, flexible workflow process.

The case management solution addressed the candidate's service via different channels. It provided a unified interface to help users to not only verify some basic details of the candidate but also help the users to raise multiple requests simultaneously. The solution was designed to also handle all sorts of exceptions.

In the resume writing process, all customer details and transactions along with customer's updated resume were extracted introduced into the workflow. There were also scenarios where the solution re-used candidate data that was collected in the resume writing process and introduced it into the workflow of the Cover Letter writing process. The solution also offered various services such as Candidate's Essay, Statement of Purpose etc. With it the client was able to achieve complete process visibility. Info Edge has built a reputation for delivering timely, excellent and effective advisory services. The solution helped the client to further enhance the efficiency of its services by allowing users to better use, manage, consolidate, share and track, and shape business processes.

The system provided flexibility to the employees to raise multiple and different kind of requests from a single email, SMS or phone call. Unlike before now an employee had the privilege of bulk emailing its customers and providing other value-added services.

The business owners got complete process visibility. System escalated the cases on burst of Turn-Around-Time (TAT) as per the defined escalation matrix. Business owners found alert messages and signals from the Business Activity Monitoring (BAM) dashboard to take pro-active decisions on upcoming opportunities or threats.

4.2 Case Handling

Info Edge India Limited wanted to automate all 5 processes.

- **Resume Writing Process** – This helps customers to develop their resume. The resulting document helped Info Edge to identify technical and operational requirements of the resume writing process. Once the resume writing service has been sold by a sales representative, all details of the customer and transaction along with customer's updated resume will be extracted by the solution and introduced into the resume writing process workflow.
- **Resume writing product definition:** A Resume is a written document that lists customer work experience, skills, and educational background. It is used as a marketing tool by job seekers. In Resume Writing, the categories are divided on the basis of the work experience of customer (Fresher, Entry, Mid, Sr.), sub categories are further made depending upon the SLA.(for e.g.: Normal, express, super express)
- **Cover Letter Process** – A cover letter is a document sent with a resume to provide additional information on the skill and experience of applicants. Cover letter writing process helps customers to develop a Cover Letter. This document helps Info Edge to identify technical and operational requirements of Cover Letter writing process.
  Cover Letter can be sold in two modes: one is combo service (Resume and Cover Letter Writing) and the second is only Cover Letter writing. Once the

Cover Letter service has been sold by sales representative, all customer details and transaction details are filled and submitted in the 'Resbilling' application along with customer's updated resume. Then Newgen's solution extracts that the requisite data and introduces the document into the workflow of the Cover Letter writing process.

- **Application Writing Process** – Application writing process helps customers to develop an application portfolio. This document helps Info Edge to identify technical and operational requirements of application writing process. It helps candidates complete their applications for applying to various universities post obtaining their GRE / GMAT scores. The service offers various combinations for GRE and GMAT candidates including essays, statement of purpose, letter of recommendations, CV, etc. based on the number of institutes they are applying to. In this process, the executive writes SOPs, LORs, Essays, etc. for aspirants who wish to secure admission to post graduate programs conducted by Universities / Institutes in India and overseas.

- **Visual Resume Process** – This process is a graphical representation of a resume. An infographic resume enables job seekers to better present his or her career history, education and skills. The solution provided enhanced analytics and pattern recognition to its client which improved the capability of this process.

- **Video Resume Script Writing Process-** This process is a document containing the script that can be used by the job seekers to get their video resume developed

System Architecture

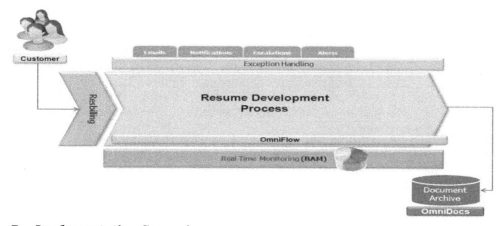

Pre Implementation Scenario

Prior to implementing the solution, the Resumepedia Process of the client was time consuming and it required extensive manual intervention across various steps. The processes needed various data entry points which led to data redundancy. Also, the manual intervention resulted in human errors which were difficult to trace and track. Earlier there was no mechanism for quality check and visibility of processes. There was no workflow system to follow the process, which lead to various manual interventions etc. There was no provision of quality check, auditing and transparency. Once the resume writing services were sold to prospective applicants by sales representative, they were forwarded to the Account Managers who worked on the requirement and closed the transaction after taking approval from the applicant. Maintaining and tracking of all the physical documents was a major challenge. It was very difficult to track all the client's details and maintain the SLAs. The client requests were tracked and responded to manually which resulted in delays services and lack-luster customer complaints.

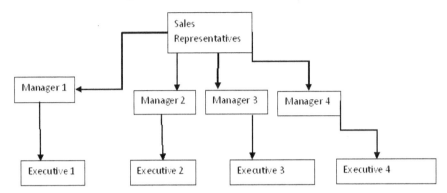

Post Implementation Scenario

The solution instantly reduced the number of steps by almost 50%. It brought all the system together on same platform linked in such a way that they could communicate with each other. Now, the entire process requires minimal manual intervention. All the physical documents are converted into digitized documents which traverse across departments and locations.

The client was able to serve its customers via subdivisions such as Sanitization desk, Pre-development chat (PDC) cell, Content design cell, Quality Audit Cell, Mail Management Cell, Application Writing cell, and Cover letter cell.

Sanitization Desk

- This group conducts a pre-allocation check to verify if the resume submitted by the client has basic details such as Work Experience and Education. They also ensure that the resume is the latest updated version.
- The Desk follows up with concern persons in case an updated resume is not available
- They manually allocate resumes to Content Designers in case of requisition above the assigned threshold
- The Flagging Team is also a part of the Sanitization Desk

Pre-development Chat (PDC) Cell

- Conducts a detailed discussion with the client after allocation (auto / manual)
- Collates inputs in a Summary of Discussion(SOD) Sheet and forwards inputs to the Content Design Cell for development of the first cut of the resume
- Responsible for the Pre-development chat till the client/applicant has been contacted

Content Design Cell

- Uses the raw resume submitted by the client, the SOD Notes and other references to develop the first draft of the resume. A Writer in the Content Design Cell might also mark queries in the document, if required, to ensure that the final resume is complete in all aspects
- Sends the first draft to the client/applicant after making changes as highlighted by the Quality Audit Cell

Quality Audit Cell

- It performs a detailed quality check of resume submitted by the Content Design Cell
- Grades each resume basis critical to quality (CTQ) parameters – Essentials & the Value Add
- Scores are mentioned in a pre-defined quality sheets, which gives the over-all quality scores earned by each writer at the end of each month's billing cycle

Mail Management Cell

- Handles all incoming & outgoing mail correspondence with the client's post sending of the First Draft. This also includes detailed discussion with the client, when/where required.
- Focuses on securing client's approval on a final resume and closure of the Resume Writing process workflow through on time iterations

Application Writing Cell

- Writes SOPs, LORs, Essays etc. for aspirants who wish to secure admission to Post graduate programs conducted by Universities/ Institutes in Indian and Foreign Universities
- Conducts detailed discussion with aspirants all across the service life-cycle

Cover Letter Writing

- Write cover letters basis first draft of the resume sent by the Content design Cell
- Also writes cover letters that have been billed as standalone products

Visual Resume

- Conducts a detailed discussion with the client after allocation (auto/manual) all across the service life-cycle
- Collates inputs in a Summary of Discussion (SOD) sheet
- Collates all data to interpret into graphical representation

Consultative approach

Processes have been analyzed at various levels:
- L1 - Distinct end-to-end processes
- L2 - Functional breakdown of Level 1 processes
- L3 - Functional Sub-Processes/Activities
- Clear identification of departments based on Job role with clear definition of work scope (E.g. Sanitization Cell, Pre-Development Chat Cell, and Content Development Cell Audit Cell, Mail Management Cell)
- Identification of all required business rules in order put clear governance and for effective monitoring and controlling
- In order to increase the productivity of transaction life cycle:
- Calculation of TAT on each cell
- Identification of real time status of transactions
- Implementation of reminders and notifications
- In order to improve the quality of real content (Resume), effective audit process has been implemented (Audit Scoring and approval)
- Checks on various levels to reduce error in transaction life cycle
- Identification of various report for effective report management
- Improve response time to customer of Info Edge by real time communication with customer through emails (E.g Movement of transaction based on response received from customer via email)
- Easy tracking of Transactions at any stage to give more transparency in system

- Better document management using various folder structures (E.g. Centralization of transaction related data for future references)

New Process – PROagile Approach

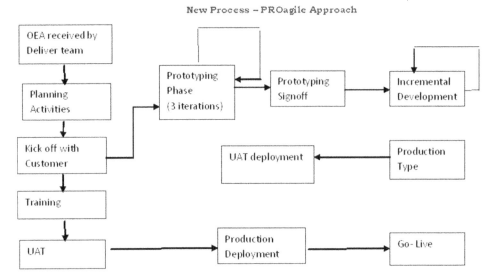

Post Implementation Diagram

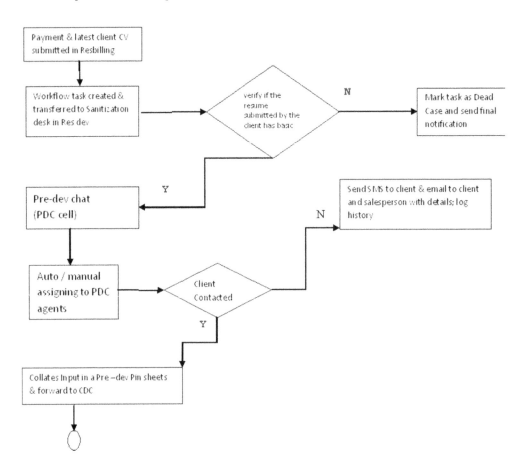

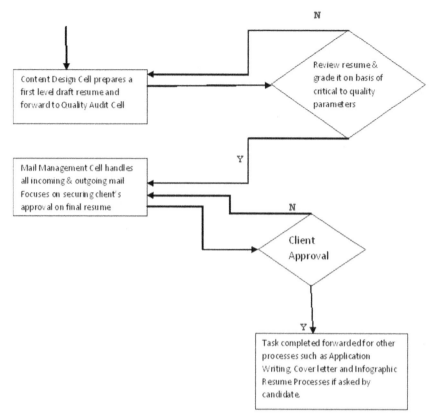

The key roles

There was a hierarchy of business owners. At the incident of TAT burst, depending upon the severity, the sales orders were escalated to the right business managers. There were three stakeholders involved in this entire project such as Executives, Team Leaders and Managers. There were 11 people who were closely related to the projects such as

- Senior Management = 3
- Process Managers = 7
- IT Manager = 1

4.3 Organization & Social

There were significant changes in the way employees at Info Edge executed their tasks. Before the solution, the concept of single account manager, who would be responsible for handling the transaction from initiation till closure. There was no facility to monitor the candidate's requests and ensure they were being closed. The candidate's resume writing and other requests were processed in the existing workflow application and were error prone.

After the solution all the five processes were automated, the process flow became dynamic and non-deterministic. The right employees used to get the right kind of cases which matched their core competency and skills. The employees at Info Edge found it easier to track the progress of the candidate's resume and the solution helped them to place the right person at right time.

Unlike before, a single account manager did not have to perform all the tasks. The case management solution automatically fetched the right candidate's information and passed on the details to the next step on submission of the tasks. With the change in the structure and implementation of the new BPM application, employees could focus on the specific task allocated to them. They were also able to handle much higher volumes of transaction, and this improved process efficiency and reduced time wastage. The customer satisfaction levels improved significantly as they found that employees were more attentive to their needs and more consultative in their approach. The unified solution screen showed not only the case data, resume writing, cover letter but also customer history and other related documents on the screen. The employees did not have to toggle between screens or search for customer records which significantly saved their time and made their job much easier than before.

5. HURDLES OVERCOME

Management

Even though the solution solved all the major business concerns, initially the management was concerned about how the solution would align with their business strategy. However, at the time of user acceptance test, the proposed solution was able to earn enough trust of the management. Within a few months after going live, the management became confident that the solution was scalable and flexible enough to align with their larger business strategy.

Business

- Integration of new application with Resbilling (Sales Dept. Application), since Naukri.com has to provide real time updates to customers and sales people
- Implementation of high frequency of alerts and notification
- Ad-hoc MIS generation, customizable dashboards
- Implementation of Norms and Compliances (DOD)

Organization Adoption

Info Edge was looking to set best-in-class operations and productivity standards. However, adopting to the change in organization structure and also a new application was a major hurdle. Initially employees took some time to understand how the solution worked. At the beginning, there were several instances where employees were unable to complete the task as described in the process. But with time and rigorous training, all the employees were able to adopt the new system and started enjoying the benefits of automation.

6. BENEFITS

6.1 Cost Savings / Time Reductions

- Savings
  - Reduced Operational Costs
  - Improvement in average daily output
- Agility
  - Decreased Time – to –Market
  - Faster Response to Market Opportunity

6.2 Increased Revenues

- Info Edge has experienced top-line growth considering all the tangible and intangible benefits that were accrued.

6.3 Quality Improvements

- All transactional data is maintained in the OmniDocs™ repository
- Bulk emails are sent to the customers as a batch process
- Greater visibility onto the work n transparency to the candidate's resume

- Tracking and monitoring of resources utilization leading to increased productivity levels
- Empowering the experts to get real time access to case documents Dashboard and everyday MIS for End to End tracking of cases Increased responsiveness via email notification to candidate's
- Access to the experts or access to the expert skills/ knowledge available in any one of the offices in India to the clients located elsewhere

7. BEST PRACTICES, LEARNING POINTS AND PITFALLS

7.1 Best Practices and Learning Points

✓ Simplicity, flexibility and robustness should be the prime focus
✓ Simple, lesser and similar interfaces across modules
✓ Transparency to clients

7.2 Pitfalls

✗ Too flashy and complex looking interfaces can be distracting
✗ The client had no clear picture about their requirement vis-à-vis the application features and the solution being offered due to which the entire project was stretched; The actual implementation team should have joined the discussion earlier to understand the requirements and guide the client about the application

8. COMPETITIVE ADVANTAGES

The Case Management provided a major step forward in terms of building its capabilities in the service industry. At Info Edge, the solution was able to provide a significant reduction in cost by automating its 5 processes. Apart from this it provided long-term improvements in User and Front office productivity.

Different approach to designing and running processes: Rather than trying to connect all paths through a process into a single, integrated end-to-end processes in one department, the solution diversified all the processes. The end-to-end workflow became a high level description of the phases associated with the work. Each phase then functioned as a component and users could use these components to support their work. This also meant that users were able to adapt their processes in real time.

Improved Transparency: The solution supported the creation of sophisticated skill-based routing which leads to easy tracking of transactions at any stage and gave more transparency in system. It gave sufficient attention to data definition, business rules and process assignments

New management behaviors: with new capabilities comes new benefits and at the same time new risks. Appropriate checks and balances must be in place to avoid misuse. To improve the quality of real content (Resume), an effective audit process has been implemented. Management practices regularly sample and review process adaptation.

Improved Security: the overall case structure provides different levels of security and flexibility. Business rules were provided at server level for routing task to different users. This setting maintained the uniformity and optimization of the entire process. This feature was highly critical in the case management solution because there were number of processes which were supposed to undergo client interaction. The solution empowered employees with full customer histories. All candidates have a full interaction history which can be used for further processes.

9. THE TECHNOLOGY AND SERVICE PROVIDERS

The client has procured the case management suite from Newgen. The case management solution comprises:

- **OmniDocs™**- an Enterprise Content Management (ECM) platform for creating, capturing, and managing, delivering and archiving large volume of documents. It provides highly scalable, unified repository for securely storing and managing enterprise content. It provides centralized repository for enterprise documents and supports rights based archival. It supports both centralized and distributed scanning with policy based upload. The platform manages complete lifecycle of documents through record retention, storage and retrieval policies. It supports exhaustive document and folder searches on date, indexes and general parameters as well as full text search on image and electronic documents.
- **OmniFlow™** a platform-independent, scalable Business Process Management engine that enables automation of organizational business processes. Built using open technologies, it has seamless integration abilities allowing it to be introduced into any IT infrastructure.

The Business Process Management Suite offers the following tools:
- **Business Process Modeler**: Used by business users to define the business process. Process is defined as set of activities in sequence, parallel or loop
- **Process Manager:** Enables efficient process management and administration using various people and process oriented real time reports
- **Process Client**: Enables manual intervention in business processes through web
- **Business Activity Monitoring Components:** Consists of a set of reporting tools for process owners, senior management, and other business users. eg: Real Time & Historic Reporting Tool and GUI Reports Builder
- **Business Analysis Monitor – BAM**
  Newgen's BPMS has a user friendly BAM module for creation of monitoring dashboards used by various stakeholders in the process including senior management, Operations manager and process participants. BAM generates customized alerts based on rules defined in the dashboards for each category of user enabling corrective action as the process is being executed.

Extensive capabilities to define KPI of tasks are available in the BAM allowing for better control over process output. Process improvement is also achieved through extensive process performance reporting. Newgen's Business Activity Monitor allows process owners to easily design reports, define KPIs, set control charts and helps them monitor the process both at real time through dashboards and offline through alerts and notifications. Alerts and notification are defined based on user roles. Using this, different stake holders can take informed decisions. With industry best reports pre-configured, the tool starts delivering from the very moment of inception and helps in Business Process Improvement. The system study, solution design and implementation were carried out by Newgen's professionals.

10. CONCLUSION

Project with Info Edge was a valuable learning experience for Newgen in order to explore its capabilities of serving the service industry. Through this implementation the Newgen team was able to explore and improvise the various features of Newgen's products which helped in the implementation of an effective workflow solution at Info Edge. Mapping of Newgen product features with requirement of Info Edge group (Service Based) helped Newgen understand the nitty-gritty (constraints, challenges, and diversified nature of processes) of service industries. With effective project methodology (Pro-Agile) and supported product features and dedication of resources, Newgen was able to successfully implement its Case Management Solution at Info Edge.

Norwegian Courts Administration, Norway

Nominated by Computas AS, Norway

1. EXECUTIVE SUMMARY / ABSTRACT

LOVISA is the ACM solution for the Norwegian Courts Administration (NCA). LOVISA supports Norwegian first and second instance courts in their case handling and court management. All court employees are LOVISA users, including judges, clerks and other staff. It facilitates communication with external stakeholders such as lawyers and lay judges through web portals, whereas police, prosecutors, the correctional services and other public bodies rely on "business to business" integration.

Supporting the complete value chain of the courts, it focuses on the active participants' decision-related parts of the juridical case handling. For each case, a work folder provides a shared work environment for the case manager (normally the judge) and other participants. These work folders provide access to worklists, case data and documents, giving users active and adaptive task support, ensuring high-quality uniform case handling in accordance with Norwegian procedural law, while leaving the specific legal contents of the case for professional judgment.

LOVISA uses a rich variety of case type templates with specific case handling functionality, ranging from simple types with short lifespans to complex types spanning over several years. The system has integrated multilingual document handling, including generating/merging documents from case data, using hundreds of document templates maintained by the NCA. It assists with delegation, deadlines, reminders and escalations—also based on task support. To assist in planning and follow-up, case folders have a generated timeline view contrasting the current state with the desired state, independently of all concurrent partial workflows operating on the case.

2. OVERVIEW

LOVISA supports juridical case management and court management. Case handling is a highly collaborative process, and LOVISA facilitates the complex interchange between court staff and external stakeholders. It is a hub for "business to business" collaboration in Norway's judicial system with integrations to police authorities, prosecuting authorities, tax authorities, public registries and correctional services.

LOVISA has around 1200 daily users; clerks, judges and administrative personnel. These users produce around 200,000 legal cases yearly, of which 37 percent are administrative cases, 29 percent are civil cases and 34 percent are criminal cases. Daily, some 7,000 documents are produced and sent to the relevant case parties.

Below is an overview of functionality:

- Work process definition, instantiation and automatic follow-up for all tasks needed to correctly handle the court cases.
- Adaptive task support for preparation of cases for trial, automated and cascading to other stakeholders where appropriate.

- Lifecycle case folders providing a complete overview of the case, including ongoing and past tasks, parties, actors, claims, documents, decisions, hearings, with drill-down into case details.
- Coordinating task-supported collaborative work through shared case folders.
- Support for the judge in reorganizing a case complex, merging and splitting and relating the cases concerned.
- Allocation of judges to court cases, based on availability and legal requirements.
- Correct drawing of lay judges for case allocation from appointed pool.
- Document templates, including automatic merging of case data and links to Microsoft Word for producing court documents.
- Interaction with a standard document management system for electronic filing, generating public document journals and encoding documents and case data for long-term archiving.
- Automated support for calculating claims, fees and costs.
- Publishing of listings and decisions/rulings/verdicts to licensed Norwegian publishers, including the Norwegian Legal Information Service (http://www.lovdata.no).
- A reporting module to serve court management with business intelligence for resource allocation planning, as well as a basis for work process improvement.

LOVISA provides adaptive task support for a wide range of case types, with a personal worklist for every user and a work folder for every case. Task templates based on declarative knowledge modeling allow for flexible task composition. Configurable process fragments and shared worklists enable an emergent and highly collaborative workflow to fit the case at hand.

Judicial cases also exist outside of LOVISA, often in a case complex with cases co-existing in several independent case management systems. LOVISA here plays the role as an adaptive collaboration hub for Norway's Judicial System. It handles tedious document production and document handling in an integrated manner, and the system also supports court management, including cross-organizational scheduling and resource management.

Right from the start of the project, subject matter experts (SME) have played a major role in process- and task-discovery, as well as setting priorities for further development. Recruited from the SME group, "super-users" assist with further organizational adoption and introduction.

LOVISA has enabled a shift from sequential to parallel court case processing, with significant benefits in terms of efficiency and quality. As an Enterprise ACM built-to-change, the system has proved its ability to adapt to major changes, to both its legislative and its organizational basis.

3. BUSINESS CONTEXT

Although it is commonplace to view the legal sector as a conservative culture with little appetite for being first to venture into new lands, let alone new technology, this has not quite been the case in Norway. Early work led to the establishment of the legislation database "Lovdata" in 1981, as a private foundation by the Ministry of Justice and the Faculty of Law at the University of Oslo. It was established on web in 1995, and has since been the main Norwegian lookup source for legal information. From the 1970s onwards, the Institute of Computers and Law, led by Professor Jon Bing, did considerable research work, and produced several Artificial Intelligence based decision support prototypes. These initiatives may have contributed to the climate in which The Supreme Court of Norway decided to develop its first electronic case management solution in 1999. Based on the experience with this solution, LOVISA was projected as an instrument to implement organizational changes in ways of working for all Norwegian courts.

A highly competent culture spanning several generations, the judges, clerks and other personnel of the courts of Norway were about to venture into a new era of electronic work. Case handling had previously been essentially manual and paper-based, albeit with a rudimentary database and text processing facility. LOVISA was going to change all that, offering active task support, providing adaptive assistance for work performance, enabling orchestrated parallel execution of case work—hiding away as much technological detail as possible.

4. THE KEY INNOVATIONS

Adaptive task support for a wide range of case types

Instead of trying to support linear and static "end-to-end" processes, LOVISA is based on supporting well-defined process fragments, known as tasks and steps. These are instantiated and recombined by events, rules and human judgment. All such tasks and steps operate on a shared data model of the particular court case, and as a side effect they update and modify the data model and the documents of the case folder. The steps in a task offer the user functionality and knowledge support for executing the work.

Case types are organized in a hierarchical structure. A particular court case is typically associated with a leaf-node in this structure, but may initially belong to a higher level and is categorized more detailed as the case proceeds. There are around 200 case types at the lowest level.

The table below reflects top-level case types covered:

Civil cases	Criminal cases	Administrative cases
Dispute resolution	Magistrate case	Notice of death
Litigation	Trial case	Notarial certification
Enforcement case	Appeal	Registration of political parties
Appeal	Verdict appeal	Registration
Appraisement / valuation	Interlocutory appeal	Legal guardian
Administration and division of estate	Compensation for unwarranted proceedings	Wedding
Bankruptcy case	Revival	Last will and testament
Debt settlement case	Private case	
Revival	Private case – court of appeal	

Table 1: LOVISA case types

NORWEGIAN COURTS ADMINISTRATION

Task templates and task library for custom execution

A task type is defined by means of a *task template*, which contains a set of steps as a general "recipe" for performing the task. These steps are subject to several conditions, defined using predicates and rules, which make it possible to derive a contextualized task template as a unique recipe for a particular instance, always reflecting its state and data. This contextualized task template is the basis for offering active task support to the user. The user selects and executes permitted steps, based on personal, professional judgment. Step conditions specify pre- and post-conditions in addition to repeat-conditions (step can be repeated), include-condition (step is made available dependent on context) and mandatory-conditions (step must be performed). The interplay between these conditions produces an appropriate set of steps for the user. Each such step will offer relevant functionality, information or tools; often including a user interface component for operating on relevant case data.

LOVISA has task definitions for more than 700 different tasks, made available and hierarchically structured through a *task library* with role based access control. For a specific case type, only valid task groups and tasks are presented to the user when a new task for the case is created. Court cases always are handled according to the legislation at the correct point in time. Hence, the task library contains tasks covering both current and earlier legislation—the task library is versioned. The first level in the task library hierarchy contains civil cases, criminal cases, administrative cases, publication of rulings, financial cases, tasks regarding lay judges and tasks dealing with deadlines and escalations.

A personal worklist for every user—a work folder for every case

Cases as well as users have worklists. For a user, the worklist represents the personal inbox component of their electronic workbench. A personal worklist contains the user's own planned and ongoing tasks, and the same task may simultaneously sit in several users' worklists, enabling easy collaboration. The tasks are also collected in the case folder worklist, maintaining a continuously updated overview of all tasks pertaining to the case at hand, indicating who is responsible for each task.

Declarative knowledge modeling—knowledge editor and task composition

In organizing these task templates, a "knowledge editor" is used to capture them as declarative models. Task-related functionality may be grouped into "standard" definitions that may be reused across higher-level definitions based on inheritance. LOVISA contains several "abstract" task templates that are not directly instantiated, but used as inheritance sources in defining variants of the task.

Emergent workflow and choreographed co-work

A particular court case may have several ongoing tasks, each operating on its data and documents. In addition to worklist access, the task library empowers users with the task types they are allowed to initiate, subject to role-based permissions. When required, a particular step of a certain task may invoke another new task for the same user or a different user. As a result, an emergent workflow is created as a side effect of the active task support.

Case complex and adaptive collaboration hub for Norway's Judicial System

A criminal case—an aggravated assault—starts off in the police and prosecution authority (case 1 in Figure 1). During investigation, several steps requiring court decisions are typically taken, such as remand detention and searches. These court decisions are outcomes of individual magistrate's court cases (cases 2 and 4). These decisions can be appealed, as shown with case 3, requiring the court of appeal to handle the appeal swiftly. The dotted line from case 2 to case 4 indicates that within the LOVISA system, information from case 2 can be used (referenced) in case 3 in order to speed the registration of information in the case. The judicial proceedings in the appeal case are kept completely independent of the originating case, although the information is shared.

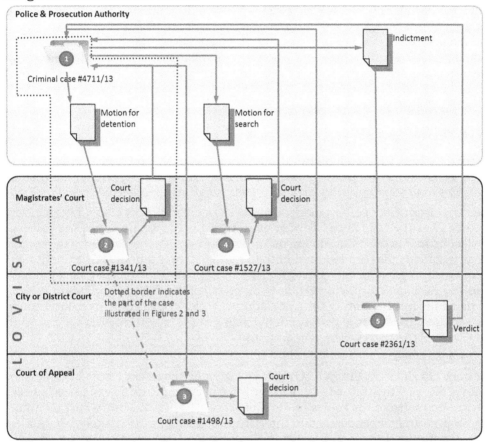

Figure 1: A case complex arising from a straightforward criminal case

Finally, when the prosecution authority has completed its investigation and the indictment is presented to the city or district court, the case is tried in court and eventually the verdict is rendered. According to this explanation, Figure 1 shows a very simple case complex from a straightforward criminal case. A similar diagram for a realistic case would be practically unreadable; especially in civil suits. All arrows between the police and prosecution authority (upper pool) and the courts (lower pool) are structured information exchanged between the respective case management systems through a secure integration bus, thus simplifying data registration.

Integrated document production and document handling

LOVISA offers advanced and adaptive functionality for integrated multilingual document production and handling. The document production is based on around 1600 templates that are being maintained by the NCA. 740 of these templates have language variants, covering the two official Norwegian written standards as well as

German, English, Swedish, French and Spanish. During automated document production, 600 different field codes, including table fields, are used for merging case data into the document. Automated personalized document production for several recipients (mass merging) is also supported. Users are allowed to make adjustments to the template, and re-merge when needed. Document versioning and archiving is handled by the archiving system—a standard product integrated through services. Document production tasks offer relevant templates only, based on case context and role-based permissions, and there are also some ad hoc tasks choosing templates based on their properties. Recipients collaborating electronically through the integrated actor portal will receive automatically generated email or SMS notice about new available documents.

Court management, cross-organizational scheduling and resource management

The business intelligence reporting module is used by the court administration officer for calculating the workload of the court and its individual roles, case handling metrics such as the handling time for a particular phase, reporting any cases violating constraints described by Norwegian procedural law. Of special interest are the strict time constraints for pre-trial detention of accused persons under-18.

The "trial-listing module" supports resource-based listing of cases for hearing. This module uses the MS Office calendar of all relevant court employees, the calendar of all courtrooms plus information about all court engagements of the lawyers and other resources that are required in the hearing. This is a critical function for efficient case progress in the courts. Furthermore, the court officials partly handle resource allocation for the prosecutors on behalf of the Public Prosecution Authority using the functionality of the trial-listing module. In civil suits the district courts are required under law to perform initial listing of the case already at the introductory stage of the court's case preparations.

4.1 Business

Through its data integration LOVISA has greatly simplified the information exchange between the various actors in the judicial system. The flow of cases between the prosecution and the courts has enabled new patterns of work, whilst maintaining their strict independence and integrity. In bankruptcy cases there is data exchange with the Norwegian Register of Business Enterprises. Whenever an individual is registered the information is checked with the Norwegian Census, and whenever a business is registered, the Business Enterprises Register is checked. The lawyers selectable as counsels are fetched from the registry of the Norwegian Supervisory Council of Lawyers'; information regarding counsel's fees is exchanged with the Tax Directorate. Significant effort has been put into ensuring data quality in order to exchange data, and good data quality has also resulted from this extensive data exchange.

4.2 Case Handling

The management of court cases is a non-linear process. Global patterns direct the overall case flows through the court instances, but due to numerous factors, complexity sets in at the level of specific work execution. A plethora of statutory rules regulate how each different type of case is to be treated. Depending on details of the specific case, different obligations or limitations may apply. The co-existence of parallel or historical cases involving the same persons or events may trigger new cases or impose restrictions or requirements for how the first case may be treated. Involvement of judicial workers across different cases may inadvertently cause partiality, and necessitate changes to the allocation of personnel to tasks. In short, a single case management event may lead a case process onto a very different track, but also simultaneously influence other related cases.

Rather than try to give an overview of all LOVISA use, we have chosen to give a summary account of one quite simple case that nevertheless demonstrates the adaptability and competence that LOVISA task support can offer to the highly competent staff of the Norwegian courts:

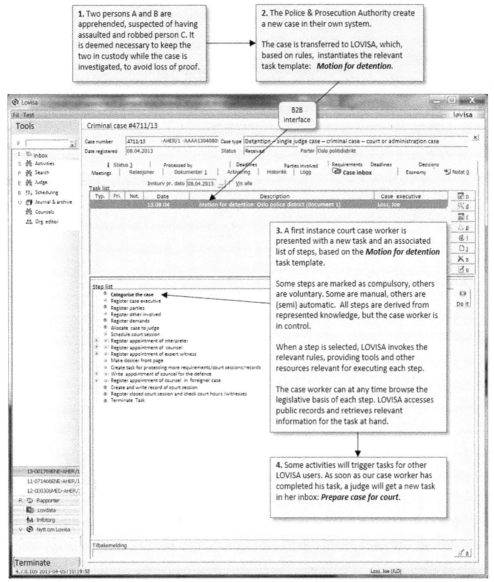

Figure 2: LOVISA case handling based on active task support, part 1

LOVISA does not delve into the juridical essence of the cases, but ensures that the management of the judicial process itself stays within the statutory requirements and makes the most out of all resources and information available. Statutory rules that apply to each type of case are therefore represented in exhaustive detail. This includes conditions for selection of correct procedures, conditions for the parties to inform at any point in the case proceedings, and the like. The scope and complexity of the legislation requires a very large number of work processes and rules in order to guarantee correct processing of all cases in "any imaginable" situation.

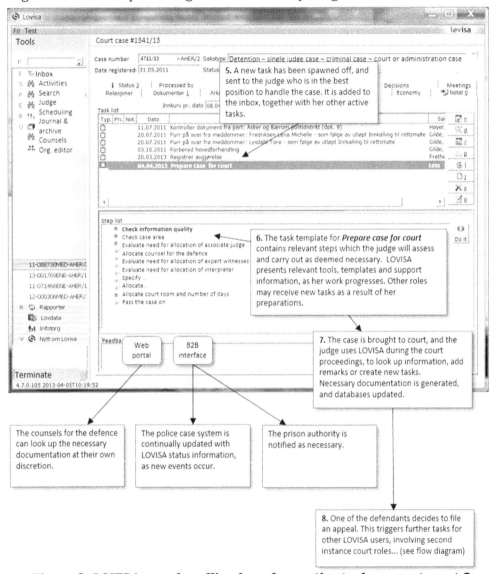

Figure 3: LOVISA case handling based on active task support, part 2

Note the main window in Figure 2 and Figure 3. It shows the LOVISA work folder, with its worklist tab window opened ("case inbox"). From this work folder, all information relevant to the particular case is available. Often, the user will prefer this view, as it has the active task support available—with the task steps shown as a "step list" to the lower left in the figures. The work folder also contains numerous other tab windows for further drilldown in case information: status, parties, actors, documents, court meetings, claims, decisions, deadlines, case history, log etc. The user can directly manipulate some of the aggregated information in these tab windows; other information is the result of the task execution and may not be manipulated directly. This work folder ties together all that is known about a particular case, and remains a calm operation center in a world of emergent workflow and parallel task execution.

The judicial system must strive for utmost perfection in its ability to piece together all relevant elements of a court case to its full legal capacity, using its limited resources to the fullest, to promote the rule of law and maintain the confidence of the general public. No two cases are alike, and managing the encounter of real world events and a complicated judicial system is the complex challenge that LOVISA must negotiate.

Today, LOVISA is a mainstay for the whole Norwegian judicial system. Judges, clerks and other knowledge workers depend on it as their daily ACM work companion. Each user role has access to a wide range of task support elements, which can be combined and put to flexible use in executing the functions of the role. It does not enforce linear task execution, but provides ample opportunity for the user to make competent decisions within allowed degrees of freedom, interspersing automatic, configurable and manual task elements in the process. Police, attorneys, prison administration and other stakeholders do not (yet) have the benefit of this ACM support, but depend on LOVISA information through B2B integration, to carry out their bits of the complex case execution that may cover periods ranging from hours to several years. They also pipeline all relevant information back to LOVISA, to keep the cases up-to-date.

Generated timeline view of cases

To assist in planning and follow-up, case folders have a generated timeline view contrasting the current state with the desired state, independently of all concurrent partial workflows operating on the case.

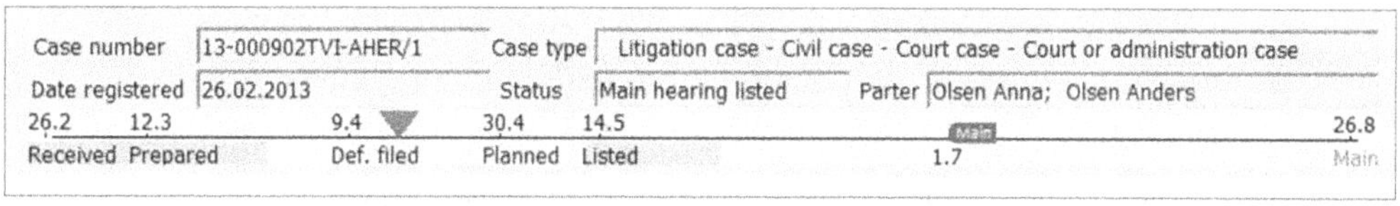

Case number	13-000902TVI-AHER/1		Case type	Litigation case - Civil case - Court case - Court or administration case		
Date registered	26.02.2013		Status	Main hearing listed	Parter	Olsen Anna; Olsen Anders
26.2	12.3	9.4 ▼	30.4	14.5	Main	26.8
Received	Prepared	Def. filed	Planned	Listed	1.7	Main

Figure 4: Timeline view of case folder

A particular case type typically proceeds through a set of states according to statutory rules. The case folder has a timeline with important dates, a sequential ordering of the main case states and an indication of which states have been reached and which remain unfulfilled. Figure 4 above shows such a timeline view for a litigation case, with main states *received, prepared, defense filed, planned, listed* and *main hearing started*. From the figure, we can see that the case has been received, prepared and listed for trial at a set date even if the defense has not been filed and the case is not planned in detail.

Delegation, deadlines, reminders, escalations

In cases dealt with by the courts, there are a number of deadlines; statutory deadlines and others. These are typically created during the court proceedings, but it is also possible to create other deadlines for follow-up. Example: If one party in the case submits an appeal, the court will send the appeal to the counterparty, awaiting a notice of intention to defend. The counterparty has 3 weeks to submit his response. LOVISA registers this deadline and links it to the affected parties. If a notice of intention to defend is received within the deadline, the deadline is deprecated. If there is no reply within the deadline, LOVISA's deadline handler creates a new task for appropriate follow up by the case owner.

LOVISA system architecture

LOVISA is data-centric in defining a shared information model for all processes, tasks, services and functionality of the system. This is a pattern shared with other ACM solutions.

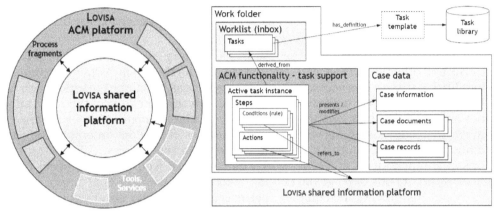

Figure 5: Data-centric design of LOVISA as an ACM solution

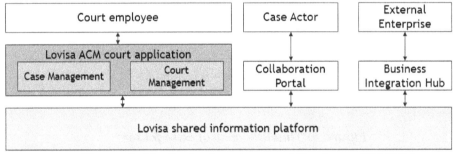

Figure 6: The logical system architecture of LOVISA

The data-centric design was chosen early on; the shared information model and the processes and tasks referring to this information model were developed in parallel from the initial project stages. The case management part of LOVISA relies upon this data-centric design, with tasks, task-steps and step-conditions operating upon the shared information platform. Later, this design proved beneficial for horizontal extensions of the system, where collaboration portals and a business integration hub were added, as depicted in Figure 6.

4.3 Organization & Social

Right from the start, the project group has included as many subject matter experts (SMEs) from the NCA and Norwegian courts as system developers. The SME group has a function similar to a BPM Center of Excellence, although there was no initial formal BPM training. Instead, an important part of their mandate has been to identify the most value generating work activities, where practical task support could best be applied. Their acknowledged common aim has been to support and enhance court work performance itself, helping court staff to comply with the statutory legal requirements of the case handling. Later on in the project, some of these SMEs have become "super users" of LOVISA and played an important part in rolling out the system to all the courts involved.

5. HURDLES OVERCOME

Management

From sequential to parallel case processing

The old "manual" case folders could not easily be shared, so each court case could only be processed one stage at a time, slowly moving from hand to hand. The information platform of LOVISA, including case documents and electronic archiving, has enabled a shift from paper-based sequential operations, to a new reality with parallel execution of several work tasks contributing to the same case, producing time savings and better use of available staff resources.

Business

Built-to-change—adapting to major changes in the "business logic"

Changes in the legislation can occur gradually or in larger steps. Whereas smaller amendments can be noiselessly assimilated into new practices, the introduction of new legislation is more demanding on the organization, in terms of altering its operations accordingly. When the new *Law on mediation and procedure in civil disputes* was introduced in 2008, LOVISA proved its eminent ability to assimilate major business logic changes. This has built confidence, both among users and the SME group responsible for maintaining the LOVISA knowledge bases. LOVISA is an enterprise ACM built-to-change, i.e. easily adapt to changes both in its internal business logic and its organizational environment.

Enabling structural changes in the organization of the court system

In parallel with the LOVISA project a significant structure change in the courts was started, resulting in a 30 percent reduction in the number of city and district courts, mainly implemented through mergers. Some of these mergers were performed simultaneously with deployment of LOVISA, but others were performed through data consolidation in LOVISA plus some transition work processes served by LOVISA itself.

Awareness and compliance boost

Providing automatic task support, LOVISA has produced an increased staff awareness concerning the details of statutory process requirements. While valuable in its own right, this also stimulates trust and adoption. The result is increased information production with acknowledged improvement of work quality.

Towards e-Government: electronic collaboration in public administration

LOVISA plays a leading role in the emerging network of collaborating institutions, with integrations to the Norwegian Register of Business Enterprises, the Norwegian Census, the Norwegian Supervisory Council of Lawyers, the Tax Directorate and the Norwegian Legal Information Service. In addition, there are extensive integrations within the judicial system. This integration includes case management systems referring to other systems' representations of the very same case.

Organization Adoption

User acceptance in a conservative work culture with rich traditions

Court clerks and especially judges are conservative when it comes to adapting new ways of working. The judiciary is a conservative body by tradition; the average age of employees is rather high and a significant number of the work processes are directly founded in procedural legislation. Many of the users were unfamiliar with IT tools, and preferred working paper-based throughout. The only way to convince these users to introduce new work practices was by demonstrating value in their daily work and making the system as easy to use as possible, whilst accepting that some users would need time to adopt the new style of work.

LOVISA's active task support contributed to the adoption, and all judges and court clerks now use LOVISA. The usage varies, as some judges use LOVISA as a real-time support for writing decisions in the courtroom, while others use it only in their office. A fundamental incentive is the fact that every workflow is modeled according to procedural regulations, thus ensuring high quality decisions and compliance with strict legislation.

Adopting LOVISA and electronic archives—two separate challenges that proved mutually synergetic

LOVISA as a case management solution was deployed in parallel with the introduction of electronic document archives. This turned out to be favorable, as it masks the technical nitty-gritty of the archiving solution for the users, again focusing on the actual work performance and performing necessary archiving transparently in the background.

Work performance focus simplifies training

With the built in task support and work performance focus, it has proven easy to introduce new users to the system and to introduce new functionality to existing users. Both new and existing users have commented that they find the system intuitive to use. Most of the training can focus on the statutory rules and case handling practice, and not on how to operate the system—which follows well-established and known patterns for creating a nice user experience. Essentially, LOVISA can be used as an instrument to "push" new work practices without always having to update training programs in parallel.

6. BENEFITS

6.1 Cost Savings / Time Reductions

The case collaboration and information exchange with external entities have contributed significantly with respect to time savings. The adaptive task support aids users in exploiting the structured data exchange both outward bound and inward bound. The path towards secure exchange of electronic documents in all situations will release even more cost savings and time reductions in the future.

The court caseloads are gradually increasing, as society grows more complex. At the same time, the average complexity of cases is increasing. It is a goal that the courts maintain—or even improve—the case handling time whilst keeping up the quality standards. Court personnel express clearly that LOVISA has been a major factor in achieving these targets. Alas, the yearly statistics from the justice sector is not easily decomposed to isolate LOVISA contribution to the targets.

All aspects of document production, handling and exchange has been significantly streamlined; the process of listing cases for trial has been streamlined, and LOVISA aids the court clerks and judges in keeping on top of the case load. At the same time as the court administration has direct access to production statistics and can reallocate staff when necessary (and admissible).

6.2 Increased Revenues

The courts do not have revenue generation as a goal, but they are obliged to collect revenue by the fees charged according to the various case and petition types, as described in the procedural legislation. The Office of the Auditor General of Norway has the auditing authority in this respect, and LOVISA offers reports for this purpose.

The LOVISA system uses a rule-based module where the fee calculation rules are implemented, thus ensuring that the case and petition attributes are considered correctly in order to stipulate the fee for each situation. The rule-based fee calculation produces a result with an attached explanation and presents it to the user, who can verify that the relevant attributes were taken into account.

6.3 Quality Improvements

The courts are proud of their high and consistent quality case handling. However, the large number of different case types and their respective statutory rules previously caused trouble, such as increased case handling time for the smaller courts who encounter less common case types very rarely. Additionally, onboarding of new court clerks and judges has been challenging because of the same variation of case types and rules. LOVISA has contributed to significant improvements in these areas.

Of particular significance are timely conclusions in cases involving detainees and adolescents where the law has strict case conclusion deadlines. Another quality effect lies in the uniform communication with the public due to the use of a central document template library for all courts and cases.

7. BEST PRACTICES, LEARNING POINTS AND PITFALLS

7.1 Best Practices and Learning Points

✓   A successful adaptive case management initiative puts together a representative and empowered group of subject matter experts (SME), typically selected amongst respected future users of the various roles in the target organization. This expert group serves as premise suppliers during the specification, development and testing phases, and they are ideally suited as super-users and instructors in the deployment phase in the organization.

✓   Do not believe that a top-down business process analysis resembles the practical case management in a knowledge organization. Your top-down analysis is probably closer to a detailed state chart of the cases handled.

✓   Focus on the most value generating work activities and center the work process and case management analysis on areas where significant simplifications of the work processes can be obtained.

✓   Make sure that the project group comprises a business analyst with value production focus—from the customer side or the vendor's side—to challenge the specifications created by the SME group for more optimal processes and data representations.

7.2 Pitfalls

✗   You can easily be driven into overly detailed support for processes that are not really crucial for the value production of the organization, simply because some experts have these as their "babies". Other areas that can consume too much focus are processes that have undergone thorough analysis in previous projects or initiatives.

✗   In the LOVISA project, some problematic situations arose when it became obvious that the standard procedure of the law in some case types turned out to be the exceptional cases, whereas most cases of the affected case types were handled by arbitration alternatives which typically cut short the case management activities and lead time. Since this was understood only after significant effort had been pursued in describing and even developing the case and work process descriptions, excess resources had already been consumed.

✗ *The underlying ACM framework allows creating very complex tasks and task steps with many logical conditions. Focusing on reuse you may be tempted to adjust a task definition for many special cases, and thus gradually increase the complexity at the cost of maintainability. In an operational solution, it is important not to exceed a certain degree of complexity and continuously keep maintainability in mind.*

8. COMPETITIVE ADVANTAGES

Rather than competing, the courts of law strive to handle their cases without unreasonable delays, and they work hard to ensure that the society in general maintains its respect for the courts, so the courts can remain the principal choice for conflict resolution, producing undisputed decisions. LOVISA has contributed significantly by making the case proceedings predictable and making the courts able to handle an increasing case load and case complexity. Even without having precise quantitative data, court officials have unofficially stated that the courts would have been completely jammed had the LOVISA system not streamlined the courts' case management in the way it does.

To maintain the services, LOVISA's rule and process definitions must be kept up-to-date with new and changed legislation. Having done that, it serves as an efficient and effective distributor of practical work support for new legislation and other process improvements.

LOVISA has gained the serious attention and interest of several foreign judicial branches in the European Union. The NCA is engaged as advisors to court administrations in other European countries, and their experience with rolling out a nationwide court ACM system is part of the attraction. The fact that it can be adapted to other legislations and languages is an advantage in this respect.

9. TECHNOLOGY

The task templates, worklists and task support functionality and engine, rule engine, work folders, xml terminologies and code- and relations-framework were implemented using a complete ACM framework developed for and used within the Norwegian public sector during the past 15 years. In LOVISA, this ACM framework was used in its Java Platform Enterprise Edition version.

10. THE TECHNOLOGY AND SERVICE PROVIDERS

Computas AS is an employee-owned Norwegian IT consulting company with around 220 consultants, which provides services and solutions for business processes and co-work. Computas AS has delivered numerous work process support applications to the Norwegian public sector and private enterprises, based on the ACM framework FrameSolutions™.

FrameSolutions™ currently has more than 100,000 users, and handles an annual cash flow of around 50 billion NOK. IT solutions based on FrameSolutions™ provide work process support and task support resulting in higher efficiency and quality in organizational processes. FrameSolutions™ is a framework for realizing bespoke process-centered case management solutions.

Assembled and authored by Thomas Bech Pettersen, Steinar Carlsen, Gunnar John Coll, Margit Matras, Tove Gråsletten Moen and Helle Frisak Sem, Computas AS.

Texas Office of the Attorney General Crime Victim Services Division, USA
Nominated by IBM

EXECUTIVE SUMMARY / ABSTRACT

The Office of the Attorney General's (OAG) Crime Victim Services Division (CVSD) legacy workflow system was implemented in 1999 to replace a paper file processing system. Victims of violent crimes in Texas can apply for eligibility for the Crime Victims' Compensation Program, which pays medical and other bills related to the crime.

All aspects of the existing system were now unsupportable by current vendors and were becoming increasingly unstable. Due to the aging infrastructure, poor architecture, and unsupported software versions, the current system was dangerously close to failure. A software change and new approach were critical to continue meeting the CVSD statutory functions. Failure to implement or improperly implementing the project could result in a delay in processing claims for victims of crime in Texas. This could also negatively impact legislatively-mandated measures, which could put future state and federal funding in jeopardy.

The OAG is using adaptive case management (ACM) to manage the victim application process, eligibility determination, case management, medical bill tracking, and the appeals procedure. The case view of the victim within the ACM solution provides knowledge workers a 360-degree view of a victim's case, with access to all received documentation and case history. Knowledge workers and other program staff can initiate pre-defined and ad hoc tasks, with email or workflow notifications to task assignees. Managers can monitor and adjust workloads, and view program productivity through reports to the individual user level. This is a cloud infrastructure deployment of ACM. Phase II of the project will include replacement of a legacy mainframe application and a potential expansion of social networking capabilities.

OVERVIEW

CVSD and the OAG Information Technology Support Division (ITS) jointly developed business and software requirements in order to implement a content management system from the selected vendor. ITS was responsible for security, operations, architecture, and development of system process requirements. CVSD was the business customer responsible for the details of the claims processing cycle. Oversight of the project was shared between ITS and CVSD management, with the final OAG approvals provided by executive sponsors.

Business Goal/Objective	Description
Upgrade Hardware/Software	Renewal and/or upgrade of all software and hardware.
Software Compatibility	Restore software compatibility with existing tools lost by using current version of workflow software.
Disaster Recovery	Increased Disaster Recovery capabilities.
Enhanced Efficiencies	Enhanced operational and system efficiencies that will improve production after initial adjustment period
Additional Flexibility	Additional supportability and flexibility to make administrative changes to the workflow.
Maximize Security	Maximize security of personal data involved in the claims management process.

The primary requirement was for a proposal that addressed the immediate needs to replace the existing document workflow management system based upon an enterprise solution that would provide the potential for additional efficiencies. Key critical success factors were:

- Hardware and software is available from the vendor on time
- Case file migration of legacy data will be completed on time and within budget constraints
- Project completed on time before end of support for legacy system

Key constraints to the project:

- Resource Availability: vendor and OAG resources with a particular skill set are required.
- Existing Budget: CVSD could only execute within available budget.
- Procurement: Timely procurement was required.
- External factors: Changes in federal and state laws or rules had to be considered while the project was active.

After reviewing proposals, a vendor was selected. Project managers from ITS and the vendor were assigned and provided the day to day project coordination. The selected vendor began validation of the OAG identified requirements in February 2012. This process included not only the validation of the needed solution to replace the legacy system, but the establishment of a foundation for continued improvements in subsequent phases of the project. The vendor-proposed solution included not only the replacement of the legacy system, but in a concept new to the OAG, an adaptive case management cloud-hosted solution with production, development, and test environments. The solution was adaptive in the sense that it provided the flexibility to support the unpredictability in some of our workflow processes and interactions. This unpredictability was very burdensome with our manual processes. Also, the cloud-hosting component offered better reliability, security and a path for future innovation.

To validate the OAG requirements, the vendor interviewed key staff at each level of management and each functional team in the current business process. Detailed process maps for each business process were created that included both visual and descriptive representations (i.e. maps). These maps were reviewed and discussed both in individual business groups and in multiple managerial levels to ascertain completeness and accuracy. The implementation team also used the actual ACM tool to model the potential environment and this allowed users to visualize and identify additional requirements. Only after the requirements were fully developed and agreed upon was work begun on the detailed implementation plan.

While the business process requirements were validated, the vendor and OAG staff developed the document conversion and transfer process. This was a phased process with a primary document conversion period and subsequent incremental conversions to capture current work in process. Over 3,100,000 documents, 750,000 cases and 700,000 bills were downloaded, converted, and uploaded to the cloud production environment.

At the end of requirements analysis phase, work began on the detailed process maps in collaboration with CVSD staff. The adaptive case management solution was moved to the test environment and tested extensively by both vendor and CVSD.

Upon completion of user acceptance testing, final document and workflow transfers were completed. From award of contract to vendor to go live which included migration of existing data, movement to a cloud solution, and creation of a new system, the project was completed in just under 13 months.

BUSINESS CONTEXT

A legacy workflow and imaging system existed, but had reached the end of its support cycle with incompatibility issues with current versions of software and hardware. All aspects of the system were unsupported by the vendors. The system had to be replaced, and the replacement had to be near seamless in order to continue to provide statutorily required services to victims in Texas.

THE KEY INNOVATIONS

The implementation of the adaptive case management solution has improved the processes used by CVSD knowledge workers and the speed and quality of work outcomes.

4.1 Business

To process cases, CVSD interacts with several key stakeholders including, among others:

- Crime victims
- Crime victims' families
- Crime victim advocates
- Law enforcement agencies
- Service providers (healthcare, funeral, counseling, etc.).

Processing an application begins with the receipt of the application plus supporting documentation. Additional documentation is required throughout the lifecycle of a crime victim's case. Requirements for documentation present a challenge to CVSD knowledge workers in that documentation does not all arrive at CVSD together. Staff must track received documentation, request missing documentation, and track those requests. All staff must have access to the status of a case as well as the status of related documentation and tasks. In addition, statutory deadlines for the completion of service milestones add to the urgency of processing cases.

The legacy system was unable to provide CVSD staff a consolidated way to view case and document information. Notifications for tasks to be completed could only be sent manually and applied to the case as a whole instead of to any individual document, process, or task associated with the case. Security governing staff access to cases and documents in the legacy system was not tracked, was not integrated with enterprise security solutions, and was no longer compliant with enterprise security standards.

The adaptive case management solution fulfilled the requirements missed by the legacy system by providing a consolidated, secure view of cases and case documents. When a victim calls about his/her application, a service provider calls about a payment, or law enforcement faxes a requested report, CVSD staff can now respond immediately. The ACM solution automates notifications and the routing of tasks based on business rules and integrates with enterprise security applications. This case management platform also provides for improved reporting, content analytics and trend analyses relative to the workload processing as well as the nature of the crime victim services required.

4.2 Case Handling

Prior to ACM, cases were not entered into the system until all documentation arrived to the Central Records office. This meant that no one outside of the Central Records office had access to information about a case while documentation was still being gathered.

The ACM solution allows cases to be entered even though CVSD has not received all the required documents. This is helpful for the staff outside Central Records as they determine eligibility and investigate related and potentially duplicate case submissions. It also brings to light data about the status of cases, which is important for service-level and productivity reporting purposes.

Prior to ACM, cases were assigned to staff for eligibility determination based on the manager's best estimate of staff workloads. With the ACM solution, business rules drive the assignment of cases, including staff availability, case type, and the degree of relatedness of a new case to existing cases.

With the legacy system, eligibility determinations that needed management review could, without diligent efforts, fall through the cracks or not be processed according to service-level goals. With ACM, the automatic routing of cases to the next step in the process mitigates this risk. Recipients of tasks within the ACM solution are immediately aware of the added item and can sort work by multiple factors, including due date. Reminder notifications and automated task escalations keep work from being overlooked. In addition, the system allows for ad hoc tasks and requests to be added to the workflow. This dynamic routing capability provides the knowledge workers with the flexibility to include new steps and approaches in resolving any case issues.

Prior to ACM, if a CVSD knowledge worker left the agency, the system administrator would create an automated script or manually reassign individually all of that person's tasks and change the security (again, individually) on all cases and related documents. With the ACM solution, case reassignments can be performed by the knowledge worker's manager without IT intervention. This can be performed on as many cases at a time as desired. This additional flexibility of the ACM system provided the benefit of being able to deploy and modify the case management application faster than previous solutions. Security is managed at the enterprise level and is role-based; meaning that replacing a staff member is done once through the enterprise standard address library.

4.3 Organization & Social

The primary organizational impact was the more robust and comprehensive role played by the case workers. The new ACM solution provided information in a more timely and complete method. This allowed the knowledge workers to be more responsive and have greater detail on the status of the case when communicating with victims and other social services organizations.

HURDLES OVERCOME

Management

The management team understood that for at least the first few months of the system rollout, the processing productivity of the team would be lower than normal. The management team appropriately set the end user expectations and those of senior management about the anticipated drop in initial productivity. With this shared understanding throughout the organization, the division anticipated appropriately the patience and support it needed to adjust to the new system. Initially, the division also chose a historically lower volume claims period to cutover to the new system. Management also implemented contingency plans for unplanned system down periods. When possible, during slow or down periods, management temporarily implemented manual processing tasks or conducted additional training.

Business

Since this was the first phase of a potentially 3-phase rollout, one of the key challenges was integrating this new solution with the current systems. This case management solution still had to interface with the existing mainframe system. In phase 2, the mainframe functionality will be incorporated into this solution. However, for approximately the next 12 – 18 months of operation, we had to determine the best approach to scope the functionality of the new solution and remain consistent with the current mainframe functions. Ultimately, this new case management system will be the official system of record.

Organization Adoption

To facilitate organizational adoption and increase user acceptance of the new system, the implementation team employed several strategies:

- There was significant involvement of the end users and their management in the design of the new processes. Detailed interviews, workshops and design reviews were held throughout the design phase. The implementation team used an online library of flow charts, swimlane diagrams and supplemental notes for the user team to review and approve.
- Several rounds of system and end user testing were held. Initially, there was a representative group of "super users" identified to be involved in over three months of systems testing which involved multiple iterations of testing and re-testing the application functionality. After the system tests were completed, two phases of user acceptance testing were held. This user acceptance testing involved all of the designated end users. The first phase was an initial acceptance test followed by a second phase of re-testing and final validation.
- Prior to and during the testing cycles, the team also conducted multiple end user and train-the-trainer instruction sessions. Working with the management team, great efforts were made by the implementation team to ensure that the training was relevant to the various user roles.
- The implementation team was also on-hand during the first days of production system "go live". The implementation team analysts were

available to assist any user requiring help with the new system functions. The training lab also remained available during the first week of production to allow for supplemental instruction.

BENEFITS

6.1 Cost Savings / Time Reductions

There are numerous cost and time-saving benefits associated with the new system. These include:

- Lower long-term operating costs using the cloud-based platform vs. a traditional capital-expensed system.
- Faster time to initiate a case since this new system supports beginning a claim process with only partial documentation and allowing additional documents to be added later.
- Improved allocation and utilization of claims processing resources because the case management system provides a comprehensive view of the workflow process and workload status.

Overall, these savings provide the ability to manage all cases with increased insight and opportunity for continuous operational improvements.

6.2 Quality Improvements

The operational quality improvements provided by using this adaptive case management solution include:

- A consolidated and comprehensive view of the all the relevant documentation related to a crime victim claim.
- The ability initially to capture and properly amend new data and documents throughout the life of the claim servicing.
- The ability to dynamically monitor and manage the claim processing volumes for distinct work groups within the division. Management can now see real-time activity of the claim processing volumes and allocate the division resources accordingly.
- Eliminating potential loss of paper-based information.
- Comprehensive audit trails for improved compliance, error-handling and resolution.
- Improved workflow management and tracking allows users to increase their ability to handle multiple claims simultaneously and decrease wait times.
- Better tracking of workflow processes which allow management to evaluate and improve the division's ability to meet service level targets and other key performance indicators.
- Workflow management and standardization that increases efficiency and enforces the use of best practices and policies.
- The system also facilitates ad-hoc workflow routing and modifications which improve the user's ability to better handle exceptions and unique case circumstances.
- This system and platform also provide the ability in subsequent phases to increase access to external partners and individual victims.

Best Practices, Learning Points and Pitfalls

7.1 Best Practices and Learning Points

Some of the best practices and lessons learned from this deployment included:

- ✓ *Ensuring senior management involvement and commitment to the project.*

- ✓ *Ensuring a high level of involvement and participation from the end users in the system design.*

- ✓ *Proactively managing the expectations of management and the users prior to issues occurring.*

- ✓ *Allocating a significant amount of time to user testing and user acceptance and supporting that with appropriate and relevant training.*

- ✓ *Using a user-friendly, online system for issue tracking and resolution in the design, testing and production deployment stages. This system greatly facilitated issue capture as well as real-time progress reporting.*

The Technology and Service Providers

The primary solution software for this adaptive case management solution was provided by the IBM Enterprise Content Management (ECM) software group (www.ibm.com/software/ecm). The software solution is known as the IBM Case Manager. It is a comprehensive advanced case management solution which also integrates with a document management repository, the IBM FileNet Content Manager.

The solution also used document capture software from a 3rd party vendor that was already implemented in the OAG environment. The document capture function was primarily the scanning and storage of the incoming victim claim data.

Adjacent Technologies, Inc. (www.adjacent-tech.com) was the system installation and development consultant used for this project. Adjacent was responsible for developing and deploying the entire system. Adjacent also provides the cloud hosting platform for the solution and the ongoing support and maintenance for the product via a multi-year agreement.

U.S. Department of Housing and Urban Development (HUD), USA

Nominated by AINS, Inc., USA

1. EXECUTIVE SUMMARY / ABSTRACT

The U.S. Department of Housing and Urban Development (HUD) is responsible for overseeing national policy and programs to address the nation's housing and community development needs, and for enforcing fair housing laws. Since 2011, approximately 10,000 staff members at HUD have relied on a highly flexible Correspondence Tracking System (CTS) to facilitate the processing of Executive Correspondence related to department-wide programs. The CTS application is built on a dynamic, configurable case management platform that was subsequently leveraged vertically within the organization to configure applications for a wide range of non-core Human Resources (HR) business process pain points. In this way, HUD was able to quickly and cost-effectively build several mission-support case management applications under a unified platform - with minimal custom software coding.

CTS, used by HUD's Executive Secretariat staff and Correspondence unit staff in all Program Offices, enables electronic collaboration across HUD for generation and approval of correspondence related to inquiries, complaints, and other matters. The system delivers routine reports on workload metrics, providing visibility to HUD managers for improved decision-making. CTS ensures that HUD's responses to controlled correspondence, including that signed by the Secretary and Deputy Secretary, are timely and accurate by creating a context for optimal performance from workers who no longer have to waste time on rote tasks such as repetitive data entry.

The HR Case Management System (HR CMS) applications bring transparency to HR operations, provide better communication, reduce opportunities for delay, allow supervisors to monitors workload, ensure accountability, and consolidate 20 disparate systems. The HR CMS is under the purview of the Office of the Chief Human Capital Officer (OCHCO) and has been configured for a variety of HR management functions such as Employee Relations/Labor Relations, Reasonable Accommodations, and Workers' Compensation.

The configurable platform approach to solving organizational case management problems has allowed HUD to consolidate legacy systems and save money on O&M; deliver new workflow-driven HR applications within 6 months from contract inception (exceeding expectations); and demonstrate the ability to make application changes in a timely manner without impacting other systems. To address their business process needs, HUD had previously required three separate contracts costing more than $1M per year, whereas it now relies on one contractor with less than $150K per year for maintenance.

2. OVERVIEW

HUD's mission is to strengthen America's communities by improving the quality and affordability of housing and protecting consumers through the enforcement of fair housing laws. In support of their operational business processes, HUD was in need of a solution to enable correspondence management and HR case management. CTS and HR CMS were configured using the same dynamic case management platform technology, a cost-effective approach to building case management applications across the organization.

CTS facilitates critical correspondence management tasks for the Office of the Executive Secretariat, while HR CMS consists of eight applications with collaborative portal capabilities for a variety of non-core human resource management processes. The goal of these systems is to empower technology-assisted people-centric interactions, providing workflow support and automation of repetitive tasks and also facilitating case ownership at a holistic level, ad hoc decision-making, and a collaborative environment.

3. Business Context

In support of its mission operations, HUD interacts on a daily basis with a wide range of contacts, including constituents, Congressional staff and Congressmen, lobbyists, the White House, and other federal departments and agencies. Therefore, HUD must adequately handle thousands of items of correspondence in numerous forms, each of which may follow a unique case workflow requiring specific approvals or concurrences depending on who an item is addressed to and its subject matter. Former manual processes created a set of challenges, including:

- The absence of status transparency and visibility into correspondence processes at the macro level made it difficult to identify workflow bottlenecks and plan ahead.
- Inadequate reporting and tracking of the workflow led to weak accountability for missed deadlines and inadequate handling of correspondence cases.
- The lack of facilitation or guidance by the existing system(s) resulted in unacceptably inconsistent and delayed responses.

Starting in late 2005 HUD implemented an enterprise office system modernization project for its records and document management (ERM) systems. In 2010, a newer, hosted case management system was leveraged enterprise-wide to enhance existing capabilities and provide greater flexibility to handle multiple application types.

The first phase of this effort was to modernize HUD's CTS. To this end, HUD implemented a complete system integration lifecycle solution for the Electronic Records Management and Correspondence Tracking System (ERM-CTS). As part of this effort, HUD correspondence business process workflows were restructured and streamlined. A Freedom of Information Act (FOIA) management solution based on the same technology was also implemented to expedite FOIA request processing in compliance with federal requirements.

The CTS was implemented to assist HUD's Executive Secretariat in its mission to ensure that HUD's responses to controlled correspondence (including that signed by the Secretary and Deputy Secretary) are responded to in a timely, accurate, and professional manner. The CTS handles multiple types of correspondence, including, but not limited to, those from: Boy/Girl Scouts of America, Cabinet-level staff, Congressional staff, elected officials, government officials, public interest groups, and the White House.

Meanwhile, HUD's HR department was facing growing challenges due to the lack of a centralized system for managing multiple HR business processes. Previously there were over 20 information technology systems being used by HUD to perform

HR operations. However, these systems were not meeting the needs of HUD's human capital programs. In fact, some managers created their own internal systems to avoid the potential errors or delays they feared would occur if they relied on the existing systems. In addition, many HR processes were to a large degree performed manually; much of the logging, tracking, and reporting of cases was handled by going through hard copy files and emails, or by using employee solutions such as Excel spreadsheets stored on SharePoint or on a shared drive or SharePoint list. The proliferation of siloed, stand-alone IT and manual systems led to process gaps, including:

- unclear accountability for critical outcomes
- inconsistent processes (with failures at key hand-offs leading to untimely delays)
- inaccurate data entered into the system
- non-compliance with internal and external policies and procedures.

These weaknesses caused delayed and "hurried" hiring actions, poor information flow for managerial decision-making, case processing errors, and, ultimately, unhappy staff, users, and customers. Therefore, HUD's Business Modernization Initiative (BMI) was designed to focus on defining, implementing, and integrating a common, enterprise-wide end-to-end HR system. The HR CMS is part of the larger HR end-to-end solution and was implemented by leveraging HUD's existing investment in the configurable case management platform used for the CTS application.

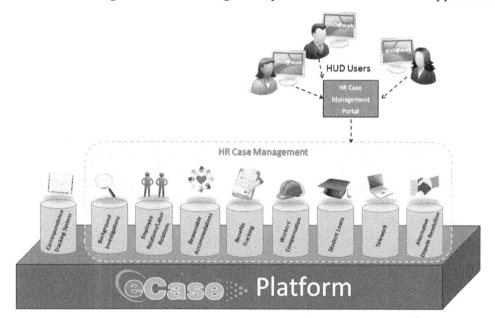

The primary purpose of the HR CMS is to track the status of a particular business process, such as hiring, benefits, reasonable accommodations, employee relations and labor relations, Pending Action Request (PAR) processing, training status, or other services that include tasks being processed by multiple parties, multiple approval channels, or transfer of responsibilities. The goals of the system are to bring transparency to HR operations, foster collaboration among staff and managers, improve service delivery, reduce opportunities for delay, and allow supervisors to monitor staff workloads.

4. THE KEY INNOVATIONS

4.1 Business

Improving the Consistency and Quality of Correspondence

To expedite communication, correspondence templates (e.g., email, letters) for frequently used boilerplate correspondence were configured within the CTS to automate several repetitive manual correspondence processes in order to free up HUD staff to focus on content and messaging, rather than on the mechanics of production. These templates also reduced the risks associated with inconsistent communication.

Whether a constituent complaint or Congressional mail, cases are not just units of information but also the human processes that initiate, produce, request, deliver, and engage with that information. As more comprehensive case ownership is encouraged over rote task fulfillment, collaboration, coordination, and consultation become increasingly important. The workflow becomes less of a point-to-point line of processing and more of a network of communication and reciprocity. Case discussion threads built into the CTS enhanced communication by increasing the awareness and group discussion regarding case matters without disturbing the more formal correspondence flow. By doing so, HUD greatly improved the efficiency of correspondence with its customers.

Utilizing a Portal for an Easier End-User Experience

To further unify HR services, HR CMS utilizes a shared end-user portal for access to each application, giving agency staff a consistent and intuitive interface and improving the experience for HUD staff interacting with the HR department. The end-user simply accesses the HR portal from their browser, fills out the electronic form for their HR request, and then submits it electronically. Key case information needs only to be entered once; this information will then auto-populate in relevant fields of the CMS during the remainder of the case life-cycle. As the form moves from the employee's supervisor for approval and to the HR department for final processing, all relevant information is tracked and stored for real-time analysis, report generation, and delivery. With an easy, centralized means of communication and information-gathering, HUD HR staff are better able to focus on meeting the needs of HUD employees, rather than paper-shuffling, email exchanges, and repetitive form data entry.

4.2 Case Handling

Conquering Case Complexity with Flexible Workflows and Process Visibility

The CTS serves as an interface between the information contained in correspondence cases, HUD staff, and HUD's contacts. However, due to the broad range of incoming correspondence types, HUD needed an agile platform that could capture widely varying interactions, often in an ad hoc or customized (and continually customizable) fashion, rather than a system that handled cases via predefined workflows. "1-2-3-A-B-C" type processing (usually associated with predictable standard workflows) derails when faced with a complex case, coming to a halt as complications must be dealt with outside of the system. In contrast, a dynamic system is flexible enough to accommodate complexity, easily adapting and restructuring itself "on the fly" to support parallel workflows, concurrencies, and ad hoc processes. At a personnel level, a dynamic system empowers workers to use their subject matter expertise so that exceptions can be handled with judgment.

In a straightforward example correspondence case, a piece of request mail is received, a correspondence technician scans it into the system as a case, a specialist processes the letter into the system as a case, and a technical representative evaluates the request and sends it to the appropriate manager for approval prior to the final response to the initial requester. But workflows are never consistently this simple. The request, for a multitude of reasons, might be disapproved at any step in the workflow and sent backwards in the process. Or the request might be completely rejected based on a failure to meet standard requirements. Or important people in the process might be unavailable, the approval process might change depending on the complexity or size of the transaction, deadlines might be modified, special circumstances might arise, exceptions might need to be made, steps might need to be bypassed or overridden, or bottlenecks might clog the system and slow the process down. In short, even a "simple" request brings with it the potential for great complexity, which means that the workflow cannot proceed linearly step-by-step when processes for approval, rejection, change, deadlines, exemptions, and exceptions add unpredictability.

As a result, the CTS needed to not only track and follow a correspondence case as it moves through the workflow, but to manage and maximize the human processes that interact with the case at each step. The CTS offers visibility into workflows and the flexibility to manage ad hoc situations. Deadlines can be changed along with relevant reminder alerts, approval requirements can be created with automatic re-routing, and ad hoc workflows can be created for special circumstances and exceptions. In addition, users can designate secondary users so that if the primary user sets her status as "unavailable", her cases will be re-routed to her selected "back-up" user for processing.

In addition, the CTS was configured to track and report on all actions associated with any workflow, down to the level of which specific user accessed a case folder and when. The system's reporting capability enhances the agility of the HUD enterprise to provide real-time information on where and how resources have been allocated, allowing HUD management to react and proceed appropriately and quickly to any exceptional circumstance.

For the HR CMS, a "case" is an interaction between a HUD employee seeking HR services and the HR staff. One of the HR applications in the CMS system is "Reasonable Accommodations," which is a service to provide equal opportunity employment for all Federal agency employees, including persons with disabilities. Employees submit reasonable accommodation requests for needs such as ergonomic keyboards, back support, and other items to ensure an optimal work environment. Federal agencies must produce a weekly report on time and funds spent on RA cases as well as produce a quarterly report on total case assignments by RA specialist, closed cases by RA specialist, and total case assignments closed. In addition, agencies must process ad hoc requests from unions regarding RA processing and respond to litigation data calls.

When HUD used manual processes to track this activity, it became extremely difficult and labor intensive to produce reports and respond to ad hoc requests. The CMS, however, automatically tracks all relevant metrics within the system by request, employee, supervisor, and HR analyst. The system's reporting module allows any HR analyst to instantly generate these reports, as well as their own custom reports, at any time. Further, it allows the agency to easily identify and address process bottlenecks.

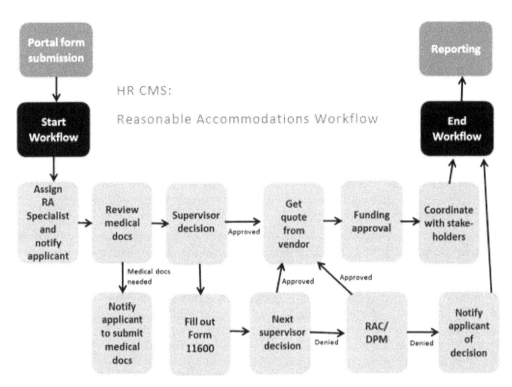

HR CMS:

Reasonable Accommodations Workflow

4.3 Organization & Social

Enabling Cross-Program Information Flow and Collaboration

The CTS and HR CMS at HUD provide robust information flow regarding case status metrics (such as all overdue cases) and user actions in the system. With the HR CMS, by unifying disparate HR process applications on a single undergirding platform HUD's HR department is able to gain real-time visibility *across* the HR department. This is critical to facilitate organizational decision-making so that the department can better forecast its human capital needs for hiring decisions.

Also, by providing full workflow tracking capabilities not found with stand-alone systems or manual processing, HUD employees are empowered to engage with cases due to the increased visibility throughout the length and breadth of the case lifecycle. Employees can better manage their resources with dashboard views into their workloads and pending/overdue tasks, and with features such as deadline alerts.

For HUD's HR employees, the full benefits of the platform are found when the end-user interacts *between* HR applications. For example, the Workers Compensation application is accessed through the same portal and interface as Reasonable Accommodation, reducing employee training time and centralizing access for end-users to these HR services. This benefit is even further realized for the HR analyst, who will use the same interface, workflow processing module, and reporting module for analysis of all the HR services in CMS.

5. HURDLES OVERCOME

5.1 Management

Prior to centralizing correspondence and non-core HR processes, HUD faced a scattered range of disparate IT systems and manual processes, which did not provide any process oversight. With case management applications configured on a single platform for processing and tracking, managerial oversight and metrics reporting were built-in, creating accountability and driving performance by monitoring the "pulse" of the system.

5.2 Business

At the start of both projects, the Executive Secretariat office and the HR department were faced with inefficient, unstandardized, or even non-documented process workflows and standard operating procedures. Both projects used the proof of concept phase for the CTS and HR CMS projects to consolidate, streamline, and standardize existing workflows and to define new and more efficient workflows as needed before incorporating them into the new systems.

HUD used the proof of concept phase for CTS and later enterprise implementation of the complete solution as an opportunity to streamline their functional workflow process, identifying numerous bottlenecks. Existing workflows at the Executive Secretariat's office were analyzed in order to create more efficient, standardized workflows for six critical external correspondence types (Congressional, White House, Elected Official, Public Interest Groups, and Appropriate Action). In addition, over 38 correspondence case types were consolidated down to 16.

The same approach was taken with the implementation of the HR CMS; many of the HR modules did not have a documented process, so "discovery sessions" allowed users to define and standardize business processes before incorporating them into the new system.

5.3 Organization Adoption

To ensure user adoption of the CTS application, contractor staff provided end-user support that included providing periodic refresher training, scanning support and related scanning analysis, producing ad hoc reports and extracts, responding to trouble calls and ERM-CTS information requests, providing a liaison with HUD's IT production support staff, maintaining user IDs and security profiles for ERM-CTS users, and monitoring and providing general support for an ERM-CTS website. Support personnel monitored HUD's Service Tracking Action Resolution System (STARS) and responded to trouble tickets from ERM-CTS users. In addition to hands-on and WebEx training, short training videos were created and shared to improve the end-user learning experience.

With HR CTS, end-users were invited to multiple "discovery sessions" to allow them to be more comfortable with the new system. End-users were also provided access to the demo/test server so that they could be included in the development process.

6. BENEFITS

6.1 Cost Savings / Time Reductions

The CTS and HR CMS systems allow HUD staff to quickly assess and digest the influx of both correspondence and HR service information and then to act appropriately. By automating and tracking workflow processes from start to finish, these systems provide greatly improved process efficiency in both time and operational costs.

Further, because the underlying case management platform of HUD's CTS and HR CMS systems supports multiple, customizable applications concurrently, HUD is realizing significant savings potential by leveraging a single solution, rather than individually acquiring or custom-developing solutions specific to each business process. This is a non-traditional, agile approach to standing up successful applications quickly. The system is highly configurable to incorporate workflow changes without custom coding, providing flexibility for both easily adapting existing work-flows as needs and requirements change and for configuring additional applications as new business processes arise.

Where HUD previously required three separate contracts costing more than $1M per year, it now relies on one contractor and with costs less than $150K per year for maintenance.

The benefits of this case management platform are such that the U.S. Office of Management and Budget as well as General Services Administration (which sponsor Shared Services initiatives that promote reuse of IT solutions across the U.S. government) are assessing the platform because it improves case management, enables rapid development, and reduces O&M costs.

6.2 Quality Improvements

Visibility: The CMS and HR CTS systems provide visibility by tracking the entire workflow movement, providing color-coded status designations, an inbox and pending folders dashboard, and automated alerts. Both systems are configurable to track and report on all actions associated with any workflow, down to the level of which specific user accessed a case folder and when. This capability enhances the ability to discover where and how resources have been allocated, allowing staff to react and proceed appropriately and quickly.

Accountability and Transparency: The CMS and HR CTS systems improve organizational transparency with in-depth reporting capabilities, both ad hoc and standard. A down-to-the-second audit trail of user actions are stored as well, providing employee accountability. Managerial oversight is also provided with the ability to re-route cases for approval or rejection by supervisors.

Flexibility and Agility: The CMS and HR CTS systems are highly configurable and easily tailored to unique organizational needs, with a customizable user interface, fields, functionality, and reporting. They can handle exceptions, special circumstances, and new patterns with ease by supporting and encouraging custom, ad hoc, and parallel workflows, as well as standard workflows.

Versatility: The underlying configuration features of the CMS and HR CTS systems can be adapted for a vast array of organizational line of business purposes. This provides a cost-effective solution for replacing the accumulation of stand-alone IT systems and manual processes that proliferate as business needs arise and change.

Connectivity. Whether for correspondence responses or HR operations, "cases" should be regarded as more than simply a unit of information, but also the human processes that initiate, produce, request, deliver, and engage with that information. Collaboration, coordination, and consultation become increasingly important. The workflow becomes less of a point-to-point line of processing and more of a network of communication and reciprocity. The CMS and HR CTS systems improve collaboration on cases by offering features such as discussion threads, memo templates, version control, task assignation, comment boxes, and integration with document management and payment solutions.

7. BEST PRACTICES, LEARNING POINTS AND PITFALLS

7.1 Best Practices and Learning Points

✓ *Business processes might differ on the details, but cases have common functional needs. Leverage technology solutions that can provide common case management functionality while still offering the configurability to tailor case types according to process-specific workflows and terminology.*

✓ When implementing new case management technology, use the planning and research phase as an opportunity to define and streamline your existing business processes and Standard Operating Procedures.

✓ Open up information flows with a robust reporting capability. Managerial visibility into case management workflows is critical for operational success, so that processes can be measured, assessed, and restructured if needed.

✓ View case management with a holistic lens. Each department might have its own set of business processes, but find ways to leverage visibility and collaboration across and between "silos."

7.2 Pitfalls

✗ Don't lock yourself into a rigid, pre-defined workflow. Flexibility is key. We live in a dynamic world and your case management approach needs the configurability to account for future process changes.

✗ Don't make the case management solution attempt to solve all type of business challenges – e.g., those associated with core financial management processes.

8. COMPETITIVE ADVANTAGES

One Platform, Many Applications

As with any large government organization, HUD manages a staggering number of unique business processes in support of their mission operations. Acquiring or custom-developing individual applications to automate each specific business process creates a bulky, expensive to maintain IT environment for agencies. Whether a case is related to White House Mail or Employee Onboarding, "cases" have common functional needs, such as approvals, task assignments, deadline alerts, form processing, and reporting. Wherever possible, government organizations should leverage technology that can power a variety of executive and mission applications with a consistent user interface and common case management functionality, while still maintaining the flexibility to configure workflows and terminology according to each specific business process.

The platform undergirding CTS and HR CMS enables IT departments such as HUD to delivery maximum value for its investment- the more solutions the tool is used for, the less costly and less time it takes to deliver each one. In today's shrinking budgets, government IT departments can't afford to custom build workflow applications for each unique case type. By leveraging a single solution to provide multiple case applications, end-users learn one tool and then can support operations across many different workflows and processes with that same knowledge. As a result, each deployment requires less training and support as it moves into the enterprise.

Comprehensive, End-to-End Capabilities

The platform tightly integrates workflow, forms, and document and/or content management; provides a portal for collaboration within the enterprise, between partners, and with the public; produces in-depth reports and graphs; and offers a down-to-the-second user action audit trail.

Low-Cost, Rapid Development

These advantages are further realized because, by providing easy-to-configure apps with productive, efficient user involvement, reusable tools for forms and interface design, extensive use of document templates, and minimal reliance on expensive developers, the CTS and HR CMS projects provide a model for cost-effective, rapid case management solution development and implementation.

9. TECHNOLOGY

HUD's CTS and HR CMS are built on the eCase platform. eCase provides a highly flexible case management framework that can power a wide range of workflow-driven business processes. eCase's innovation is in its configurability; unlike traditional development platforms, the platform's powerful configuration options allow agencies to manage diverse business processes and quickly adapt to change – in their processes or in their IT environment – without custom coding. This approach helps agencies produce or replace ad hoc workflow applications under a single unified platform to streamline architecture, decreasing O&M costs and reducing time to upgrade multiple applications. In addition, the eCase platform has well-defined APIs to provide ease of integration with other applications, providing further flexibility.

eCase: Architecture

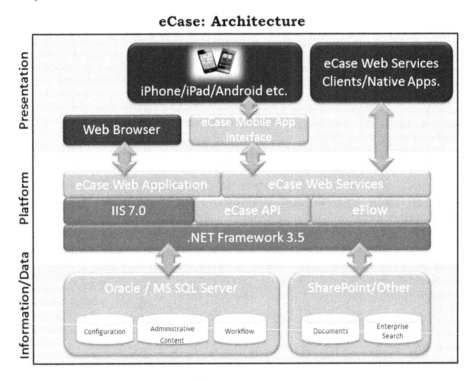

10. THE TECHNOLOGY AND SERVICE PROVIDERS

eCase is a product of AINS Inc., a small IT business specializing in innovative solutions for Enterprise Information Management (EIM). Based on EIM industry demand and tailored to customer-specified features, AINS has developed a family of advanced COTS solutions for case management, with integrated document and records management, electronic Freedom of Information Act management, workflow management, and related functions. eCase is built on case management technology that is currently used by over 150 client organizations with over 20,000 users around the world, all of which are fully supported and maintained by AINS. eCase is both hosted and supported at AINS as well as deployed and supported at client sites.

UBS Bank, Worldwide

Nominated by Whitestein Technologies

1. EXECUTIVE SUMMARY / ABSTRACT

Our submission is based on the successful adoption of Adaptive Case Management by UBS Wealth, a division of UBS Bank. UBS is enhancing their global operations with client-centric collaboration, operational visibility, adaptive process improvement, through the 'PM1' portfolio management suite built with the Living System's Process Suite (LSPS).

LSPS is designed for cases in which adaptive changes to data state are made by a goal-oriented software controller. This ensures that cases evolve in coordination with events and situational change in order to adapt in real-time to a goal-focused execution path.

In partnership with Whitestein, PM1 was built by Expersoft Systems, a global vendor of Portfolio and Wealth Management applications for retail and private banks, independent wealth managers, and asset management providers. LSPS provided Expersoft with the ability to model a comprehensive set of goal-oriented processes that form the core of their portfolio management system.

PM1 with LSPS integrates and extends UBS' complex ecosystem of banking applications, supporting the achievement of transversal goals within a flexible, integrated, and intuitive environment for both the bank and their customers. Each case follows a goal-driven pathway defined by the customer's specific objectives, while meeting both the unique local requirements that vary between regions, yet ensuring that each region complies with the bank's global goals and policies.

2. OVERVIEW

UBS AG is a Swiss global financial services company headquartered in Basel and Zürich, Switzerland. It provides investment banking, asset management and wealth management services for private, corporate and institutional clients worldwide, as well as retail clients in Switzerland. The name "UBS" was originally an abbreviation for the Union Bank of Switzerland, but it ceased to be a representational abbreviation after the bank's 1998 merger with Swiss Bank Corporation. The company traces its origins to 1856, when the earliest of its predecessor banks was founded.

UBS is the largest bank in Switzerland, operating in more than 50 countries with about 63,500 employees globally as of 2012. It is considered the world's largest manager of private wealth assets, with over CHF2.2 trillion in invested assets, a leading provider of retail banking and commercial banking services in Switzerland.

UBS is enhancing their global wealth management operations with client-centric collaboration, operational visibility, adaptive process improvement, through the 'PM1' portfolio management suite built with the Living System's Process Suite (LSPS). In partnership with Whitestein Technologies, PM1 was built by Expersoft Systems, a global vendor of Portfolio and Wealth Management applications for retail and private banks, independent wealth managers, and asset management providers. LSPS provided Expersoft with the ability to model a comprehensive set of goal-oriented processes that form the core of their portfolio management system.

PM1 with LSPS integrates and extends UBS' complex ecosystem of banking applications, supporting the achievement of transversal goals within a flexible, integrated, and intuitive environment for both the bank and their customers. Each case follows a goal-driven pathway defined by the customer's specific objectives, while meeting both the unique local requirements that vary between regions, yet ensuring that each region complies with the bank's global goals and policies.

3. Business Context

As the global economy begins to emerge from several years of economic crisis, UBS is embarking on a strategy to establish, and in some cases re-establish, presence in multiple global emerging markets spanning Latin America, MENA, and APAC. A component of this is launching a single, modular, client-centric front office platform for wealth management that can be deployed and integrated rapidly with any existing application infrastructure. The initial state in each market is this either greenfield or brownfield with a mixture of applications to be either preserved or obsoleted.

The emerging markets strategy demands software that is flexible and oriented toward managing clients as adaptive cases. Success of the emerging markets strategy will have an influence on the evolution of UBS strategy beyond emerging markets to established core markets.

4. The Key Innovations

4.1 Business

Wealth management is by definition a client-centric business where the focus of all activities is on building valued and sustainable relationships with individuals of high net wealth.

This new banking front- and middle- office solution is focused on automating the phases of client case management including prospecting (seeking new candidate clients), onboarding (transitioning a prospect into a bank client), and advisory (building an asset portfolio). This satisfies various needs including ensuring that the prospect/client is managed properly and efficiently, that staff tasking is focused on priority issues, and that regulatory and compliance issues are appropriately observed.

However, the key impact on business is derived from the solution's ability to optimize and govern the processing of client cases in terms of mandated and ad-hoc goals associated with prospect/client requirements, with local operational, performance, and compliance obligations (spanning multiple client cases), and with global corporate strategy. By actively combining these objective factors, differentiated market advantages are created which help UBS to attract key clients and establish long-lasting, sustainable relationships.

4.2 Case Handling

Cases are handled primarily by local user resources. Generically, Client Advisors handle individual cases, report to a 'Desk Head' and are supported in administrative duties by Client Advisor Assistants. However, this structure is variable according to location. Client Advisors are responsible for the lifetime of individual cases from prospecting through off-boarding. Client Advisor Assistants support one or more Client Advisors in performing certain tasks according to their right of access to client data.

Before the solution common working modality spanned a range of paper-based activities with various disconnected user interfaces onto legacy applications. Significant efficiency gains and improved comfort of use is achieved with the new unified front-office system that is built on a modern Java-based technology stack with tiered delineation between data, logic, and Web-client presentation. Comprehensive integration is supported at all levels, and separation of concerns ensures that different databases can be supported reducing the need for large scale data migration for brownfield deployments.

Managers at local, regional, and global offices have the ability to inspect ongoing cases according to their information security rights, and to influence the goals that drive case efficiency. For example, a regional manager can set a weighting factor on a goal to emphasize the necessity of accelerating onboarding cases for individuals of net wealth above a set threshold, with a specific domicile, and during a specific period of the year. This goal then directly influences case task distribution patterns, including optimizing task ordering to circumvent bottlenecks and increase work throughput.

With regard to client interaction, the new user interface supports ad-hoc annotations to client case history, collaborative decision making on case state to progress a workflow, attachment of documents associated with a case, access control for edit vs. view rights on client data, and more.

Real-time case reporting dashboards allow all stakeholders, including the client when appropriate, to monitor case progress and track all dependencies from a unified perspective.

4.3 Organization & Social

For many markets into which the solution is being deployed, the impact is a radical step-change in usage modality from working with a complex mixture of paper-based activities with legacy infrastructure, to a unified front-office interface that directly supports collaborative work. Feedback from users is universally positive as they are able to now flexibly manage prospect/client accounts throughout their entire lifecycle, working in close collaboration with colleagues.

In particular data annotations made by users allow client cases to automatically transition state or (shared) ownership, while ensuring that pertinent trace information is recorded for audit purposes. Moreover, the interface supports/case task delegation, escalation, and collaborative effort. The latter is assisted by integrated social chat widgets supporting dialog-based negotiation over how to resolve specific issues.

Tasks are assignable to individuals or role groups; the latter of which is dynamic according to authoritative administration. Tasks may be shared, and automatically shifted between user work queues according to measurable performance goals. Each user has task lists from which they can pick work items. Priorities are indicated, as is ownership and status. Work obligations are clearly specified in terms of who bears final responsibility for task completion.

Full email and mobile device support is integrated, including task completion via email when feasible and appropriate.

5. HURDLES OVERCOME

A central hurdle overcome was the efficient translation of business requirements into solution features. This was amplified by the necessity to meet requirements sourced from the needs of different deployment locations when seeking to build a unified, modular solution. Contributing to this was the identification of a common lexicon of business terminology and semantic mapping to regional differences.

Another major hurdle was achieving consensus on the overall solution approach. Once management approval for the global initiative was agreed the selection of solution was driven by various factors including an older incumbent use case and the significant attraction of business to the adaptive case management focus of the client-centric approach taken. IT was particularly positive due to the strongly integration-focused architecture and usage of new technology, including model-driven application design.

Lastly, a key challenge is presenting new technology, new user interfaces, and new collaborative work modalities, in such a way as to support the user in recognizing their own position as a stakeholder. This is a varying challenge across different cultures and strong local support is critical to achieving good results. User adoption is ongoing in many regions of the world, with response to the new solution being resoundingly positive.

6. Benefits

6.1 Cost Savings / Time Reductions

The solution improves efficiency in the organization of internal staffing resources around the management of individual clients. In particular activity transitions are faster and more seamless with consequent reductions in time spent on collaboration and task execution. Decisions related to compliance suitability, restriction checks, product matching, and other topics including approvals are considerably accelerated, more accurate, and auditable. Transparency is improved. Performance control is now central to the evolution of cases which enforces time/cost constraints and more efficient governance.

6.2 Increased Revenues

Creating a modular, adaptive, case-driven solution supports deployments that can be rapidly configured for specific regional requirements and variations such as those relating to regulatory compliance and language. This reduces capital investment in standing up new deployments, encourages reusability, and consequently provides a basis for improvement in operational margins.

Moreover, goal-driven governance and optimization of case management within and between regional banks significantly improves cost saving potential by encouraging more efficient task distribution and resource management while offering a better client experience that competing banks.

6.3 Quality Improvements

Users of the solution, e.g., client advisors and client advisor assistants, become more efficient in managing their client cases, in particular in terms of task distribution to balance workload and achieve improved prioritization, approval, and escalation management.

Automatic auditing of all actions performed by users provided full accountability and decision tracing. This is critical for ensuring verifiable, non-repudiable regulatory compliance.

Goal-driven governance provides measures and optimization control points not only related to the activities of individual cases, but across cases, and across offices spanning regions and global operations.

7. BEST PRACTICES, LEARNING POINTS AND PITFALLS

7.1 Best Practices and Learning Points

- ✓ *Delivering a modular solution requires that a principled approach is taken to configuration and deployment; particularly that opportunities to extend functionality are properly preserved.*
- ✓ *LSPS offers a modernization framework that allows the offset of legacy functionality with an efficient model-driven replacement value well in excess of 10:1. This incorporates the ability to manage logic at model level, rather than code level.*
- ✓ *In deployments where the solution operates alongside existing systems, best practice is to utilize LSPS as an integration framework spanning all systems, e.g., a user interface can unify access to multiple applications via integrated tabs, portlets, specialized dashboard widgets, etc.*
- ✓ *Non-standard functionality can, if required, be added ad-hoc onto individual cases, or groups of cases, using real-time transfer of model updates to execution contexts.*
- ✓ *Users may be enthusiastic about adopting the solution, but nevertheless need to be provided sufficient opportunity to properly adapt their working modality toward sharing tasks according to priority, workload, and the attainment of goal metrics.*

7.2 Pitfalls

- ✗ *Uptake must support both greenfield deployments, but most critically brownfield deployments where supporting migration from traditional work methods is critical to encourage a seamless transition.*
- ✗ *The definition of goals must be undertaken judiciously in order to avoid competing and conflicting goals when possible, although resolution mechanisms are available.*
- ✗ *The new solution encourages collaboration which implies the necessity of exposing work activities to co-workers. Any resistance to this change in modality must be offset through demonstration of efficiency gains and reduction in risk of error.*

8. COMPETITIVE ADVANTAGES

The global banking industry is seeking opportunities to reestablish credibility, with wealth divisions of banks competing to attract and retain high net wealth clients. A modern, client-centric approach to this is critical and the foundational principal driving the choice of LSPS built case management technology by UBS.

By encoding operational and governance goals into the performance of cases and spanning multiple cases at regional and global level, LSPS technology is helping to realize the true potential of ACM by connecting action with objective. This approach is new, and powerful when used to coordinate action across multiple levels or organization from team, through department, to inter-organizational value chains.

Sustaining established competitive advantage is achievable due to the solution design supporting rapid inclusion of new features, and (real-time) adaptation of current features, to meet the evolving needs of existing clients and new means to target and attract new clients, e.g., reaching out via new forms of communication media.

9. TECHNOLOGY

The solution is built with the Living System's Process Suite (LSPS) from Whitestein Technologies. LSPS is explicitly designed to manage cases in which adaptive changes to data state drive collaborative work streams; these changes are managed intelligently by a goal-oriented case controller. This mechanism ensures that cases evolve in coordination with events and situational change in order to adapt in real-time to a goal-focused execution path.

10. THE TECHNOLOGY AND SERVICE PROVIDERS

In partnership with Whitestein, PM1 was built by Expersoft Systems, a global vendor of Portfolio and Wealth Management applications for retail and private banks, independent wealth managers, and asset management providers.

Appendix

Author Appendix

ILIA BIDER

Lecturer and researcher at the department of Computer and System Sciences of Stockholm University and co-founder of IbisSoft AB, Sweden

Dr. Ilia Bider is Software Engineer, Business Analyst, IS-researcher and Teacher with long experience in several IT-related fields. He has MS in Electronic Engineering and PhD in Computer and System Sciences, and combined experience of over 30 years of research (in the fields of IS, SE, DB, and computational linguistics), and practical work (business analysis, and software design, coding, sales, and marketing) in five countries (Norway, Russia, Sweden, United Kingdom, and United States). Dr. Bider has published over 50 research papers as well as a considerable number of articles for practitioners. His main specialty is finding research topics in business practice, and testing research results in business practice. Dr. Bider is an inventor of the state-oriented approach to business process modeling and control that is based on the application of the conceptual ideas of the Mathematical system theory to the realm of business processes. This approach has been successfully tested in business analysis and software application development practice of IbisSoft and its partners. Dr. Bider puts a lot of effort in bridging the gap between the academics and practitioners.

STEINAR CARLSEN

Chief Engineer, Computas AS, Norway

Dr. Steinar Carlsen is a recognized Norwegian expert within business processes and workflow technology. He is a senior advisor specializing in adaptive case management, business process management, knowledge management, social technologies, with more than 20 years of experience in different approaches to the modelling of work processes. His focus is on realizing work support systems, as well as baselining "organizational implementation/enactment". Steinar has a background from applied research within business process modelling, enterprise modelling, enterprise architecture and requirements engineering. Steinar is the product owner of FrameSolutions™ - Computas AS' framework for realizing operational ACM solutions.

GUNNAR JOHN COLL

Senior Advisor, VP, Computas AS

Gunnar John Coll represents a behavioural approach to technology, organization and knowledge. He assists customers in corporate process initiatives, including knowledge management and organizational learning. His main area of work is where business process and human competence meet with new technology, to answer the need for change. He provides perspectives, facilitates and manages initiatives in close cooperation with customer's key personnel. Gunnar has more than 25 years of experience in IT projects related to organizational processes. Due to his combined background as a psychologist and an IT professional, he provides a complementary perspective on system development and organizational adoption.

LAYNA FISCHER

Publisher, Future Strategies Inc., USA

Ms Fischer is Editor-in-Chief and Publisher at Future Strategies Inc., the official publishers to WfMC.org. She was also Executive Director of WfMC and BPMI (now merged with OMG) and continues to work closely with these organizations to promote industry awareness of BPM and Workflow.

Future Strategies Inc. (www.FutStrat.com) publishes unique books and papers on business process management and workflow, specializing in dissemination of information about BPM and workflow technology and electronic commerce. As such, the company contracts and works closely with individual authors and corporations worldwide and also manages the renowned annual Global Awards for Excellence in BPM and Workflow and the new annual Adaptive Case Management Awards.

Future Strategies Inc., is the publisher of the business book series *New Tools for New Times*, the annual *Excellence in Practice* series of award-winning case studies and the annual *BPM and Workflow Handbook* series, published in collaboration with the WfMC. Ms. Fischer was a senior editor of a leading international computer publication for four years and has been involved in international computer journalism and publishing for over 20 years.

KEITH HARRISON-BRONINSKI
CTO, Role Modellers

Keith has been regarded as an IT and business thought leader since publication of his 2005 book "Human Interactions: The Heart And Soul Of Business Process Management". Building on 20 years of research and insights from varied disciplines, his theory provides a new way to describe and support collaborative human work. Keith speaks regularly in keynotes to business, IT and academic audiences at national conferences, most recently in Poland, India, the Netherlands, the UK, Finland and Portugal.

Keith Harrison-Broninski is CTO of Role Modellers, a Gartner Cool Vendor. The company's product, **HumanEdj**, is cloud software for Virtual Team Planning that provides unique support for large-scale, complex collaboration across multiple organizations.

More information about HumanEdj is available at www.rolemodellers.com and about Keith at http://keith.harrison-broninski.info.

PAUL JOHANNESSON
Professor, Stockholm University

Paul Johannesson received his BSc in Mathematics, and his PhD in Computer Science from Stockholm University in 1983 and 1993, respectively. He holds a position as professor at Stockholm University, where he works in the area of information systems. Johannesson has published work on federated information systems, translation between data models, languages for conceptual modelling, schema integration, the use of linguistic instruments in information systems, process integration, e-commerce systems design, and analysis patterns in systems design. He is the co-author of a text book on conceptual modelling, published by Prentice Hall. He has been a member of several EU projects on knowledge based systems and requirements engineering. He has been the project leader of and participated in several national projects on information integration, the use of IT in teaching information systems design, process modelling and integration, and IT in health care. Johannesson is and has been a member of several international program committees; among these are the ER conference and the CAiSE conference.

MANUELE KIRSCH PINHEIRO
Maître de Conférences at the University of Paris 1 Panthéon-Sorbonne

Manuele Kirsch Pinheiro is Associate Professor in the Computer Science Research Center (*Centre de Recherche en Informatique*) of the University of Paris 1 Panthéon-Sorbonne. Previously, she occupied a post-doctoral position on the Computer Science of the Katholieke Universiteit Leuven, where she contributed to the IST-MUSIC Project. She received her PhD in computer science from the University Joseph Fourier – Grenoble I in 2006, Grenoble, France. Her expertise include Context-Aware Computing, and notably context modeling. Additionally, her research interests include Ubiquitous computing, Service-Oriented Computing, Cooperative Work (CSCW) and Information Systems.

BENEDICTE LE GRAND
Full Professor at Université Paris 1 Panthéon-Sorbonne, France

Bénédicte Le Grand is a full Professor at Université Paris 1 Panthéon – Sorbonne since September 2012. She is a telecommunication engineer and has been Associate Professor at Université Pierre et Marie Curie for 10 years. Her research area is data mining and the analysis of real-world complex networks such as the Internet or social networks. She has published her work in international journals and conferences and has contributed to several books. She has been working since 2004 as an expert for the European Commission, for the evaluation of research project of the 6th and 7th Framework Programmes (FP6 and FP7).

ALBERTO MANUEL
CEO of Process Sphere, Portugal

Alberto Manuel has over 10 years of hands-on experience helping companies to improve, redesign and implement business process, in order to become more agile and lean over and over again, working as a mentor, coach and consultant helping companies to reach successful outcomes.

Previously, for seven years, he was committed to R&D of consumer goods products and improving manufacturing operations.

He is involved with the BPM community helping to bring innovation to this field of practice. He is Vice President of the *Association of Business Process Management Professionals - Portuguese Chapter*, member of the task force on Process Mining, and various working groups of the Workflow Management Coalition and World Wide Web Consortium. He is the Chair of BPM Conference Portugal. His blog is at http://ultrabpm.wordpress.com

NATHANIEL PALMER
VP & CTO, Business Process Management, Inc. and Executive Director, Workflow Management Coalition

A noted author, practitioner and one of the early originators of Adaptive Case Management, Nathaniel Palmer has been the Chief Architect to some of the world's largest BPM, SOA and ACM projects, involving investments of $200 million or more. He is currently VP & CTO, Business Process Management, Inc., as well as the Executive Director of the Workflow Management Coalition. Previously he was the BPM Practice Director at SRA International, Director, Business Consulting for Perot Systems Corp, and spent over a decade with Delphi Group serving as Vice President and Chief Technology Officer. He frequently tops the lists of the most recognized names in his field, was identified through independent market research as #1 among the most influential thought leaders in BPM, and was the first individual named as Laureate in Workflow.

ERIK PERJONS
Lecturer and researcher at the department of Computer and System Sciences of Stockholm University, Sweden

Dr, Erik Perjons holds a position as senior lecturer (assistant professor) at the Department of Computer and Systems Sciences (DSV), Stockholm University. He has worked at the department since 1999. His research and teaching interest includes areas such as enterprise modeling, conceptual modeling, business process management, model-driven development, service oriented architecture, system integration, enterprise systems, knowledge management, decision support systems and qualitative research methods. A main focus has been to design methods based on modeling techniques and scientific approaches for analyzing practical problems in organizations, and designing business and IT solutions addressing these problems. He has published around 40 publications in international journals, and conferences, participated in several domestic and international research projects in domains such as health care, e-government and telecom. He has also a university exam in journalism and has worked as journalist at several Swedish newspapers, and as a media analyst, analyzing how organizations or products are portrayed and covered in different media such as newspapers, television and the internet.

THOMAS BECH PETTERSEN
CTO, Computas AS, Norway

Thomas is an experienced information system architect and knowledge management specialist with an emphasis on active business process and case management systems; i.e. adaptive case management systems that go all the way to knowledge supported business process execution in the daily workplace. "Why be satisfied with just mapping business processes? Go all the way to activate the processes for each individual employee and associate!" Thomas is a Division Director in Computas with more than 20 years of experience with workflow technology, process-based and rule-based solutions. He has worked with clients such as the Norwegian courts and the police and prosecuting authority, and served also as a functional adviser on the NFSA MATS project. Thomas has been a key player in the Computas FrameSolutions initiative that has brought forward FrameSolutions as an ACM framework product. He has also spoken at OOPSLA and several national conferences.

IRINA RYCHKOVA
Associate Professor at University Paris 1, Panthéon-Sorbonne, France

Irina Rychkova is a senior lecturer in Computer Science and a researcher at Centre de Recherche en Informatique of the University Paris 1. Her research interests are in the areas of strategic alignment, enterprise and business process modeling. Irina holds a PhD in System modeling and Enterprise Architecture from Suisse Federal Institute of Technology at Lausanne (EPFL), a MSc in Applied Mathematics and Physics from Moscow Institute of Physics and Technology, in Russia, and an Engineer degree in Information Systems from Samara State Aerospace University, in Russia. Prior to joining CRI - Paris 1, Irina was a research assistant at EPFL, Laboratory of Systemic Modeling (LAMS). She also spent six months working as Enterprise Architect at adidas Global IT, in Germany.

HELLE FRISAK SEM
Chief Architect, Computas AS, Norway

Dr. Helle Frisak Sem is a Chief Architect in Computas, specializing in solution architecture and requirements engineering. With more than 20 years of experience, Helle leads functional teams towards the realization of operational ACM solutions, in collaboration with customer and user. She is a senior advisor in knowledge management, work process support, enterprise modelling, estimation of software projects and user interface design. From a background in research and education, Helle combines deep technical knowledge with experience on how customers' problems may be met by an operational solution. Helle is the functional architect behind the MATS solution described in this book, and over the last 15 years she has been a main contributor to FrameSolutions™ - Computas AS' framework for realizing operational ACM solutions.

KEITH SWENSON
Vice President of R&D, Fujitsu America Inc., USA

Keith Swenson is Vice President of Research and Development at Fujitsu North America. As a speaker, author, and contributor to many workflow and BPM standards, he is known for having been a pioneer in collaboration software and web services. He is currently the Chairman of the Workflow Management Coalition. He has led agile software development teams at MS2, Netscape, Ashton Tate & Fujitsu. In 2004 he was awarded the Marvin L. Manheim Award for outstanding contributions in the field of workflow. Co-author on more than 10 books. In 2010 his book "Mastering the Unpredictable" introduced and defined the field of adaptive case management and established him as one of the most influential people in the field of case management. He blogs at http://social-biz.org/.

WfMC Structure and Membership Information

WHAT IS THE WORKFLOW MANAGEMENT COALITION?

The Workflow Management Coalition, founded in August 1993, is a non-profit, international organization of BPM and workflow vendors, users, analysts and university/research groups. The Coalition's mission is to promote and develop the use of BPM and workflow through the establishment of standards for software terminology, interoperability and connectivity among BPM and workflow products. Comprising more than 250 members worldwide, the Coalition is the primary standards body for this software market.

WORKFLOW STANDARDS FRAMEWORK

The Coalition has developed a framework for the establishment of workflow standards. This framework includes five categories of interoperability and communication standards that will allow multiple workflow products to coexist and interoperate within a user's environment. Technical details are included in the white paper entitled, "The Work of the Coalition," available at www.wfmc.org.

WORKFLOW MANAGEMENT COALITION STRUCTURE

The Coalition is divided into three major committees, the Technical Committee, the External Relations Committee, and the Steering Committee. Small working groups exist within each committee for the purpose of defining workflow terminology, interoperability and connectivity standards, conformance requirements, and for assisting in the communication of this information to the workflow user community.

The Coalition's major committees meet three times per calendar year for three days at a time, with meetings usually alternating between a North American and a European location. The working group meetings are held during these three days, and as necessary throughout the year.

Coalition membership is open to all interested parties involved in the creation, analysis or deployment of workflow software systems. Membership is governed by a Document of Understanding, which outlines meeting regulations, voting rights etc. Membership material is available at www.wfmc.org.

COALITION WORKING GROUPS

The Coalition has established a number of Working Groups, each working on a particular area of specification. The working groups are loosely structured around the "Workflow Reference Model" which provides the framework for the Coalition's standards program. The Reference Model identifies the common characteristics of workflow systems and defines five discrete functional interfaces through which a workflow management system interacts with its environment—users, computer tools and applications, other software services, etc. Working groups meet individually, and also under the umbrella of the Technical Committee, which is responsible for overall technical direction and co-ordination.

ACHIEVEMENTS

The initial work of the Coalition focused on publishing the Reference Model and Glossary, defining a common architecture and terminology for the industry. A major milestone was achieved with the publication of the first versions of the Workflow

API (WAPI) specification, covering the Workflow Client Application Interface, and the Workflow Interoperability specification.

In addition to a series of successful tutorials industry wide, the WfMC spent many hours over 2009 helping to drive awareness, understanding and adoption of XPDL, now the standard means for business process definition in over 80 BPM products. As a result, it has been cited as the most deployed BPM standard by a number of industry analysts, and continues to receive a growing amount of media attention.

Workflow Reference Model

The Workflow Reference Model was published first in 1995 and still forms the basis of most BPM and workflow software systems in use today. It was developed from the generic workflow application structure by identifying the interfaces which enable products to interoperate at a variety of levels. All workflow systems contain a number of generic components which interact in a defined set of ways; different products will typically exhibit different levels of capability within each of these generic components. To achieve interoperability between workflow products a standardized set of interfaces and data interchange formats between such components is necessary. A number of distinct interoperability scenarios can then be constructed by reference to such interfaces, identifying different levels of functional conformance as appropriate to the range of products in the market.

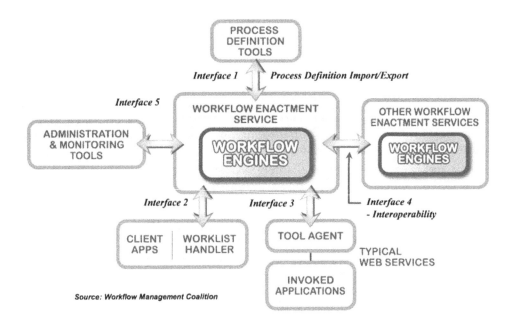

WORKFLOW REFERENCE MODEL DIAGRAM

XPDL (XML Process Definition Language)

An XML based language for describing a process definition, developed by the WfMC. Version 1.0 was released in 2002. Version 2.0 was released in Oct 2005. The goal of XPDL is to store and exchange the process diagram, to allow one tool to model a process diagram, and another to read the diagram and edit, another to "run" the process model on an XPDL-compliant BPM engine, and so on. For this reason,

XPDL is not an executable programming language like BPEL, but specifically a process design format that literally represents the "drawing" of the process definition. Thus it has 'XY' or vector coordinates, including lines and points that define process flows. This allows an XPDL to store a one-to-one representation of a BPMN process diagram. For this reason, XPDL is effectively the file format or "serialization" of BPMN, as well as any non-BPMN design method or process model which use in their underlying definition the XPDL meta-model (there are presently about 60 tools which use XPDL for storing process models.)

In spring 2012, the WfMC completed XPDL 2.2 as the *fifth* revision of this specification. XPDL 2.2 builds on version 2.1 by introducing support for the process modeling extensions added to BPMN 2.0.

BPSim

The Business Process Simulation (BPSim) framework is a standardized specification that allows business process models captured in either BPMN or XPDL to be augmented with information in support of rigorous methods of analysis. It defines the parameterization and interchange of process analysis data allowing structural and capacity analysis of process models. BPSim is meant to support both pre-execution and post-execution optimization of said process models. The BPSim specification consists of an underlying computer-interpretable representation (meta-model) and an accompanying electronic file format to ease the safeguard and transfer of this data between different tools (interchange format).

Wf-XML

Wf-XML is designed and implemented as an extension to the OASIS Asynchronous Service Access Protocol (ASAP). ASAP provides a standardized way that a program can start and monitor a program that might take a long time to complete. It provides the capability to monitor the running service, and be informed of changes in its status. Wf-XML extends this by providing additional standard web service operations that allow sending and retrieving the "program" or definition of the service which is provided. A process engine has this behavior of providing a service that lasts a long time, and also being programmable by being able to install process definitions.

Awards

The Workflow Management Coalition sponsors three annual award programs.

1. The **Global Awards for Excellence in BPM & Workflow**[1] recognizes organizations that have implemented particularly innovative workflow solutions. Every year between 10 and 15 BPM and workflow solutions are recognized in this manner. WfMC publishes the case studies in the annual Excellence in Practice series.

2. WfMC inaugurated a Global Awards program in 2011 for **Adaptive Case Management**[2] case studies to recognize and focus upon ACM use cases. Adaptive Case Management, also known as Dynamic or Advanced Case Management, is a new technological approach to supporting knowledge workers in today's leading edge organizations. These awards are designed to highlight the best examples of technology to support knowledge workers. In 2012 nine teams were awarded top honors at the ACM Live Event and are featured in the book, "How

---

[1] www.BPMF.org

[2] www.adaptivecasemanagement.org

Knowledge Workers Get Things Done.[3] In 2013, WfMC updated the program to "WfMC Awards for Excellence in Case Management" to recognize the growing deployment of Production Case Management.

3. The **Marvin L. Manheim Award For Significant Contributions** in the Field of Workflow is given to one person every year in recognition of individual contributions to workflow and BPM standards. This award commemorates Marvin Manheim who played a key motivational role in the founding of the WfMC.

WHY YOU SHOULD JOIN

1. Gain Access to Members-Only Research and Q&A Forums
2. Participate in Members-Only "Brown Bag" Networking Sessions and Industry Speaker Series
3. Receive Free Admission to Business Process Focused Events and Programs (a Benefit Worth $1,000s Annually)
4. Access to the Industry's Largest Research Library on Business Process Modeling, Workflow, BPMS
5. Assistance in Product Certification and Conformance, as well as Requirements Analysis and Procurement Strategy

Being a member of the Workflow Management Coalition gives you the unique opportunity to participate in the creation of standards for the workflow industry as they are developing. Your contributions to our community ensure that progress continues in the adoption of royalty-free workflow and process standards.

BENEFITS OF MEMBERSHIP

Membership offers exclusive visibility in this sector at events and seminars across the world, enhancing your customers' perception of you as an industry authority, on our web site, in the Coalition Handbook and CDROM, by speaking opportunities, access to the Members Only area of our web site, attending the Coalition meetings and most importantly within the workgroups whereby through discussion and personal involvement, using your voting power, you can contribute actively to the development of standards and interfaces.

Full member benefits include:

*   Web Visibility: your logo on WfMC pages, inclusion in the WfMC web banner network, a detailed company profile in online member directory as well as in all WfMC publications.
*   User RFIs: (Requests for Information) is an exclusive privilege to all full members. We often receive queries from user organizations looking for specific workflow solutions. These valuable leads can result in real business benefits for your organization.
*   Publicity: full members may choose to have their company logos including collaterals displayed along with WfMC material at conferences /expos we attend. You may also list corporate events and press releases (relating to WfMC issues) on the relevant pages on the website, and have a company entry in the annual Coalition Workflow Handbook
*   Speaking Opportunities: We frequently receive calls for speakers at industry events because many of our members are recognized experts in their fields. These opportunities are forwarded to Full Members for their direct response to the respective conference organizers.

---

[3] *How Knowledge Workers Get Things Done.* Published 2012 by Future Strategies Inc. http://www.futstrat.com/books/HowKnowledgeWorkers.php

ASSOCIATE MEMBERSHIP

Associate and Academic Membership is appropriate for those (such as IT user organizations) who need to keep abreast of workflow developments, but who are not workflow vendors. It allows voting on decision-making issues, including the publication of standards and interfaces but does not permit anything near the amount of visibility or incentives provided to a Full Member. You may include up to three active members from your organization on your application.

INDIVIDUAL MEMBERSHIP

Individual Membership is appropriate for self-employed persons or small user companies. Employees of workflow vendors, academic institutions or analyst organizations are not typically eligible for this category. Individual membership is held in one person's name only, is not a corporate membership, and is not transferable within the company. If three or more people within a company wish to participate in the WfMC, it would be cost-effective to upgrade to corporate Associate Membership whereby all employees worldwide are granted membership status.

HOW TO JOIN

Complete the form on the Coalition's website at www.wfmc.org or contact the Coalition Secretariat, at the address below. All members are required to sign the Coalition's "Document of Understanding" which sets out the contractual rights and obligations between members and the Coalition.

THE SECRETARIAT

Workflow Management Coalition (WfMC)

Nathaniel Palmer, Executive Director,

+1-781-923-1411 (t), +1-781-735-0491 (f)

nathaniel@wfmc.org

Glossary of Terms
Adaptive Case Management

To have a meaningful discussion, we must start with clear definitions.

- **activity**—A description of a piece of work that forms one logical step within a process. It is the basic unit of work within a process. Presumably, work could be subdivided into units smaller than a given activity, but it is not meaningful for the organization to track the work to that level of detail. Synonyms include node, step, and task.
- **adaptive case management (ACM)**—A productive system that deploys not only the organization and process structure, but it becomes the system of record for the business data entities and content involved. All processes are completely transparent, as per access authorization, and fully auditable. It enables nontechnical business users in virtual organizations to seamlessly create/consolidate structured and unstructured processes from basic predefined business entities, content, social interactions, and business rules. It moves the process knowledge gathering from the template analysis/modeling/ simulation phase into the process execution phase in the lifecycle. It collects actionable knowledge—without an intermediate analysis phase—based on process patterns created by business users. ACM differs from business process management (BPM) and from human interaction management (HIM) in that the case information is the focus and the thing around which the other artifacts are organized. And it is the case information that persists for the long term.
- **ad hoc process**—See emergent process.
- **agile methodology**—To move quickly and lightly. In reference to solution development, it is a method where many short iterations are used, with many quick (internal) releases, so that the nontechnical customer of a solution can be more actively involved in guiding the course of development. The agile approach to development is known to produce solutions that better meet the needs of the customer, and it also allows for greater responsiveness to external changes in requirements.
- **analytics**- A mechanism for collecting and processing statistics. Process analytics will gather and process statistics about the running of processes in such a way that it is useful for evaluating how well the process is running.
- **best practice**—An approach to achieving a particular outcome that is believed to be more effective than any other approach in a particular condition or circumstance.
- **business operations platform (BOP)**— A next-generation technology platform oriented toward continuously designing, executing, monitoring, changing, and optimizing critical business processes proposed by Fingar (2009).
- **business process**— A set of one or more linked activities which collectively realize a business objective or policy goal, normally within the context of an organizational structure defining functional roles and relationships.

- **business process execution language (BPEL)**—A standard executable language, based on XML, for describing a process that uses web service calls to communicate with the outside world.
- **business process management (BPM)**—The practice of developing, running, performance measuring, and simulating business processes to effect the continued improvement of those processes. Business process management is concerned with the lifecycle of the process definition. BPM differs from adaptive case management (ACM) and from human interaction management (HIM) in that its focus is the process, and it uses the process as an organizing paradigm around which data, roles, and communication are organized. Process models are prepared in advance for particular situations, and the performance can be measured and monitored so that over time the process will be improved.
- **business process management suite/soft ware/system (BPMS)**—A soft ware system designed to support business process management. The acronym BPMS is used to distinguish the technology product from the management practice of BPM.
- **business process modeling notation (BPMN)**—A standard set of graphical shapes and conventions with associated meanings that can be used in modeling a business process.
- **business process orientation (BPO)**—A concept that suggests that organizations could enhance their overall performance by viewing all the activities as linked together into a process that ultimately produces a good or service.
- **business rules engine (BRE)**—A soft ware system for managing and evaluating a complex set of rules in a business processing environment. A business rule is a small piece of logic that is separated from the application logic so that it may be managed separately from the application code. Rules are oft en expressed in a language that is more accessible to non-programmers.
- **case**—The name given to the specific situation, set of circumstances, or initiative that requires a set of actions to achieve an acceptable outcome or objective. Each case has a subject that is the focus of the actions—such as a person, a lawsuit, or an insurance claim—and is driven by the evolving circumstances of the subject.
- **case file**—Contains all of the case information and processes, and it coordinates communications necessary to accomplish the goal for a particular case. A case file can contain information of any type including documents, images, video, etc.
- **case management**—A method or practice of coordinating work by organizing all of the relevant information into one place—called a case. The case becomes the focal point for assessing the situation, initiating activities and processes, as well as keeping a history record of what has transpired. Beyond this generic definition, case management has specific meanings in the medical care, legal, and social services fields. For this book, we see case management as a technique that could be used in any field of human endeavor.
- **case owner**—A person (or group of people) who is responsible for the outcome of a case. The case owner can change any aspect of a case and is actively involved in achieving the goals of the case.

- **clinical pathway**—a method that medical professionals use to standardize patient care based on accepted practice guidelines.
- **commercial-off -the-shelf (COTS)**—Describes software or hardware products that are ready-made and available for sale to the general public. This term is used to distinguish such product from custom software and hardware made specifically for a purpose that is presumed to be more expensive to produce and maintain.
- **crowdsourcing**—Identify evolving trends and best practices through continuous analysis of social interactions and conversations[2]
- **customer relationship management (CRM)**—Technology to manage a company's interactions with customers and sales prospects.
- **dynamic case management**—support real-time, incremental and progressive case-handling in response to changing events by leveraging collaborative and information-intensive BPM.[2]
- **emergent process**—A process that is not predictable. Emergent processes have a sensitive dependence upon external factors outside of the control of the process context, which is why they cannot be fixed according to their internal state. Workers involved in an emergent process will experience it as planning and working alternately or at the same time, such that the plan is evolved as the work evolves. Synonyms include *ad hoc* process and unstructured process.
- **enterprise content management (ECM)**—Strategies, methods, and tools used to capture, manage, store, preserve, and deliver content and documents related to organizational processes. ECM strategies and tools allow the management of an organization's unstructured information, wherever that information exists.
- **enterprise resource planning (ERP)**—Computer system used to manage resources including tangible assets, financial resources, materials, and human resources.
- **extended relationship management (XRM)**—a discipline of mapping and maintaining relationships between any type of asset in very flexible ways, for the purpose of leveraging those relationships in business rules or business processes.
- **goal-oriented organization design (GOOD)**—The change management methodology associated with human interaction management (HIM), which defines 3 standard Stages: Design (scope definition, business motiation modeling, benefits definition), Delivery (requirements management, stakeholder management, operational transition, risk management) and Optimization (marketing & communications, benefits realization). Each Stage has associated Roles, Activities and Deliverables.
- **human interaction management (HIM)**—The practice of describing, executing and managing collaborative human activity according to 5 standard principles (effective teams, structured communication, knowledge management, time management and dynamic planning) so as to achieve optimal results. HIM differs from business process management (BPM) and adaptive case management (ACM) in that its focus is definition of goals, assignment of associated responsibilities, and management of the resulting knowledge. Templates describing Stages, Roles, Activities and

---

[2] Forrester Research, USA

Deliverables are used to generate executable Plans that evolve during usage and may be re-used as new templates.

- **knowledge work**—A type of work where the course of events is decided on a case-by-case basis. It normally requires a person with detailed knowledge who can weigh many factors and anticipate potential outcomes to determine the course for a specific case. Knowledge work almost always involves an emergent ACM/BPM process or HIM Plan template.
- **knowledge workers**—People who have a high degree of expertise, education, or experience and the primary purpose of their job involves the creation, distribution, or application of knowledge. Knowledge workers do not necessarily work in knowledge intensive industries.
- **lifecycle**—This book uses lifecycle only in regard to the work of creating a solution. The development lifecycle of a solution might start with definition of requirements, development of a process definition, development of forms, testing, deployment of the solution into production, use of the solution by many people, and finally the shutting down of the solution. The lifecycle of a solution may involve monitoring the running process instances and improving those process definitions over time. Note: A solution has a lifecycle that takes it from start to finish; a case has a process or processes that take it from start to finish.
- **model**—A simplified summary of reality designed to aid further study. In the business process field, a process model is a simplified or complete process definition created to study the proposed process before execution time.
- **node**—See activity.
- **online transaction processing (OLTP)**—A class of systems where time-sensitive, transaction-related data are processed immediately and are always kept current.
- **organizational agility**—That quality of an organization associated with sensing opportunity or threat, prioritizing its potential responses, and acting efficiently and effectively.
- **predictable process**—process that is repeatable and is run the same way a number of times. Synonyms include definable process, repeatable process, and structured process.
- **process definition**—A representation of a business process in a form that supports automated manipulation, such as modeling or enactment by a process management system. The process definition consists of a network of activities and their relationships, criteria to indicate the start and termination of the process, and information about the individual activities, such as participants, associated IT applications, and data. Synonyms include process diagram and workflow.
- **process diagram**—A visual explanation of a process definition. Synonyms include process definition, process model, and process flowchart.
- **process flowchart**—See process diagram.
- **process instance**—A data structure that represents a particular instance of running of a process. It has associated context information that can be used and manipulated by the process. A process instance plays a role in a business process management suite (BPMS) that is very similar to but not exactly the same as a case in a case management system. A particular case may have more than one process instance associated with it.

- **process model**—A simplified or complete process definition created to study the proposed process before execution time. Synonyms include process diagram.
- **records management**—Management of the information created, received, and maintained as evidence and information by an organization in pursuance of legal obligations or in the transaction of business.
- **role**—An association of particular a user, or users, with a particular set of responsibilities in a particular context. In this case, responsibility means the expectation to perform particular activities for that context. routine work— Work that is predictable and usually repeatable. Its predictability allows routine work to be planned to a large extent before the work is started. As the name implies, routine work is considered normal, regular, and it is not exceptional.
- **scientific management**— An early twentieth century school of management that aimed to improve the physical efficiency of an individual worker by carefully recording precisely what must be done for a particular task, and then training workers to replicate that precisely. It is based on the work of Frederick Winslow Taylor (1856–1915).
- **scrum**—An agile software development methodology emphasizing iteration and incremental development. Originally referred to as the *rugby approach.*
- **service-oriented architecture (SOA)**—An approach to system design where the software functionality is deployed to a specific logical location (a service) and programs requiring that soft ware functionality make use of communications protocols to access the service remotely. SOA has oft en been discussed together with business process management (BPM), but this connection is coincidental. While BPM might benefit from SOA the way that any program/system would, there is no inherent connection between managing business processes and the system architecture that supports them.
- **social business**—An organization that has put in place the strategies, technologies and processes to systematically engage all the individuals of its ecosystem (employees, customers, partners, suppliers) to maximize the co-created value.
- **social BPM**—Leverage social networking tools and techniques to extend the reach and impact of process improvement efforts.
- **social network analysis**—Pinpoint historical activity patterns within social networks through the statistical mining of complex behavioural data sets.
- **social process guidance**—Apply crowdsourcing and social network analysis techniques to deliver real-time contextual advice and guidance for completing a process task or activity.
- **social software**—A class of software systems that allows users to communicate, collaborate, and interact in many flexible ways. Generally, such software allows users to form their own relationships with other users and then exchange messages, write notes, and share media in different ways.
- **solution**—A package of artefacts (configurations, forms, process definitions, templates, and information) that have been prepared in advance to

help users address particular kinds of recurring situations. A solution may embody best practices for a particular kind of situation.

- **sphere**—a collection of people or other assets. Inclusion in a sphere can be based on business rules or can be a nested collection of other spheres. Spheres can represent nodes in a network of relationships or process flow in a workflow system
- **step**—See activity.
- **straight-through processing (STP)**—The practice of completely automating a process and eliminating all manual human tasks. This term is typically used in the financial industry.
- **subject (of a case)**—An entity that is the focus of actions performed in the context of a case. For example, a person, a lawsuit, or an insurance claim.
- **task**—See activity.
- **template**—The general concept of something that is prepared in advance approximately for a particular purpose with the anticipation that it will be modified during use to more exactly fit the situation. A process template does not define a process in the way that a process definition does.
- **unstructured process**—See emergent process.
- **work**—Exertion or effort directed to produce or accomplish something. Organizations exist to achieve goals and work is the means to achieve those goals. The smallest recorded unit of work is an activity. Activities are combined into procedures and processes.
- **workflow**—The automation of a business process, in whole or part, during which documents, information, or tasks are passed from one participant to another for action according to a set of procedural rules. Synonyms include process definition.

These definitions are licensed under Creative Commons—you are free to copy and use them in any way that helps the pursuit of knowledge. It is not strictly necessary to reference this glossary, but we would appreciate a link back to this book. The bulk of this glossary is derived from the work done by Keith Swenson at http://social-biz.org/glossary and was originally assembled for inclusion in *Mastering the Unpredictable*[3]."

Accreditation guide if you quote from this glossary: "Empowering Knowledge Workers" 2014 published by Future Strategies Inc. Lighthouse Point, FL. www.FutStrat.com

---

[3] Mastering the Unpredictable: How Adaptive Case Management Will Revolutionize the Way That Knowledge Workers Get Things Done, published by Meghan-Kiffer Press, April 2010

Index

Additional Resources

Download PDF immediately and start reading.

- Introduction to BPM and Workflow
  http://store.futstrat.com/servlet/Detail?no=75

- Financial Services
  http://store.futstrat.com/servlet/Detail?no=90

- Healthcare
  http://store.futstrat.com/servlet/Detail?no=81

- Utilities and Telecommunications
  http://store.futstrat.com/servlet/Detail?no=92

NON-PROFIT ASSOCIATIONS AND RELATED STANDARDS RESEARCH ONLINE

- AIIM (Association for Information and Image Management)
  http://www.aiim.org
- BPM and Workflow online news, research, forums
  http://bpm.com
- BPM Research at Stevens Institute of Technology
  http://www.bpm-research.com
- Business Process Management Initiative
  http://www.bpmi.org *see* Object Management Group
- IEEE (Electrical and Electronics Engineers, Inc.)
  http://www.ieee.org

Institute for Information Management (IIM)
http://www.iim.org

- ISO (International Organization for Standardization)
  http://www.iso.ch
- Object Management Group
  http://www.omg.org
- Open Document Management Association
  http://nfocentrale.net/dmware
- Organization for the Advancement of Structured Information Standards
  http://www.oasis-open.org
- Society for Human Resource Management
  http://www.shrm.org
- Society for Information Management
  http://www.simnet.org
- Wesley J. Howe School of Technology Management
  http://howe.stevens.edu/research/research-centers/business-process-innovation
- Workflow And Reengineering International Association (WARIA)
  http://www.waria.com
- Workflow Management Coalition (WfMC)
  http://www.wfmc.org
- Workflow Portal
  http://www.e-workflow.org

TAMING THE UNPREDICTABLE

http://futstrat.com/books/eip11.php

The core element of Adaptive Case Management (ACM) is the support for real-time decision-making by knowledge workers.

Taming the Unpredictable presents the logical starting point for understanding how to take advantage of ACM. This book goes beyond talking about concepts, and delivers actionable advice for embarking on your own journey of ACM-driven transformation.

Retail #49.95 (see discount on website)

HOW KNOWLEDGE WORKERS GET THINGS DONE

http://www.futstrat.com/books/HowKnowledgeWorkers.php

How Knowledge Workers Get Things Done describes the work of managers, decision makers, executives, doctors, lawyers, campaign managers, emergency responders, strategist, and many others who have to think for a living. These are people who figure out what needs to be done, at the same time that they do it, and there is a new approach to support this presents the logical starting point for understanding how to take advantage of ACM.

Retail $49.95 (see discount offer on website)

DELIVERING BPM EXCELLENCE

http://futstrat.com/books/Delivering_BPM.php

Business Process Management in Practice

The companies whose case studies are featured in this book have proven excellence in their creative and successful deployment of advanced BPM concepts. These companies focused on excelling in *innovation*, *implementation* and *impact* when installing BPM and workflow technologies. The positive impact includes increased revenues, more productive and satisfied employees, product enhancements, better customer service and quality improvements.

$39.95 (see discount on website)

DELIVERING THE CUSTOMER-CENTRIC ORGANIZATION

http://futstrat.com/books/Customer-Centric.php

The ability to successfully manage the customer value chain across the life cycle of a customer is the key to the survival of any company today. Business processes must react to changing and diverse customer needs and interactions to ensure efficient and effective outcomes.

This important book looks at the shifting nature of consumers and the workplace, and how BPM and associated emergent technologies will play a part in shaping the companies of the future.

Retail $39.95

BPMN 2.0 Handbook SECOND EDITION

(see two-BPM book bundle offer on website: get BPMN Reference Guide Free)

http://futstrat.com/books/bpmnhandbook2.php

Updated and expanded with exciting new content!

Authored by members of WfMC, OMG and other key participants in the development of BPMN 2.0, the BPMN 2.0 Handbook brings together worldwide thought-leaders and experts in this space. Exclusive and unique contributions examine a variety of aspects that start with an introduction of what's new in BPMN 2.0, and look closely at interchange, analytics, conformance, optimization, simulation and more. **Retail $75.00**

BPMN MODELING AND REFERENCE GUIDE

(see two-BPM book bundle offer on website: get BPMN Reference Guide Free)

http://www.futstrat.com/books/BPMN-Guide.php

Understanding and Using BPMN

How to develop rigorous yet understandable graphical representations of business processes.

Business Process Modeling Notation (BPMN) is a standard, graphical modeling representation for business processes. It provides an easy to use, flow-charting notation that is independent of the implementation environment.
Retail $39.95

iBPMS - INTELLIGENT BPM SYSTEMS

http://www.futstrat.com/books/iBPMS_Handbook.php

"The need for Intelligent Business Operations (IBO) supported by intelligent processes is driving the need for a new convergence of process technologies lead by the iBPMS. The iBPMS changes the way processes help organizations keep up with business change," notes Gartner Emeritus Jim Sinur in his Foreword.

The co-authors of this important book describe various aspects and approaches of iBPMS with regard to impact and opportunity. **Retail $59.95 (see discount on website)**

Social BPM

http://futstrat.com/books/handbook11.php
Work, Planning, and Collaboration Under the Impact of Social Technology

Today we see the transformation of both the look and feel of BPM technologies along the lines of social media, as well as the increasing adoption of social tools and techniques democratizing process development and design. It is along these two trend lines; the evolution of system interfaces and the increased engagement of stakeholders in process improvement, that Social BPM has taken shape.
Retail $59.95 (see discount offer on website)

Get 25% Discount on ALL Books in our Store.

Please use the discount code **SPEC25** to get **25% discount** on ALL books in our store; both Print and Digital Editions (two discount codes cannot be used together).

www.FutStrat.com

www.ingramcontent.com/pod-product-compliance
Lightning Source LLC
Chambersburg PA
CBHW080407060326
40689CB00019B/4157